Tolley
VAT in Europe

Third Edition

INTERNATIONAL

Edited by John Voyez

Tolley

A Member of the LexisNexis Group

Members of the LexisNexis Group worldwide

United Kingdom	LexisNexis Butterworths Tolley, a Division of Reed Elsevier (UK) Ltd, Halsbury House, 35 Chancery Lane, LONDON, WC2A 1EL, and 4 Hill Street, EDINBURGH EH2 3JZ
Argentina	LexisNexis Butterworths, BUENOS AIRES
Australia	LexisNexis Butterworths, CHATSWOOD, New South Wales
Austria	LexisNexis Verlag ARD Orac GmbH & Co KG, VIENNA
Canada	LexisNexis Butterworths, MARKHAM, Ontario
Chile	LexisNexis Chile Ltda, SANTIAGO DE CHILE
Czech Republic	Nakladatelství Orac sro, PRAGUE
France	Editions du Juris-Classeur SA, PARIS
Hong Kong	LexisNexis Butterworths, HONG KONG
Hungary	HVG-Orac, BUDAPEST
India	LexisNexis Butterworths, NEW DELHI
Ireland	Butterworths (Ireland) Ltd, DUBLIN
Italy	Giuffré Editore, MILAN
Malaysia	Malayan Law Journal Sdn Bhd, KUALA LUMPUR
New Zealand	LexisNexis Butterworths, WELLINGTON
Poland	Wydawnictwa Prawnicze LexisNexis, WARSAW
Singapore	LexisNexis Butterworths, SINGAPORE
South Africa	Butterworths SA, DURBAN
Switzerland	Stämpfli Verlag AG, BERNE
USA	LexisNexis, DAYTON, Ohio

© Nexia 2002

A CIP Catalogue record for this book is available from the British Library.

ISBN 07545 16407

Typeset by YHT Ltd, London
Printed and bound in Great Britain by Hobbs the Printers Ltd, Totton, Hampshire

Visit Butterworths LexisNexis *direct* at www.butterworths.com

Preface

Tolley's VAT in Europe is a general guide to the Value Added Tax (VAT) implications of commercial activities in the member states of the European Union (EU) and some of the countries which may be joining in the near future and/or with which the EU has regular business activity.

VAT in Europe has been produced by Nexia International, the twelfth largest international network of accounting firms in the world. It is represented by around 250 offices in 76 countries worldwide. Country-specific information has been compiled by a Nexia member firm in each country concerned, and co-ordinated under general chapter introductions by John Voyez, editor and VAT specialist at Smith & Williamson, Nexia's member firm in the United Kingdom.

VAT in Europe is not exhaustive and is not intended to cover VAT law and practice in detail, although its structure is based on the *EC Sixth Directive*, which is the main body of European VAT legislation. The book aims to give a brief guide to the basic rules governing VAT in each country. Whilst VAT in Europe aims to provide accurate and up-to-date information up to and including 30 April 2002, the book is no substitute for international tax advice, which should be sought from an international tax practitioner before any action is taken or decision made.

Every effort has been taken to ensure the accuracy of the contents of this book. However, neither the authors nor the publishers can accept any responsibility for any loss occasioned to any person acting or refraining from action in reliance on any statement contained in the book.

The reader should contact in the first instance his nearest Nexia office (details are shown at the end of the book).

Structure of the book

Each chapter of the book is divided into two parts. The first explains the EU legislation on a particular topic and the second highlights differences of interpretation and treatment within each member state.

The topics covered are as follows:

(1) Taxable persons
(2) Taxable activities
(3) Place of supply
(4) Exemptions
(5) Basis of taxation
(6) Tax rates
(7) Credit for input tax
(8) Administrative obligations
(9) Liability

(10) Penalties
(11) Objections and appeals
(12) Special VAT regimes

Chapter 13 deals with non-EU countries as follows:

As at 30 April 2002 there are fifteen member states of the European Union, namely:

(i)   Austria
(ii)   Belgium
(iii) Denmark
(iv)   Finland
(v)   France
(vi)   Germany
(vii) Greece
(viii) Ireland
(ix)   Italy
(x)   Luxembourg
(xi)   The Netherlands
(xii) Portugal
(xiii) Spain
(xiv) Sweden
(xv)   United Kingdom

What is Value Added Tax?

VAT is a European tax. Although its theoretical origins date back to the beginning of the twentieth century, it was first introduced in France in 1953 as TVA, '*taxe sur la valeur ajouté*'. It has spread throughout the European Union, new members being obliged to introduce it when they join.

VAT is gradually spreading to other parts of the world and most developed countries have a turnover tax, whether it is called VAT, gross sales tax (GST) or is known by another name.

VAT is a general tax on consumption and is added to the value of supplies of goods and services en route to the final consumer. The principle is based on a tax credit system which allows every taxable person in the chain of production to recover the VAT on costs incurred. In this way it is the final consumer which ultimately bears the burden of the tax.

Within the European Union, neutrality is achieved by means of exempting (or zero rating) supplies of goods to other EU member states and taxing 'acquisitions' in the EU member state of destination. Thus, the VAT paid by the final consumer in any member state is the same whether he obtains the goods from his own country or from another EU member state.

A single market within the European Union

The idea of forming a united Europe goes back to 1951 when Belgium, the Netherlands, Luxembourg, Germany, Italy and France signed a treaty forming the European Coal and Steel Community.

In 1957, these six countries signed two further treaties in Rome: the *European Economic Community (EEC) Treaty* and the *European Atomic Energy (EURATOM) Treaty*. The EU was extended to nine countries in 1973 when the United Kingdom, Ireland and Denmark joined. On 1 January 1981, Greece joined the EU and on 1 January 1986, Spain and Portugal became members. On 1 January 1995 Austria, Finland and Sweden became members.

The goal of the EEC *Treaty of Rome* is the removal of economic barriers between the members countries and the attainment of a single common market. In order to accelerate the completion of the internal market, the European Commission proposed a complete legislation programme setting 1 January 1993 as the target date to achieve the common market.

As part of the harmonisation of VAT legislation within the European Community, the Council of Ministers issued several Directives for member countries to implement in their national legislation. The process started in 1967 when the Council of Ministers adopted two Directives which resulted in the implementation of VAT by all member states.

Further harmonisation was required to provide the EU with a basis for its own income by a Directive introducing a uniform basis of taxation (the EU receives a part of all VAT levied). This was the *Directive 77/388 or the Sixth Directive on the harmonisation of the Laws of the Member States relating to turnover taxes – common system of value added tax: uniform basis of assessment*. It is now generally known as the *Sixth Directive*. However, this Directive did not require harmonisation of VAT rates and did not eliminate fiscal frontiers. In order to achieve that, the Council of Ministers reached agreement in 1991 for a transitional system from 1993 to 1997. It was intended that this system be replaced by a definitive system in 1997. However this has yet to be achieved in full and it now seems likely that the transitional system will continue for the immediate future. While there has been considerable simplification, the convergence of VAT rates around Europe which was expected has not happened.

Under the transitional system, from 1993 the fiscal borders between the EU member states were removed: the 'export' to another EU member state is an 'intra-Community supply' and the 'import' in the other member state is an 'intra-Community acquisition'.

The basic rule is that for intra-Community supplies to (taxable and exempt) business and non-taxable corporate entities, VAT will be levied in the destination member state. This rule applies for exempt business and non-taxable corporate entities when the acquisitions from any one other EU member state exceed a set monetary amount not less than 10,000 euros, or they opt for this rule. If the customer does not opt for taxation in the member state of destination, then VAT is levied in the member state of supply.

The sale to individuals is generally taxable in the country of supply. However, special rules apply in certain cases: the purchase of 'new vehicles' is always taxable in the EU member state of destination. For 'mail order supplies' special rules also apply.

The Council of Ministers also reached agreement in 1991 on minimum rates for VAT. Accordingly, member countries must provide for a normal rate of at least 15% and a minimum reduced rate of 5%.

Modernisation of the EC Sixth E-Directive

The existing VAT framework is now beginning to show its age, and steps are being taken at European level to update the legislation in line with modern technology and working practices. The main change is expected in July 2003 when the e-commerce Directive will come into force requiring non-EU suppliers to register in the EU for supplies made to individuals in the EU. There is also discussion on the need for conformity on the requirements for a VAT invoice, electronic invoicing and storage, a review of the Tour Operators Margin Region Scheme, the need to review the operation of simplification rules, and a move towards a single standard rate within the EU. In short, it is to be expected that there will be a number of changes to the operation of VAT within the EU in the coming years.

Contents

Contents

Contents

Chapter 1

Taxable Persons

Taxable persons: EU rules

General

1.1   A taxable person is any legal entity which independently carries out economic activities. These include the activities of producers, traders and persons supplying a range of services including the activities of the professions. In general, economic activities should be ongoing rather than on a one-off or on an occasional basis. Wage earners as employees under contract to their employer are not treated as taxable persons.

The exploitation of tangible or intangible property, for the purpose of obtaining income there from on a continuing basis, is also considered an economic activity.

A profit motive is not required to qualify as a taxable person. However, a person who always provides services free of charge or consistently below cost may not be regarded as a taxable person. Actions preparatory to the carrying on of a business form part of the business.

A taxable person can be a resident or non-resident, an individual, an association of individuals (e.g. a partnership), a company, or any other legal economic entity.

A holding company which only holds the shares of subsidiaries and is not engaged in any other activity is not treated as a taxable person.

[EC Sixth Directive 77/388, Art 4].

Public bodies

1.2   State, regional and local government bodies are not considered taxable persons in respect of the activities or transactions in which they are engaged as public authorities. This is also the case if the above bodies collect dues, fees, contributions or payments in connection with these activities.

However, if the 'public' activities would lead to significant distortions of competition, the government bodies may be considered taxable persons in relation to the activities undertaken.

Public bodies are usually considered taxable persons if they make supplies in the following fields:

(*a*)   telecommunications;

(*b*)   water, gas, electricity and steam;

(*c*)   the transport of goods;

(*d*)   port and airport services;

(*e*)   passenger transport;

(*f*)   new goods manufactured for sale;

(*g*)   certain agricultural activities pursuant to regulations on the common organisation of the market of these products;

(*h*)   the running of trade fairs and exhibitions;

(*i*)   warehousing;

(*j*)   the activities of travel agencies;

(*k*)   the running of staff shops, co-operatives and industrial canteens and similar institutions;

(*l*)   commercial activities by radio and television bodies.

Many of the above supplies now made in the EU are commonly made by privatised bodies.

[*EC Sixth Directive 77/388, Art 4(5) and Annex D*].

Group registration

1.3   EU countries may treat as a single taxable person entities which, while legally independent, are closely bound to one another by financial, economic and organisational links.

The EU member states are free to dictate conditions for forming a fiscal unity.

Importers

1.4   The importation of goods into the EU is generally subject to VAT in the EU country of importation, whether or not the importer fulfils the requirements set out above. The VAT liability at importation arises when the goods pass through Customs at the frontier.

If goods are transported from one EU country to another this is not considered an 'export' or 'import' of goods but rather an EU dispatch or acquisition.

[*EC Sixth Directive 77/388, Art 7*].

Persons treated as taxable persons

1.5   The concept of a taxable person is extended to all circumstances in which any person (including a private individual) effects an intra-Community acquisition of a new means of transport and to any person who also occasionally arranges an intra-Community supply of a new means of transport.

Non-taxable legal persons (e.g. public bodies, pure holding companies) and fully exempt businesses are in principle treated as taxable persons for intra-Community acquisitions of goods.

For further discussion on these points, see Chapter 2.

Specific rules in the various EU countries

Austria

General

1.6   A taxable person is any person or legal entity which independently carries on continuous commercial or professional activities. A profit motive is not required. A business comprises of all commercial or professional activities undertaken by a specific person or legal entity.

If an activity does not yield profits in the long term, it may be regarded as a hobby rather than a commercial or professional activity.

Employees who receive income independently from their employment, e.g. a doctor employed at a hospital who earns income from his independent work, are regarded as taxable persons.

Public bodies

1.7   Public legal entities are only taxable in respect of any commercial business and agricultural and forestry activities.

Group registration

1.8   In Austria it is possible to treat special partnerships such as joint ventures as a group for VAT purposes where the relevant companies do business under a single business name. This form of fiscal unity (*Arbeitsgemeinschaft*) is often found in the building industry.

Furthermore, groups of dependent companies may be covered by a single VAT registration number if the following conditions are met:

(*a*)   all entities must be corporate bodies resident in Austria;

(*b*)   one company must control all the others, as follows:

    (i)   it must hold more than 75% of voting rights;

    (ii)   it must exercise a controlling influence on the managing board; and

    (iii)   the (majority-owned) subsidiaries must be economically dependent, in that they are all integrated in the production process of the parent company.

If a single business carries out more than one activity, it must be registered as one taxable person, provided that the activities are not carried out through separate legal entities.

Foreign businesses

1.9   Foreign businesses making taxable supplies of goods or services in Austria must register for VAT. Businesses which are not resident in Austria and do not have a permanent establishment for VAT purposes there, are included in this category. However, a permanent establishment includes a fixed place of business at which there is economic activity, for example, office space, premises for the storage of stock or a construction site in existence for more than twelve months are all fixed establishments.

If foreign businesses make taxable supplies in Austria the VAT liability may be transferred to the customer. However, this scheme does not apply if the customer is not a resident of Austria, in which case the supplier is responsible for payment. In this case, the foreign business must register for VAT with the authorities in Graz-Stadt and file tax returns accordingly. The foreign business may appoint a person resident in Austria to deal with all correspondence with the authorities.

Belgium

General

1.10   A taxable person is anyone whose activities consist of making, consistently and independently, with or without a profit motive, as a principal or agent, taxable supplies of goods or services.

Those not considered to be taxable persons include individuals acting as private persons, public bodies and authorities, pure holding companies and real estate companies which undertake no entrepreneurial activity, as well as a certain number of specific professions such as doctors, lawyers, etc.

Particularities

1.11   In certain circumstances, private individuals and non profit organisations may opt to become VAT taxpayers.

This applies, for example, in the case of an individual who pays VAT on the acquisition of a newly constructed building and transfers the building, in whole or part, for consideration, either before or after construction but not later than 31 December of the year following that in which the property tax is registered for the first time.

Such an individual, although not a VAT taxpayer, may elect to be subject to VAT for the specific transaction, whereby the VAT originally paid on the construction becomes deductible.

Private individuals may also be required to apply VAT on certain private transactions, including:

(*a*)   rental of garages and parking facilities where these are not rented together with an apartment or house occupied as a private dwelling;

(*b*)   construction work performed by a private individual for his own benefit;

(*c*)   rental of furnished flats.

Registration requirement

1.12   A VAT taxpayer must obtain a VAT identification number before commencing any taxable activity.

An application must be filed with the VAT office local to the registered head office or the residence.

There is no requirement to apply for VAT registration where the annual turnover, subject to VAT, does not exceed € 5,580, although the local VAT tax office must be notified and an annual statement must be made.

As from 1 January 2002, new rules have been established for non-resident EU businesses. They now have the choice:

(*a*)   either to appoint a responsible VAT representative under the same conditions as available for non EU foreign entities; or

(*b*)   to request directly a Belgian VAT registration number without having to appoint a Belgian VAT representative or provide a bank guarantee ('direct identification'); or

(*c*)   to waive the application for a Belgian VAT registration and to opt for a VAT deferral system whereby the Belgian client will have to declare the VAT in its own monthly or quarterly statements.

A VAT registration will however be compulsory in certain circumstances including:

(a)   keeping up of a warehouse in Belgium;

(b)   activities involving intra-Community acquisitions and deliveries.

The 'direct identification' system will avoid the expenses related to the appointment of a tax representative. However, the foreign entity will have to comply with all regulations which are imposed on Belgian tax-payers such as keeping separate incoming and outgoing invoice ledgers, separate numbering of invoices to Belgian clients, filing monthly or quarterly statements, electing a place in Belgium where inspections can take place etc.

Only French, Dutch or German language may be used in respect of communication with the authorities. In this system, the foreign entity will not be allowed to use the deferral system, and will be responsible for paying the VAT to the tax authorities.

The extension of the VAT deferral system – originally only granted to foreign entities with a VAT representative and in respect of certain transactions – will simplify the procedure in those cases where foreign entities do not have frequent transactions giving rise to Belgian VAT, and do not have to recover large amounts of VAT on invoices from Belgian suppliers.

For the recovery of input VAT, businesses will have to apply the special procedure of application for reimbursement, whereby the reimbursement will be obtained usually after a 3 to 6 month delay.

Non-EU businesses are required to appoint a responsible VAT repre-sentative and to provide a bank guarantee, at a level fixed by the VAT office, which is usually the equivalent of at least three months VAT due.

The application should contain the following required information:

(a)   the personal details of the individuals;

(b)   for companies, a complete set of articles, the deed of incorporation and a copy of any trade registration;

(c)   for foreign firms, a statement from the foreign VAT authorities confirming that the entity is subject to VAT in its country of resi-dence;

(d)   an estimate of annual turnover.

A Belgian bank account must be opened. It should be noted that obtaining a VAT registration for a foreign entity, which does not have registered offices in Belgium, often takes up to three months.

Group registration

1.13   The concept of fiscal unity does not exist under Belgian law, therefore it is not permitted for legally independent companies to be treated as a single VAT taxpayer.

Nor is it possible for a company to obtain a separate VAT registration for one or several of its branches, as it is the single legal entity which is registered.

An exception exists in the case of a joint venture, whereby the partners may opt for a separate common VAT registration for the activities performed under the joint venture agreement, on the understanding that each party will nevertheless maintain its own VAT registration.

Denmark

General

1.14   A taxable person is any person or legal entity making taxable supplies in the course of business.

'Business' comprises any activity, including any trade, profession or vocation, carried on with a reasonable degree of continuity and organisation, whether profitable or not. Hobbies and the provision of services by an employee to his employer are excluded.

Registration limit

1.15   Danish and foreign companies with a turnover within a twelve month period from the sale of goods and services up to and including DKK 20,000 are not required to register, nor are they required to charge VAT.

Group registration

1.16   If a taxable entity owns more than one business, these are in principle considered as one taxable entity for VAT purposes. However, on request, each business may be registered as a separate taxable entity, provided that separate accounts are kept for each business.

Independent legal entities and those which are not owned by the same person may be permitted to register as a single taxable entity if so requested. If permission is granted, no VAT will be due on supplies of goods and services between these businesses. Companies with a joint registration will have joint and several liability for the payment of VAT.

Alternatively, a company may register in divisions. For example, companies dealing in exports may register their export department separately and thereby obtain a refund of export related input VAT on a monthly or weekly basis.

Foreign business

1.17   Foreign companies that have no fixed establishment in Denmark, but which are subject to taxation in Denmark on the sale of goods or services, must register through a resident individual or a company domiciled in Denmark.

This only applies if the country in which the company is located is a country outside the EU and Denmark has not entered with the country into a mutual assistance agreement equivalent to the one applicable between EU member states.

Finland

General

1.18   All persons engaged in the selling of goods and services in the course of business in Finland are subject to VAT. Taxable persons can be individuals, enterprises, non-profitable organisations, foreigners and public bodies.

Businesses not engaged in taxable activities, such as not for profit organisations, banks or insurance companies, may be obliged to register for VAT depending on the level of acquisitions from other EU member states.

The area of Finland comprises the Republic of Finland. The islands of Åland are not part of the EU for VAT and excise duty purposes.

Public bodies

1.19   To ensure neutrality of competition, public utilities are subject to VAT on business related activities.

Group registration

1.20   This is available only for businesses carrying on mainly exempt financial or insurance activities and their closely linked companies. The group members must have close economic, financial and administrative relations with each other.

Importers

1.21   A business that does not have a permanent establishment in Finland may register using a representative approved by the regional tax office. The representative is responsible for completing returns, but not for the payment of VAT.

France

General

1.22   The French VAT system divides all transactions into two categories:

(*a*)   transactions outside the scope of VAT and certain transactions performed by public bodies;

(*b*)   transactions within the scope of VAT, these include:

(i)   exempt supplies;

(ii)   taxable supplies;

(iii)   optional taxable supplies.

A taxable person is any person who independently carries out any economic activity, whether on an occasional or regular basis, whatever the purpose or results of that activity and whatever the status of that person as regards other taxes.

Persons not considered as taxable persons

1.23   Apprentices, theatrical artists, journalists, press agents, fashion models, travelling salesmen and workers from home are generally not considered to be taxable persons as they do not act independently.

Employees and other people who are bound by a work contract concerning working conditions, remuneration and employer liability are not considered to be taxable persons.

The chairman and managing director of a private or public establishment whose remuneration is comparable to a salary, are not considered to be taxable persons.

Public bodies/public services

1.24   The activities of statutory bodies will be liable for VAT if they would lead to a competition imbalance.

The public services activities, for which non-competition is presumed, are not taxable (e.g. transactions closely bound to social aid and Social Security, supplies of goods and services closely bound to childhood protection, cultural and sport services, etc.).

All other activities are liable for VAT (e.g. golf ranges, amusement parks, cinemas).

Certain activities, as provided by French law, are mandatorily subject to VAT (e.g. telecommunications, supply of water in towns of at least 3,000 inhabitants, gas and electricity distribution, etc.).

Local collectives can opt for VAT for the following activities:

(*a*)   waste collection;

(*b*)   supply of water;

(*c*)   all transactions connected with these activities.

Group registration

1.25   If a person owns more than one business, the businesses are treated as one taxable business unless they are legally distinct. It is not possible to treat a group of legally independent companies as a fiscal unit for VAT purposes.

Germany

General

1.26   As a rule, taxable persons are businesses within the meaning of the VAT legislation. A person is in business when that person independently carries on commercial activities with the intention of continuing those activities, whether or not a profit is realised.

Public bodies

1.27   If a public body is engaged in activities of a commercial nature, it is considered to be a taxable person. This includes all establishments carrying on a business activity with a view to generating income. In general, a business is deemed to be of a commercial nature if its turnover exceeds € 127,822 in any year or if it consistently exceeds € 30,678.

For certain activities, public bodies always qualify as taxable persons, e.g. distribution of spectacles by social security institutions, municipal health resorts, cemeteries, swimming pools and the supply of staff by government bodies.

Group registration

1.28   Provided businesses are integrated financially, by structure **and** economically, they may be regarded as a fiscal unit for VAT. Therefore a holding company may reclaim VAT if at least one of its subsidiaries is a business within the meaning of VAT law. Intra-group transactions are not subject to VAT.

A profit-pooling agreement is not required. The establishment of the parent or the subsidiary of a fiscal unit, is decided by the location of the headquarters of the business.

Greece

General

1.29 The term 'taxable person' includes every person or entity making taxable supplies in Greece in the course of its business.

Small businesses are exempt from all VAT obligations if annual turnover is less than € 5,282.47 (GRD 1,800,000) for the supply of goods or € 1,760.82 (GRD 600,000) for the supply of services.

Group registration

1.30 A group of dependent companies may not be treated as a fiscal unity for VAT purposes.

Foreign businesses

1.31 In principle, the VAT provisions for resident businesses apply also to foreign businesses.

Foreign businesses which make supplies in Greece, are required to appoint a fiscal representative to comply with administrative obligations and pay any VAT due.

Ireland

General

1.32 A taxable person is a person who, otherwise than as an employee, makes a supply, within Ireland, of taxable goods or services in the course or furtherance of business, and whose annual turnover is in excess of certain thresholds.

The term 'person' includes companies, partnerships, individuals and all other business entities.

Under Irish VAT legislation the term 'business' includes farming, the promotion of dances and any trade, commercial activity, manufacturing enterprise or any venture or concern in the nature of trade, and any profession or vocation whether for profit or otherwise.

Group registration

1.33   The term 'fiscal unity' is not used in Irish legislation.

Where the authorities are satisfied that two or more taxable persons, established in the State, are closely bound by financial, economic or organisational links, they may agree to a group registration. This will allow one member of the group to make a single VAT return on behalf of all of the members of the group. The condition 'closely bound by financial economic or organisational links' is interpreted very widely.

Each person within the group must register for VAT and will be allocated an individual VAT registration number. However, when group registration is granted, only one VAT return is required to be remitted for the group as a whole. One company will be nominated as the group representative.

An Irish VAT group may not include a company or a branch located outside the State.

Group registration is usually applied for by a number of taxable persons, but occasionally a group registration may be imposed.

A group registration for VAT has the following implications:

(*a*)   members of a group need not charge VAT on inter-group supplies, other than supplies of property;

(*b*)   only one VAT return is required for all the members of the group. This means that if one company in the group is due a VAT repayment, the repayment can be offset against any liability outstanding of the group as a whole;

(*c*)   the members of a group registration are jointly and severally liable for each member of the group.

When forming a VAT group, there is no need to include all companies which would qualify. For example, if one company is in a constant VAT repayment position it may be preferable to leave that company out of the group registration.

The inclusion of a company which makes VAT exempt supplies may have an adverse effect on the VAT recovery of the group as a whole.

It is possible to have two separate groups, but a company may only be a member of one group.

Intra-Community acquisitions of new means of transport

1.34   Where a person has become a taxable person only as a result of the intra-Community acquisition of a new means of transport, that person will not be required to comply with all the obligations for VAT (e.g. keeping accounts).

Italy

General

1.35   A taxable person is any individual carrying on a business activity on a continuing basis, even if such activity is not the sole or the main activity carried on by the business. Companies and business partnerships are always deemed to be taxable persons. Artists and professional persons or partnerships are considered to be taxable persons for VAT purposes if their activities are on a continuing basis.

Group registration

1.36   Where a person owns more than one business, he must disclose to the tax authorities for each business the following information:

(*a*)   the nature of the activity engaged in by the enterprise;

(*b*)   its location; and

(*c*)   the place where its accounting books and other documents are kept.

If a person owns more than one business, or exercises substantially different business activities in the same company, VAT is calculated on the basis of the total supplies, but he may opt that each of his businesses, or each of his activities, be registered separately for VAT. The option is effective for a minimum of three years.

Where a person owns a business and also has separate professional or artistic activities, each entity is treated separately for VAT purposes.

To a limited extent, group registration may be permitted for VAT purposes. The group can only comprise a holding company and all limited liability companies in which the former owns and has owned, directly or indirectly, the majority (greater than 50%) of voting rights from the beginning of the taxable year prior to the one in which the grouping takes place.

No grouping is possible for individuals and partnerships and no foreign entity may be part of a group. The election for this special regime must be made each year before 16 February. Group registration enables the holding company to offset VAT credit and debit positions. Transactions within the group remain taxable and VAT is computed by each company according to the normal rules.

There is, therefore, no particular advantage in including an exempt entity in the group. The holding company is jointly and severally liable for the VAT due from any member of the VAT group.

Public bodies

1.37 Public bodies may be considered to be making supplies in the course of a business with the exception of the following situations:

(*a*) trading in gold and foreign currency, provided one of the parties is the Italian Central Bank, the Italian Exchange Bureau or banks which act as their agents;

(*b*) the running of canteens by the military and police administrations for their personnel.

Foreign businesses

1.38 Foreign businesses without a permanent establishment in Italy, but which make taxable supplies in Italy, are not required to register with the Italian tax authorities. They may appoint a fiscal representative who will register the company and fulfil all VAT obligations. This representative is personally liable for VAT due, together with his principal. If no Italian representative is appointed, the Italian customer must issue the invoices and calculate the VAT due which can then be deducted as input tax.

Luxembourg

General

1.39 A taxable person is any person engaged in economic activities on a regular basis and in an independent manner, regardless of the aims or results of those activities and regardless of where the activities take place. Independence may be refuted on various grounds, particularly:

(*a*) being subject to the instructions of an employer in relation to work;

(*b*) being registered for wage tax purposes; or

(*c*) receiving a fixed payment.

Public bodies

1.40 Public bodies are not regarded as taxable persons in respect of:

(*a*)   exploitation of state property, except supplies from agricultural or forestry activities;

(*b*)   activities involving a collective interest or of a social, cultural, educational or sporting nature, except the renting out of skating rinks and swimming pools;

(*c*)   certain public services, e.g.:

    (i)   supplies by educational bodies of an educational nature;

    (ii)   holiday camps, day nurseries, crèches, etc;

    (iii)   ambulance and fire-fighting services;

(*d*)   abattoir services including the supply of animal carcasses;

(*e*)   certain health and hygiene services (including the collection and distribution of waste and industrial pollutants);

(*f*)   the processing of animal carcasses;

(*g*)   work on roads and urbanisation;

(*h*)   the sale of topographic and urban plans;

(*i*)   the granting of rights to perform road and construction work;

(*j*)   the granting of rights to park on public roads;

(*k*)   the granting of rights to land and park at airports;

(*l*)   services connected with weighing, measuring and gauging;

(*m*)   the granting of rights to use collective antenna receivers;

(*n*)   the supply of funeral and undertaker services;

(*o*)   the granting of rights to use cemeteries/crematoria.

Public bodies are considered to be taxable persons for the supply of gas, electricity, transport etc. However, if the annual turnover from one of these supplies does not usually exceed € 5,000, the public body may, upon request, be treated as not a taxable person for that supply.

Group registration

1.41   VAT grouping of affiliated companies is not possible in Luxembourg.

Foreign businesses

1.42   Foreign businesses which have a permanent establishment in Luxembourg are, in all respects, treated in the same manner as resident businesses. They must be registered and they have the same rights and obligations as resident businesses.

Foreign businesses which do not maintain a permanent establishment in Luxembourg, but make supplies within Luxembourg which are within the scope of VAT, are normally required to appoint a VAT representative who will be responsible for fulfilling their administrative obligations and for payment of tax due.

If the foreign business does not have a VAT representative, liability is transferred to the recipient of the goods or services. Under certain conditions the tax authorities allow the foreign business to register itself without appointing a fiscal representative in Luxembourg. In such cases the foreign business must provide security and meet certain criteria set down by the tax authorities.

The Netherlands

General

1.43   A taxable person is someone who conducts a business or profession independently. The exploitation of goods (e.g. the leasing of immovable property) and the supply of services is deemed to be a business activity. A taxable person may also be someone who does not directly conduct business, e.g. any person who imports goods or acquires new vehicles via an intra-Community acquisition.

Management companies and partnerships

1.44   A management company which supplies staff to another business is usually regarded as a taxable person, although the tax authorities may take a different view where the director of the management company is also a director of the other business.

An association which acts only on behalf of its members is not, in principle, engaged in economic activity. If a partnership is formed, the partnership, rather than the individual partners, will be regarded as a taxable person for VAT purposes. It follows that transactions between partners are not supplies for VAT purposes.

Group registration

1.45   Two or more Dutch resident businesses, or businesses with fixed establishments in the Netherlands, may be registered as a group for VAT purposes if they are closely integrated financially, organisationally and economically.

Financial integration means that more than 50% of the shares are in the hands of one person or company. Organisational integration means that one person or company controls the group, and economic integration means that the members all operate in, or direct their efforts toward, the same market.

Businesses wishing to form a group must make a formal request to the tax authorities who will then give written approval.

A holding company which does no more than own the shares of the subsidiaries cannot form a fiscal unity with its subsidiaries. A company which merely exploits tangible or intangible assets may not be part of a group for VAT purposes.

From the moment a group is created all businesses within the group become jointly and severally liable for the payment of any VAT due from the group.

If a company wishes to leave the group, it must send a written request to the tax authorities.

If a business is split into divisions, there is no effect for VAT purposes. The supplies of one division to another are not subject to VAT, which is due only when goods and services are supplied to other third parties.

Foreign businesses

1.46 A foreign business without a permanent establishment for VAT purposes in the Netherlands, but which makes taxable supplies there, is required to register as a taxable person with the tax authorities responsible for foreign businesses (in Heerlen).

If the foreign business supplies goods or services to a Dutch resident business or legal entity which is liable for VAT, the VAT liability may be transferred to the recipient. Under these circumstances, the foreign business is not required to be registered as a taxable person.

Portugal

General

1.47 In general, a taxable person for VAT purposes is any person who is subject to corporate tax or income tax on his business or professional activities. If a business carries on its activities through more than one establishment, its head office must keep accounting records relating to the transactions carried out in all the branches, together with supporting documentation. Records relating to transactions carried out between branches should also be kept. VAT is then due on the aggregate of positive rated supplies.

Group registration

1.48 It is not permitted to treat a group of dependent companies as a fiscal unity for VAT purposes.

Foreign businesses

1.49   Generally, foreign businesses are treated in the same way as resident businesses. A foreign business is not required to have a permanent establishment or representative in Portugal, but if a representative is appointed, that representative must fulfil all obligations in respect of VAT payable by the principal.

The appointment of a resident representative must be notified to the Portuguese purchaser or customer before a transaction takes place. The representative is then jointly and severally liable for VAT payments. If the foreign business does not have a representative in Portugal, the VAT obligations must be fulfilled by the resident business that purchases the goods or services.

Spain

General

1.50   All businesses, trades or professionals carrying out activities subject to Spanish VAT are obliged to register as taxable persons.

Group registration

1.51   A group of dependent companies may not be treated as a group for VAT purposes. When a business has more than one activity, it must be registered as a single taxable person, unless the activities are carried out through separate legal entities. In that case, each separate entity must have its own VAT registration.

Foreign businesses

1.52   Foreign businesses with no permanent establishment for VAT purposes in Spain are not treated as taxable persons for VAT purposes and do not have to register.

Sweden

General

1.53   A taxable person (an 'entrepreneur') is any person who independently and from any place in the world carries out an economic activity for the purpose of obtaining income and gaining a profit. Organisations and individuals whose activities are similar to this may be deemed to be taxable persons, if their annual turnover exceeds SEK 30,000, excluding VAT. Non-profit making organisations are not taxable persons when excluded from income tax liability.

Group registration

1.54 Upon application to the tax authorities, legally independent entities providing financial services or insurance services may, together with a taxable person who supplies them with goods or services, be treated as a single taxable person for VAT purposes. The same applies to two companies that are closely linked and where one company is entitled to account for income tax on behalf of both of them.

United Kingdom

General

1.55 In the UK, a taxable person is a person who makes or intends to make taxable supplies while he is, or is required to be, registered for VAT. However, as a result of case law and EU legislation, the authorities should allow registration to legal entities who can demonstrate they are engaged in any economic activity. Only corporate bodies may have more than one registration through the divisional registration system.

1.56 Registration applies to any legal entity operating in the course or furtherance of business whose taxable turnover in any twelve-month period has exceeded the threshold or if taxable turnover is expected to exceed the limit in the next 30 days. The threshold is normally set each year and is currently GBP 55,000. Businesses may register voluntarily if their turnover is below the limit, or as an intending trader if they expect to make taxable supplies in the future. The threshold is one of the highest in the EU. Certain businesses not otherwise required to be registered, may need to register in cases where assets used in the business are sold and on which VAT has been recovered on acquisition.

Group registration

1.57 Groups of companies may be covered by a single VAT registration number provided certain conditions are met.

To qualify, a business must:

(*a*) be a corporate body resident in the UK;

(*b*) be a fixed establishment in the UK; and

(*c*) satisfy the control requirements.

One company must control all the others to be grouped or the same third party (a corporate body, an individual or partnership) must control them all.

'Control' is defined as:

(i) holding more than 50% voting rights; or

(ii) having the right to appoint or remove a majority of a company's board of directors (those directors holding the majority of control or voting rights) as a member of that company; or

(iii) being a member of another company and controlling alone pursuant to an agreement with the other shareholders or members, a majority of voting rights in it; or

(iv) being a subsidiary of a company which is itself a subsidiary of that other company.

In a group registration, all supplies are treated as made by or to one of the companies treated as the representative member.

The Single Market

1.58   EU acquisitions are included in taxable turnover. If a business is not already VAT registered, the turnover limit applies to acquisitions in a calendar year. Where a supplier from another EU member state supplies goods to non-registered UK customers and arranges delivery, the supplier must register for UK VAT as soon as turnover exceeds the prescribed limit, which has been set at GBP 70,000.

Chapter 2

Taxable Activities

Taxable activities: EU rules

General

2.1   VAT is levied on the following activities:

(*a*)   the supply of goods and services in an EU member state;

(*b*)   the importation of goods;

(*c*)   the acquisition of goods.

Supplies of goods

Definition

2.2   'Supply of goods' means the transfer of the right to dispose of tangible assets as the owner. Each EU member state is obliged to consider electricity, gas, heat, refrigeration and the like as tangible assets.

[*EC Sixth Directive 77/388, Art 5*].

Obligatory extensions to the supply of goods

2.3   Furthermore, in each EU member state the following supplies are deemed supplies of goods:

(*a*)   the transfer of the ownership of goods as a result of expropriation by or on behalf of the government;

(*b*)   the actual handing over of goods pursuant to a hire-purchase agreement or the sale of goods on deferred terms;

(*c*)   the transfer of goods pursuant to a contract under which commission is payable on purchase or sale;

(*d*)   the private use of goods, e.g. the transfer of goods from a business for private use, shall be treated as a supply made for a consideration. However, the provision of samples or gifts of small value for the purpose of the taxable person's business are not to be so treated.

[*EC Sixth Directive 77/388, Art 5(4), 5(6)*].

Optional extensions to the supply of goods

2.4   Each EU member state is entitled to consider the following transactions as the supply of goods:

(*a*)   the supply of certain interests in immovable assets;

(*b*)   the supply of rights giving the holder thereof a right to use immovable assets;

(*c*)   the supply of shares, or interests equivalent to shares, giving the holder thereof rights of ownership or possession of immovable assets;

(*d*)   the handing over of certain works of construction;

(*e*)   the self-supply of goods (i.e. the use for business purposes, by a business, of goods manufactured in the business itself) but only if the business would not have been entitled to a full credit for the VAT previously paid if it had purchased the goods instead of manufacturing them. Goods produced by a third party upon request of the business using goods belonging to that business are deemed to be goods manufactured in the business' own enterprise;

(*f*)   the application of goods by a business for the purposes of a non-taxable activity, but only if the business was entitled to deduct VAT wholly or partly on the acquisition of such goods;

(*g*)   the retention of goods by a taxable person when he ceases to carry out a taxable economic activity where the VAT on such goods was wholly or partly deductible on their acquisition.

[*EC Sixth Directive 77/388, Art 5(3), (5), (7)*].

No taxable supply of goods

2.5   In the event of a transfer of a business as a going concern, each member state may consider that no supply of goods or services has taken place and in that event the recipient shall be treated as the successor to the transferor.

Supplies of services

2.6   A service is any transaction for consideration which does not otherwise qualify as a supply of goods. If there is no consideration, the service is not taxable. The supply of services also includes the transfer of rights such as patent rights, copyrights, licences, etc., with the exception of rights over immovable property which are classified as supplies of goods.

[*EC Sixth Directive 77/388, Art 6*].

Services may include inter alia:

(*a*) assignments of intangible property whether or not it is the subject of a document establishing title;

(*b*) obligations to refrain from an act or to tolerate an act or situation;

(*c*) the performance of services in pursuance of an order made by or in the name of a public authority or in pursuance of the law.

Each member state must consider as supplies of services:

(i) private use of goods where VAT was deductible;

(ii) the self-supply of services by a taxable person.

Although EU countries may derogate from this provision provided that such derogation does not lead to distortion of competition. The taxable amount is the full cost of the service.

[*EC Sixth Directive 77/388, Art 6(2)*].

Where a taxable person acting in his own name but on behalf of another takes part in a supply of services, he shall be considered to have received and supplied those services himself.

[*EC Sixth Directive 77/388, Art 6(4)*].

Imports of goods

2.7 Importation of goods is the entry of goods into free circulation in the territory of a member state of the EU. Since 1993, the term 'import' no longer applies to trade within the EU. Cross-border transactions between EU countries will be considered 'exempt' intra-Community supplies and taxable intra-Community acquisitions.

The territory of the EU for VAT purposes does not include:

(*a*) the Island of Heligoland and the territory of Busingen (Germany);

(*b*) Faroe Islands and Greenland (Denmark);

(*c*) Livigno, Campione d'Italia and the Italian waters of Lake Lugano (Italy);

(*d*) Canary Islands, Ceuta and Melilla (Spain);

(*e*) the overseas departments of the French Republic;

(*f*) Agio Oros (Mount Athos in Greece);

(*g*) Åland Islands (Finland).

Monaco and the Isle of Man are treated as part of the French Republic and the United Kingdom respectively.

[*EC Sixth Directive 77/388, Art 3*].

Acquisitions of goods

General

2.8   Since 1993 the scope of VAT has been extended to intra-Community acquisitions of goods for a consideration. Intra-Community acquisition of goods means acquisition of the right to dispose as owner of movable tangible property dispatched or transported to the person acquiring the goods by or on behalf of the vendor, or the person acquiring the goods to a member state other than that from which the goods are dispatched or transported.

Intra-Community acquisitions of goods by exempt or taxable businesses and non-taxable legal entities (e.g. government bodies) are in principle taxable in the EU member state of destination. If the purchaser is an exempt business or a legal entity which is not a business and purchases have not exceeded a certain level, in the current or previous calendar year, the acquisition is not taxable in the state of acquisition but VAT is levied in the state of supply. Every country can determine its own limit but this should be at least € 10,000. However, the purchaser can opt for taxation in the EU member state of destination.

[*EC Sixth Directive 77/388, Art 28A*].

Fictitious acquisitions

Internal transfers of goods

2.9   The intra-Community acquisition of goods includes the use by a taxable person for the purpose of his business of goods dispatched or transported by or on behalf of that taxable person from one EU member state to another.

The exceptions are explained below:

(*a*)   Flat rate scheme farmers — an intra-Community acquisition of goods is not subject to VAT when it is made by a flat rate scheme farmer for the purpose of his agricultural, forestry or fisheries undertaking. A flat rate scheme farmer is a farmer whose sales are subject to a certain flat rate compensation.

(*b*)   Taxable persons making only exempt supplies — an intra-Community acquisition of goods is not subject to VAT when it is made by a person who makes only exempt supplies of goods and services as they do not give rise to any right to deduction of input tax. The supply, in such cases, is usually taxed in the country of origin.

(*c*)   Non-taxable legal entities — an intra-Community acquisition of goods is not subject to VAT when it is made by a non-taxable legal entity. Non-taxable legal entities are, for example, state, regional and local authorities and other bodies governed by public law in respect of activities or transactions in which they are engaged as public bodies. The definition covers also legal entities which are not engaged in activities which fall within the scope of VAT because they cannot be qualified as 'economic', e.g. a pure holding company.

Acquisitions by the categories of persons mentioned above in (*a*) to (*c*) are not subject to VAT provided these acquisitions do not exceed a minimum threshold of € 10,000, excluding VAT, in a given calendar year. The threshold does not include acquisitions of 'new means of transport' or products subject to excise duties. If the threshold with regard to intra-Community acquisitions of goods is reached during the calendar year by one of the above types, the acquisitions are automatically taxable in the member state where the person is established.

Taxation of the intra-Community acquisition in the Member State of establishment is a consequence whenever the threshold was exceeded in the previous calendar year.

Businesses affected may also opt for taxation in the country of acquisition so long as they remain registered for a minimum period of at least two years.

In the following cases no acquisition takes place:

(i)   the transfer of goods from one EU member state to another where a service is performed for the taxable person involving work on the goods in question which are then returned by him to the EU member state where he is registered for VAT purposes;

(ii)   the transfer of goods for temporary use in the EU member state of arrival for the purpose of the supply of services by the taxable person;

(iii)   the transfer of goods to another EU member state for temporary use for a period not exceeding 24 months, within another EU member state.

[*EC Sixth Directive 77/388, Art 28A*].

25

Special rules for new means of transport

Intra-Community acquisitions of new means of transport

2.10   VAT is due on the intra-Community acquisition of new means of transport by anyone including taxable persons, non-taxable legal entities which are 'exempt from acquisition' and any other non-taxable person (e.g. private persons).

'Means of transport' are defined as:

(*a*)   vessels exceeding 7.5 metres in length;

(*b*)   aircraft, the take-off weight of which exceeds 1,550 kilograms; and

(*c*)   motorised land vehicles, the capacity of which exceeds 48 cubic centimetres or the power of which exceeds 7.2 kilowatts.

Some vessels are excluded from this definition, e.g. certain sea-going vessels used for navigation on the high seas and carrying passengers for reward or used for the purpose of commercial, industrial or fishing activities; and the supply of sea-going vessels used for rescue or assistance at sea, or for inshore fishing.

The supply of aircraft used by airlines operating for reward chiefly on international routes are also excluded from the above definition. International routes include routes between EU member states.

Means of transport are new if:

(i)   they were supplied within three months (six months for vehicles) of the date they were taken into use for the first time; or

(ii)   they have travelled not more than 6,000 km in the case of land vehicles, sailed for not more than 100 hours in the case of vessels, or flown not more than 40 hours in the case of aircraft.

[*EC Sixth Directive 77/388, Art 28A(2)*].

Intra-Community supplies of means of transport

2.11   Any person who, from time to time, supplies a new means of transport to a person acquiring it in another member state, must be regarded as taxable, subject to the normal registration rules.

Specific rules in the various EU countries

Austria

General

2.12 Supplies of goods are defined as transfers by one business to another in the course of business. It is not necessary for the buyer to become the legal owner of the goods.

The following transactions are treated as supplies of goods:

(*a*)   transfer of movable and immovable tangible goods;

(*b*)   intangible supplies, e.g. gas or electricity;

(*c*)   transfer of aggregated objects, e.g. a business unit.

Although the transfer of real property is normally exempt from VAT the supplier may opt for taxation.

Supplies of services

2.13 Generally, all transactions other than supplies of goods are considered to be supplies of services. The transfer of rights is always treated as a supply of services.

Territory

2.14 VAT applies to the whole territory of Austria. A special tax rate of 16% is levied in the Mittelberg and Jungholz areas.

Private use

2.15 The private use of goods and services is a deemed supply, subject to VAT.

Finance leases and hire-purchase agreements

2.16 If goods are hired with an option to purchase, each transaction must be reviewed on its merits to decide whether a supply of goods or services has been effected.

Thresholds for intra-Community acquisitions

2.17 Non-business entities and exempt business entities are subject to VAT for their intra-Community acquisitions above a limit of € 11,000.

Chain transactions

2.18   Each business within a chain shall be deemed to have conducted a taxable transaction in the form of a supply of goods.

Agents and auctioneers

2.19   A transfer of goods conducted by an agent in his own name but on behalf of his client is treated as a supply of goods both to and by the agent.

Goods for sale at auction are first deemed to be delivered by the supplier to the auctioneer and then from the auctioneer to the customer.

Belgium

Supply of goods

2.20   This includes all transfers or disposals, as owner or transferor, pursuant to a contract and usually for an agreed consideration, of movable tangible assets, including supplies of electricity, gas, heat and refrigeration, as well as the delivery of consumables by way of rental agreement.

The following are also treated as supplies of goods:

(*a*)   taking movable goods out of the business for private use or non-business purposes;

(*b*)   transfers of goods without consideration, except in the case of free commercial samples or low priced commercial gifts;

(*c*)   the use for investment purposes of goods originally acquired for resale;

(*d*)   the transfer for consideration of new constructions, provided the sale takes place before 31 December of the year following that during which the real estate tax is registered for the first time;

(*e*)   transfer of goods to another EU member state or export of goods;

(*f*)   transactions made by a commission agent on behalf of a principal.

Certain items such as securities (shares, bonds) are not included here.

Supplies of services

2.21   This covers all transactions which are not considered to be supplies of goods, including:

(*a*)   intellectual services;

(*b*)   secondment of personnel in exchange for payment;

(*c*)   acting as a representative, agent or commission agent;

(*d*)   business activities in exchange for payment;

(*e*)   rental of parking facilities and furnished premises;

(*f*)   access to cultural activities, sports, etc.;

(*g*)   banking services;

(*h*)   services provided by travel agencies, etc.

Supplies of immovable property

2.22   A supply of immovable property takes place where a professional building contractor supplies a new building and transfers title before, during or after construction, but not later than 31 December of the third year following that in which the property tax (12%) is recorded on the tax register for the first time. If the building is not transferred within the required period, there is to be a deemed transfer for private use. Individuals who occasionally construct or contract for the construction of a building are not normally taxable, but may opt for taxation. It is important to note, however, that the sale of land is never subject to VAT.

Private use

2.23   If movable goods are taken from a business for private use, or more generally for non-business purposes or for disposal free of charge, there is a deemed taxable supply. However, supplies of samples and low value gifts are not subject to tax.

The private use of services is generally not taxable.

Finance leases and hire-purchase agreements

2.24   Finance leases constitute supplies of services whereas hire-purchase agreements are supplies of goods.

Agents and auctioneers

2.25   The purchase of goods by a commission agent, and their resale to another party, represent two transactions both subject to VAT even if the goods are transferred directly to the ultimate buyer.

Any sale or purchase through an auctioneer is treated as a sale to, and subsequently a sale by, the auctioneer if the auctioneer issues documentation in his own name. VAT is due on both transactions.

Denmark

Territory

2.26   Danish VAT law covers the whole Kingdom of Denmark except Greenland, the Free Port of Copenhagen and the Faroe Islands.

Supplies of goods

2.27   VAT is levied on the supply of all new and second-hand goods.

The supply of goods includes:

(*a*)   gas, water, electricity, heating etc.;

(*b*)   coins, if sold as collectors' items;

(*c*)   live animals and plants.

The following items are not regarded as goods and are therefore not subject to VAT:

 (i) bonds, shares, other securities and lotteries;

(ii) real estate.

VAT on expenditure attributable to the private use of goods is not reclaimable.

When goods are sold successively by a number of businesses, each of the sales is treated as a taxable transaction, even if the goods are actually transferred by their original owner directly to the last customer in the chain.

Hire-purchase agreements are regarded as taxable supplies of goods.

Supplies of services

2.28   VAT is chargeable on all services other than those specifically listed as exempt under Danish VAT legislation.

Where a business uses services from its own resources, they are subject to VAT in the same way as goods put to private use.

Agents and auctioneers

2.29   If an agent stores and distributes products for his principal, he will normally be regarded as a taxable person. The taxable value attributable to the agent's account will be the entire consideration received by the agent from the principal.

Auctioneers are also taxable persons. Therefore, items sold at an auction will in general be taxable.

Finland

Supply of goods

2.30   VAT is payable on supplies of goods within Finland made in the course of business, on importation of goods from non-EU countries and on intra-Community acquisitions.

Goods include movable objects and real estate. Also, electricity, gas, heat, refrigeration and other similar energy commodities are considered to be goods. The sale of goods means the transfer of the right of ownership for consideration.

Sales to taxable persons and public bodies subject to VAT in other member states are exempt from VAT in Finland provided the VAT registration number of the purchaser is obtained and proof of dispatch has been kept.

A transfer by a business of its own goods to another member state without a sale, e.g. to create stock in the other member state, is treated as an intra-Community supply. The following are not considered to be intra-Community supplies:

(*a*)   transfer of goods in order for work to be carried out on those goods in another member state and returned to Finland;

(*b*)   temporary transfer to another member state of goods in order to supply services;

(*c*)   transfer of goods to be supplied on board ships, aircraft and trains during transport in the EU;

(*d*)   transfer of goods to be installed or assembled in another member state;

(*e*)   transfer of goods for distance sales;

(*f*)   certain other temporary transfers.

For goods sold to private individuals in other member states the Finnish business must account for VAT unless, under the 'distance selling' rules, registration is required in the other member state.

Installation/assembly

2.31   Goods sold with installation or assembly are deemed to be supplied in Finland if the installation or assembly is performed in Finland. If the project lasts for up to nine months the reverse charge applies, but for projects over nine months a foreign supplier must register in Finland.

Supply of services

2.32   VAT is payable on supplies of services made by businesses. These are defined as any commercial activity for consideration other than a supply of goods. Cross-border services are also liable to VAT if the place of supply is Finland.

Import of goods

2.33   Goods imported from non-EU member states are subject to customs duty and VAT on importation. VAT paid is recoverable through the VAT return if the goods are used in activities subject to VAT.

Acquisitions of goods

2.34   VAT on the acquisition of goods from another EU member state is accounted for through the VAT return of the business. The same amount is deductible in the month of acquisition provided the goods are used for a taxable purpose.

New means of transport

2.35   The transfer to Finland from another EU member state of new means of transport is always taxable as an intra-Community acquisition regardless of the status of the supplier or the purchaser.

France

General

2.36   The supply of goods is defined as the transfer of ownership of any goods even those requisitioned by a public authority.

The following transactions are also deemed to be taxable transactions:

(*a*)   purchase of capital assets;

(*b*)   part-exchange transactions;

(*c*)   in-kind loans;

(*d*)   the transfer of own goods by a taxable person to another EU member state.

The supply of immovable property is generally exempt, but taxable in certain cases, including construction services, transactions carried out by property companies, transactions carried out by persons who subdivide land into separate sections, and transactions carried out by intermediaries.

There is a taxable supply when goods are put to private use. However, the private use of goods by a sole proprietor for his normal requirements and those of his family are not subject to VAT. In such cases, the input VAT must be repaid.

Mandatory or optional taxable activities

2.37 The following activities are mandatorily taxable under French law:

(*a*) self-supply of goods and services, meat products;

(*b*) supplies of certain products to a person who is not liable for tax, e.g. alcohol, canned foods;

(*c*) operations undertaken by an estate agent;

(*d*) building supplies;

(*e*) supplies of goods and services by co-operatives;

(*f*) television licence fees.

Individuals or legal entities who carry on exempt activities or activities outside the scope of VAT, can elect to be subject to VAT, but only for certain activities specified by French law, as follows:

(i) leasing of commercial buildings;

(ii) leasing of agricultural property;

(iii) sales of building land to a private individual by the local community;

(iv) certain operations undertaken by banking and financial establishments (e.g. transferable security transactions, bills of exchange transactions);

(v) associations for blind persons and for handicapped workers.

Chain transactions

2.38 In the case of chain transactions, every time a business sells positive rated goods, it must charge VAT on the selling price.

Hire-purchase agreements/finance leases

2.39 The hire-purchase of goods is defined as the actual supply of goods pursuant to a contract for the hire of goods for a certain period of time. The hire purchase is considered as a supply of goods at the time they are physically transferred to the purchaser.

Finance leasing is a contract under which a person leasing goods from another person may (after expiration of the contract) elect to purchase the goods. Finance leasing is a supply of services.

Intermediaries

2.40   Intermediaries, e.g. commission agents and general agents who act as intermediaries in the supply of goods or services, normally render a service and are only taxable on the fees they receive as consideration for such services, provided they meet certain conditions (e.g. the fee must be a percentage of the price of the transaction arranged).

If any of these conditions has not been fulfilled, the intermediary will be subject to VAT on the total transaction price as if he was acting as a principal.

The intermediary must act in the name of and on behalf of the principal (transparent intermediary) and not in his own name (non-transparent intermediary).

Threshold for EU acquisitions by exempt businesses or non-business legal entities

2.41   In order to benefit from exemption, the non-taxable legal person must not have carried out in the previous year, nor carried out in the current year, intra-Community acquisitions amounting to € 10,000, or more, exclusive of VAT.

Germany

General and territory

2.42   German VAT applies within the territory of the Federal Republic of Germany, excluding the so-called *Freihäfen* (harbours with duty free zones), Büsingen (the German enclave in Switzerland) and the island of Helgoland. Special rules apply for the *Zollanschlüsse* of Mittelberg and Jungholz in Austria. The region of Germany and of all other member states of the EU is referred to as the 'common territory', for which special rules apply. The rest of the world is referred to as 'third countries territory'. VAT is only due on the supply of goods and services if they are rendered for consideration, and if the place of supply is within the territory of Germany.

Supplies of goods

2.43   Supplies of goods are defined as transfers from a business to another person, directly or indirectly, of the right to dispose of an item in the recipient's own name. It is not necessary for the recipient to become the legal owner of the goods.

German VAT legislation uses the term 'objects' instead of 'goods', in relation to supplies. Goods include:

(*a*)   movable and immovable tangible goods;

(*b*)   aggregated items, e.g. combinations of various separate tangible goods to form one new unit;

(*c*)   intangible goods, e.g. water, gas, electricity.

Transfers and assignments of rights are not considered to be supplies of goods.

The supply of immovable property is exempt. However, if a business supplies immovable property to another business, the supplier may opt for taxation.

Supplies of services

2.44   A supply of services is defined as any supply which is not a supply of goods. This includes cases where the business merely agrees to refrain from or tolerate an act, as well as the leasing of goods and the transfer of rights, and services by travel agencies.

Where a business undertakes to carry out a process or work on goods, the procurement of the materials constitutes a delivery, provided that at least one of these materials is supplied by the business itself *(Werk-Lieferung)*. If, however, none of the materials is supplied by the business this is a supply of services *(Werk-Leistung)*.

Private use

2.45   The private use of goods and/or services is a deemed supply and is therefore subject to VAT. This use is only taxable if the tax on acquisition in respect of the acquired goods and/or services has been partly or fully recovered.

Intra-Community acquisitions

2.46   Intra-Community acquisitions are subject to German VAT. An intra-Community acquisition comprises the supply of goods from one member state of the EU to Germany, if the recipient is a German business purchasing on its own behalf, or a non-business legal entity purchasing for non-business reasons, and the supply is made by a business.

Intra-Community acquisition is also assumed, if a business transfers its own goods from a member state to Germany for permanent use.

An intra-Community acquisition has not taken place where:

(*a*)   the recipient performs only tax-free activities;

(*b*)   is a small business; or

(*c*)   the recipient is either an agricultural or forestry enterprise or a legal entity purchasing for non-business reasons on behalf of another non-business legal entity.

In addition, the purchase value must have been less than € 12,500 in the preceding year, and will be less than € 12,500 in the current year. In all cases, the recipient may opt for taxation on the basis of intra-Community acquisition and the option is binding for two years.

An intra-Community acquisition is not taxable if margin scheme rules have been applied to the supply in another member state.

Import from countries outside of EU

2.47   The import of goods from a non-member state to Germany is subject to VAT.

Intra-Community acquisition of new cars, ships or planes

2.48   Where any of the following purchases new vehicles, i.e. cars, ships or planes meeting certain usage rules within the first months of being new, this is considered to be an intra-Community acquisition if the vehicle is delivered from a member state to Germany:

(*a*)   a business for non-business use;

(*b*)   a private person;

Transfer of a business as a going concern

2.49   the transfer of a business as a going concern is not subject to VAT.

Greece

Supplies of goods

2.50   Supplies of goods are any transactions by which the owner's right to dispose of tangible movable goods and immovable property is transferred to another person.

For there to be a taxable supply of goods, the following conditions must be met:

(*a*)   the supply must be made by a taxable person acting in the course of a business;

(*b*)   there must be a bilateral agreement, transferring the ownership of goods; and

(*c*)   the goods must be removed to the customer's possession, so that the customer is in a position to exercise control over the goods as owner.

The supply of real property is a taxable transaction if the following apply:

(i)   the transfer relates specifically to buildings, and not to immovable property in general;

(ii)   the transfer must include the necessary building land;

(iii)   the buildings must be new, i.e. the transfer must take place prior to first occupation; and

(iv)   a building permit must have been issued.

Supplies of services

2.51   Supplies of services are broadly defined as any transactions which do not constitute supplies of goods.

Territory

2.52   VAT applies to the whole territory of Greece, except the area of Mount Athos which is outside the EU for VAT purposes.

Private use

2.53   The private use of goods and services is a deemed supply subject to VAT.

Finance leases

2.54   If the finance lease provides for the transfer of ownership of goods, then it is considered a supply of goods.

Agents

2.55   In cases where a taxable person acts as an intermediary in a supply of services, acting in his own name but on behalf of another person, the taxable person is considered to have received and supplied those services as principal.

Thresholds for intra-Community acquisitions

2.56   The limit over which exempt businesses or non-business legal entities are subject to VAT for their intra-Community acquisitions is € 29,347.03 (GRD 10,000,000).

Ireland

Supplies of goods

2.57   A taxable supply of goods includes the normal transfer of ownership of goods on payment by one taxable person to another person. Goods are defined as all movable and immovable objects with a few minor exceptions. There is no supply by the owner until the buyer signifies his approval or acceptance or otherwise indicates that he is taking the goods.

The following are also treated as supplies of goods:

(*a*)   transfer of ownership of goods by agreement, whether or not accompanied by a transfer of possession;

(*b*)   the seizure of goods by a sheriff or other person acting under legal authority;

(*c*)   the provision of electricity, gas and any form of power, heat, refrigeration or ventilation;

(*d*)   the provision of goods under a hire-purchase contract;

(*e*)   the provision by a contractor of goods made up from materials in whole or part provided by his customer;

(*f*)   the application or appropriation of materials or goods to some private or exempt use.

When a taxable person makes a supply of goods or services liable to VAT at different rates for a single charge, then VAT is chargeable on the entire supply at the highest rate of VAT applicable to any of the goods in the package. This is known as the 'package' or the 'cocktail' rule. An example is where a book is sold with an audio tape for a single price; the sale is liable at the standard rate, even though the book would be liable at the zero rate of VAT, if sold separately.

The Revenue however does, by concession, allow certain traders to split a package into component parts and to charge VAT at the different VAT rates on different items. An application for such a concession must be approved by the Revenue first.

Supplies of services

2.58   The supply of services is defined as the performance or omission of any act or the toleration of any situation other than the supply of goods. In addition, Irish law lists various transactions which would ordinarily be considered supplies of goods but are deemed supplies of services (e.g. supplies of food and drink in hotels, restaurants etc.).

Software

2.59   The supply of standardised software is regarded as a supply of goods. The supply of customised software is considered to be a taxable service.

Private use/self-supply

2.60   If a business transfers goods for a non-business or non-taxable use, in cases where the person was entitled to a deduction of the VAT incurred on the purchase, acquisition or import of the goods transferred, there is a taxable supply for VAT purposes. The only self-supply of services currently taxable is catering.

Hire-purchase agreements and finance leases

2.61   Hire-purchase agreements are considered to be supplies of goods.

The leasing of movable goods including means of transport is a supply of services.

Contract work

2.62   The handing-over of goods which have been developed, constructed, manufactured, produced or extracted from goods entrusted in whole or part by the customer is a supply of goods.

Repair and maintenance services and building services

2.63   Repair and maintenance services and building services are generally liable to VAT at the rate of 12.5%. However, where the cost of goods (to the person making the supply) used in the provision of a service, exceeds two-thirds of the charge for the service, the transaction is regarded as a supply of goods, rather than the supply of a service. VAT is then chargeable at the rate applicable to the goods. This is known as the 'two-thirds' rule.

Auctioneers and agents

2.64   Auctioneers and agents are treated as if they buy and sell goods as principals where they make arrangements for the sale of goods.

Transfer of a business

2.65   The transfer of ownership of goods in connection with the transfer of a business or part thereof to another taxable person is deemed not to be a supply for VAT purposes.

Thresholds for intra-Community acquisitions

2.66   The annual limit over which exempt businesses or non-business legal entities are subject to VAT for their intra-Community acquisitions is € 41,000. However, the registration turnover limit for a person who is in business but not established in Ireland is nil.

Italy

General

2.67   Only transactions which are performed in the course or furtherance of a business are subject to VAT. Transactions carried out by certain persons will always be performed in the course of a business. Those persons include stock companies, limited liability companies, limited partnerships and limited partnerships with share capital, partnerships, co-operatives, mutual insurance companies, de facto companies and non-resident companies. For transactions conducted by other persons, the exclusive or principal aim of the transactions should be the carrying on of a business enterprise.

The following transactions are not considered to be transactions exercised in the course or furtherance of business:

(a)   the provision by consortia and cooperative societies of mutual guarantees with respect to the quality of products and the checking thereof, as well as the application of quality marks to products by them on behalf of their members;

(*b*)   the delivery of goods and the rendering of services relating to the advertising of political parties, provided such political parties are represented in Parliament.

Supplies of goods

2.68   The supply of goods is defined as the transfer of ownership to the acquiring party pursuant to a contract for consideration or the creation or transfer of rights in property of any kind. In order for there to be a supply, it is essential that there is a contract for the transfer of ownership of goods.

Supplies of services

2.69   Generally, all transactions other than supplies of goods, carried out in exchange for consideration, are considered to be services. Services usually consist of the obligation to perform or refrain from performing acts, or the granting of permission to perform acts.

Certain transactions are *inter alia* not considered to be taxable services:

(*a*)   transfer, licensing or sublicensing of copyrights by authors;

(*b*)   writing of articles by authors for newspapers, periodicals, and encyclopaedias;

(*c*)   granting of bond loans;

(*d*)   transfer of contracts to supply currency, to supply a business enterprise or an independent working branch of an enterprise, and to supply unimproved land;

(*e*)   transfer of contracts under a merger contract, or following the change in the corporate form of a business;

(*f*)   services supplied by agents and intermediaries to authors relating to copyrights of a literary or other artistic character and services supplied to protect such copyrights;

(*g*)   services supplied by a commission agent if he acts in his own name on behalf of another person, and the services supplied by an agent if the services relate to a transfer which is deemed not to be a supply of goods.

Territory

2.70   The territory of Italy for VAT purposes does not include the municipalities of Livigno and the Campione d'Italia situated in an enclave in Switzerland near Lugano, and the national waters of Lake Lugano.

Leasing of immovable property

2.71   The leasing and renting of immovable property for business purposes is generally subject to VAT. However, certain types of leasing and renting of agricultural land, agricultural businesses and areas not designated for construction are exempt from VAT.

Agents and auctioneers

2.72   If an agent conducts a transaction on behalf of someone else, the agent is considered to have supplied a service, and commission will be subject to VAT.

An agent who buys or sells goods in his own name, but on behalf of someone else, is considered to have made a supply of goods.

Private use

2.73   Allocation for private use is deemed to be a supply of goods and therefore subject to VAT. The private use of services is also taxable.

Hire-purchase agreements and finance leases

2.74   Hire-purchase contracts are considered to be supplies of goods, whereas finance leases are supplies of services.

Chain transactions

2.75   Each business within a chain shall be deemed to have conducted a taxable transaction in the form of a supply of goods.

Thresholds for intra-Community acquisitions

2.76   The annual limit above which exempt businesses or non-business legal entities are subject to VAT for their intra-Community acquisitions is € 8,263.00.

Luxembourg

Supplies of goods

2.77   A supply of goods is defined as the transfer of the right to dispose of goods. For VAT purposes, the transfer is determined from an economic point of view.

Supplies of services

2.78   Services are broadly defined as all supplies which do not constitute supplies of goods or imports. Services normally include the granting of rights, obligations to permit or to refrain from doing something and services performed by law or under an order issued by or in the name of a public authority.

Chain transactions

2.79   In chain transactions, goods are deemed to have been delivered to and supplied by each person in the chain.

Private use

Goods

2.80   If goods are removed from a business free of charge for non-business purposes, there is a deemed taxable supply. Private use in the form of gifts of small value and of samples for business purposes are not considered taxable supplies. The private use of business assets is subject to VAT.

Services

2.81   Private use of services in general is not a taxable supply.

Hire-purchase contracts

2.82   Hire-purchase contracts for goods are deemed supplies of goods.

Supplies and leasing of immovable property

2.83   The supply of immovable property is exempt from VAT, unless all or part of it has been developed by the business under a sale or construction agreement. A business which supplies immovable property to another business may opt for taxation.

The leasing of immovable property is normally exempt from VAT. However, a business which leases immovable property to another business may opt to waive the exemption and request that the supply be subject to VAT.

Agents and auctioneers

2.84   If a business, acting in its own name but on behalf of a third party, arranges the supply of services which are actually provided by that other party, it will be treated as having supplied those services itself. Thus, there are two deemed supplies of services: one from the person actually providing the services to the agent and one from the agent to the final consumer. If an agent does not act in its own name, VAT is due only on the commission fee it charges.

Thresholds for intra-Community acquisitions

2.85   The annual limit above which exempt business or non-business legal entities are subject to VAT for their intra-Community acquisitions is € 10,000.

The Netherlands

Supplies of goods

2.86   The supply of goods includes the transfer of ownership pursuant to a contract. The following transactions are deemed supplies of goods:

(*a*)   transfer of legal ownership of property by contract;

(*b*)   actual delivery of goods pursuant to a hire-purchase agreement;

(*c*)   actual transfer of goods to a customer from a business which has manufactured the goods from materials owned by and supplied to the business by the customer;

(*d*)   transfer of ownership of goods as a result of expropriation by or on behalf of a government body;

(*e*)   disposal of business assets;

(*f*)   transfer of goods under an agreement to install them or incorporate them into other goods;

(*g*)   establishment, assignment, alteration and cessation of certain rights in immovable property.

Supplies of services

2.87   Taxable supplies of services are any taxable supplies which are not taxable supplies of goods.

Territory

2.88   The territory of the Netherlands includes for VAT purposes the European territory of that country, but excludes the Dutch Antilles and Aruba.

Finance and operating leases

2.89   For VAT purposes, finance lease transactions are deemed to be supplies of goods according to a resolution of the Dutch Ministry of Finance. The supply takes place when the goods become the property of the purchaser. Finance leases include all transactions in which goods are supplied to the user for a stipulated period of time during which the user pays periodic amounts and at the end of which the lessee has an option to buy the goods. The current value of all lease payments, exclusive of the finance costs, must be equal to the purchase price of the goods. If the user does not wish to apply the resolution of the Dutch Ministry of Finance, the finance lease is deemed to be a supply of services.

Operating leases are deemed supplies of services and include all transactions whereby the property is leased to the user in the ordinary sense, i.e. use of the property must conform to an agreement which may be terminated at any time, and pursuant to which periodic payments are made.

Supplies of real estate

2.90   The supply of 'new' real estate is a taxable supply for VAT purposes. This includes the supply of real estate up to two years after it has been brought into use for the first time.

A supply of real estate after this period is taxable provided both the supplier and purchaser opt for taxation. In this case the VAT liability is transferred to the customer and the customer must pay the VAT due to the tax authorities. This option to tax must take place before the supply is made.

The supply of real estate takes place when economic ownership is transferred to the purchaser.

Private use of goods and services

2.91   There is a taxable supply of goods put to private use only if effected by individuals. Other taxable legal entities do not make taxable supplies in such cases, e.g. when gifts are given to employees. In such cases, credit for input tax will not normally be given (see Chapter 7).

Auctions

2.92   Goods for sale at auctions are first deemed to be delivered by the supplier to the auctioneer and then from the auctioneer to the customer.

Triangulation

2.93   The Dutch Ministry of Finance has published a resolution to implement the simplification provisions of the EU Directive for triangular transactions as follows:

The first supplier is deemed to make an intra-Community supply to the second supplier which is deemed to make an intra-Community acquisition in its own country followed by an intra-Community supply to the final customer.

The final customer is deemed to make an intra-Community acquisition in the arrival country and must file VAT returns accordingly.

The scope of this resolution is widened by a ministerial decree. Accordingly, the simplified procedure may be used even where not all the conditions of the simplification directive are met. For example, it is not necessary for the first supplier to arrange transportation; the second supplier may do so.

Even if the second supplier is registered in the EU member state of final arrival, the simplified measures may be used. However, where that company is located outside the EU, and is not registered in any EU member state, the benefits of the simplified measures are not available. Such a non-EU company may, however, register for VAT purposes in the Netherlands. In practice, the Dutch VAT authorities allow a registration in order to apply the simplified measures for triangular sales even if the intermediary does not perform any VAT relevant activities in the Netherlands.

Commission agents

2.94   If a business, acting in its own name but on behalf of a third party, arranges the supply of services which are actually provided by that other party, it will be treated as having supplied them itself. Thus, there are two deemed supplies of services: one from the person actually providing the services to the agent and one from the agent to the final consumer. Where an agent does not act in its own name, VAT is due only on the commission fee charged.

Telecommunications

2.95   Telecommunication services provided by the Dutch KPN Telecom are subject to VAT. The place where the service is deemed to have been rendered is where the consumer is located, unless the consumer is an individual located in an EU member state, in which case the supplier accounts for the tax. The interpretation of the category 'telecommunications' is broad and includes internet and e-mail etc.

Sale of goods on a consignment basis by foreign (EU) businesses

2.96   The Dutch Ministry of Finance has issued a resolution allowing suppliers resident in another EU member state, who send goods to consignment holders in The Netherlands in expectation of onward sales by the consignment holders, to treat the transaction as an intra-Community sale.

The Dutch consignment holder pays the VAT due as an intra-Community acquisition of the goods in the Netherlands and will be held liable for onward sales.

The above system avoids the necessity for the foreign supplier to register in the Netherlands.

Supplies of goods to other EU countries with local VAT

2.97   The Dutch Ministry of Finance has reached a further agreement in a resolution regarding supplies of goods to other EU countries.

If a Dutch supplier makes supplies to other EU countries (e.g. Germany), it is possible to charge German VAT to the German customers instead of treating the sale as a normal intra-Community supply. In this case, the Dutch supplier must be registered for VAT in Germany. The Dutch supplier pays German VAT on the company's German VAT return in respect of the transfer of goods in the course of the company's business from the Netherlands to Germany, and this qualifies as a fictitious intra-Community acquisition in Germany. The Dutch supplier may deduct this German VAT as input tax. The intra-Community acquisition is followed by a normal domestic supply by the Dutch supplier in Germany.

Thresholds for intra-Community acquisitions

2.98   The annual limit above which exempt businesses or non-business legal entities are subject to VAT for their intra-Community acquisitions is € 10,436 (NLG 23,000).

Portugal

Supplies of goods

2.99   Supplies of goods are defined as the transfer for consideration of the right to dispose of tangible property as owner.

In addition, the following transactions are treated as supplies of goods:

(*a*)   the delivery of movable goods under a sales contract in which the seller retains the ownership until total or part payment is made by the purchaser;

(*b*)   goods retained by the customer of the supplier of merchandise placed on consignment (sale or return) which have not been sold within twelve months of the date on which the delivery was made;

(*c*)   the production by a business of movable goods to be assembled or processed for a certain purpose.

Supplies of services

2.100   Any transaction involving a supply for consideration which is not a supply or importation of goods is treated as a supply of services.

2.101   *Taxable Activities*

Territory

2.101   The Portuguese territory for VAT purposes includes the mainland in the Iberian Peninsula and the autonomous regions of Madeira and Azores.

Private use

2.102   The appropriation of goods by a business for private use and business gifts is subject to VAT where the business claims a credit for input VAT on acquisition.

Supplies of samples and gifts of relatively low market value (up to € 14.96 per item) are not subject to VAT. The private use of services is usually taxable.

Supplies of immovable property

2.103   The supply (including finance leasing) of real property is not subject to VAT. However, the vendor may opt for taxation, provided that both he and the purchaser are in business.

Chain transactions

2.104   Where several businesses enter into a series of transactions in respect of the same goods, but the actual right of disposal as owner is transferred directly from the first business to the last recipient in the chain, then each business is treated as having conducted a taxable transaction in the form of a simultaneous supply of goods.

Hire-purchase agreements

2.105   Hire-purchase agreements are considered to be taxable supplies of goods.

Finance leases of movable property

2.106   Finance leases of movable property are subject to VAT.

Agents and auctioneers

2.107   If an intermediary or agent conducts a transaction on behalf of another person, he is considered to have supplied a service and his commission is then subject to VAT. Where the supply of services is made through an agent who acts in his own name, the agent is considered first as purchaser and then as supplier of such services. No special provisions apply to auctioneers.

Thresholds for intra-Community acquisitions

2.108   The annual limit above which exempt businesses or non-business legal entities are subject to VAT for their intra-Community acquisitions is € 8,978.36.

Spain

General

2.109   VAT is charged on supplies of goods or services which are taxable and made by taxable persons in the course or furtherance of business.

Supplies of goods

2.110   For VAT purposes, finance leases with an option to acquire are considered to be supplies of goods from the moment the parties involved in the contract agree to exercise the contract, or on such date as the option is compulsorily exercisable by either party.

The construction or the refurbishment of a building may also be treated as a supply of goods for VAT purposes, where the contractor supplies materials with a value exceeding 20% of the total value of the finished work.

The supply of standardised computer products, including support and programs or information incorporated in it, is also treated as a supply of goods.

Supplies of services

2.111   Operating and finance leases that are not considered to be supplies of goods must be treated as supplies of services.

Territory

2.112   The Spanish territory for VAT purposes includes the mainland and the Balearic Islands but excludes the Canary Islands and the North African territories of Ceuta and Melilla.

Thresholds for intra-Community acquisitions

2.113   Non-registered entities must register for VAT in Spain if their annual intra-Community acquisitions exceed € 10,000.

Sweden

Supplies of goods and services

2.114   A taxable person levies VAT on all sales of goods and services, except where these are specifically exempted (see Chapter 4).

The services of intermediaries are subject to VAT notwithstanding the VAT liability of the goods or services which are the subject of the arrangements, unless exemption for such is explicitly stated in the law, e.g. the services of insurance intermediaries (see Chapter 4).

United Kingdom

General

2.115   VAT is charged on any supply of goods or services which is a taxable supply made by a taxable person in the course or furtherance of any business carried on by the person. The term 'supply' is not defined in legislation, but includes all forms of supply, but not anything done other than for consideration.

Certain transactions are considered supplies of neither goods nor services, such as the transfer of a business as a going concern or supplies within a VAT group.

Supplies of goods

2.116   A taxable supply of goods generally covers the normal transfer of goods on payment by one taxable person to another. Goods are defined as all movable and immovable objects with minor exceptions. The following are also treated as supplies of goods:

(*a*)   any transfer of the whole property in goods (the transfer of an undivided share in property is a supply of services);

(*b*)   the transfer of possession of goods under an agreement for the sale of the goods or under agreements which expressly contemplate the future transfer of the property (this includes hire-purchase and conditional sale agreements);

(*c*)   the supply of any form of power, heat, refrigeration or ventilation;

(*d*)   the grant, assignment or surrender of a major interest in land;

(*e*)   the disposal of business assets (except a gift of goods made in the course of business where the cost to the donor is less than GBP 50).

Supplies of services

2.117 Under UK legislation, anything which is not a supply of goods but is done for a consideration is a supply of services. Where services are received from abroad by a person, which would be taxable if supplied in the UK, the taxable person is deemed to have supplied those services in the course of furtherance of his business.

Territory

2.118 For the purpose of VAT legislation relating to the making of taxable supplies, the UK consists of the territories of the United Kingdom, including the Isle of Man but excluding the Channel Islands.

Finance and operating leases

2.119 Goods sold under hire or lease purchase contracts involve both a taxable supply of goods and a supply of credit or finance which is exempt from VAT where a separate charge is made for this and it is disclosed to the customer. If no such charge is made or disclosed, then the whole consideration is treated as a taxable supply. Operating leases and hiring of goods are supplies of services.

Real estate

2.120 The supply by means of a grant, assignment or surrender of a major interest in land is a supply of goods. The term 'major interest' in relation to land means the freehold or a tenancy or leasehold exceeding 21 years (a slightly different definition applies to property in Scotland).

The grant of any other interest in, or right over land, or any licence to occupy land, constitutes a supply of services. The grant of any interest in land is generally exempt unless specified.

Private use/self-supplies of goods and services

2.121 Where specific goods or services received, produced or provided by a person in the course of furtherance of his business are neither supplied to another person nor incorporated in other goods produced in the course of the business, but are used by him for the purpose of the business, there is provision for it to be deemed that the goods or services are supplied by him for the purpose of the business and to him in the course of it.

In the UK, self-supply provisions exist for stationery and construction services.

Agents and auctioneers

2.122   Supplies arranged by a disclosed agent or auctioneer are made by or to the principal he represents, and the liability to account for VAT remains with the principal, although special rules may apply.

An agent/principal relationship exists if both parties agree that it does and the agent has agreed with the principal to act on his behalf in relation to the particular transaction concerned. It must always be clearly established that the agent is disclosed and arranging transactions on behalf of the principal rather than trading on his own account.

Amendments were made in the UK to bring the accounting by agents into line with the EU treatment, as in certain cases EU principals incurred UK VAT which put UK agents at a competitive disadvantage.

Thresholds for intra-Community acquisitions

2.123   Under certain circumstances, an acquisition of goods is a taxable supply in the member state in which it takes place. Provided the acquisition is a taxable acquisition, i.e. where the goods are acquired by a person in the course or furtherance of a business carried on by him, and where the supplier is a taxable person in another member state at the time of the transaction, and also provided the goods are not acquired in the making of an exempt supply, then VAT is due on such an acquisition.

Where a person not registered for VAT acquires goods in the UK from a taxable person in another member state in the course of furtherance of his business he is liable to register under the same registration regulations as govern taxable persons in the UK. The registration threshold for taxable supplies within a twelve-month period has historically been increased each financial year. The current limit is GBP 55,000 and for intra-Community acquisitions, the limit applies to a calendar year.

Chapter 3

Place of Taxable Transactions

Place of taxable transactions: EU rules

General

3.1   According to the general principles, supplies of goods and services are subject to VAT if they are performed inside the territory of an EU member state. The question of whether an activity is performed within (or outside) an EU member state is not always straightforward.

Since 1993, for intra-Community trade, a temporary destination system has applied. Supplies to EU member states are exempt with credit in the EU member state of departure, and the acquisition of goods in the EU member state of destination is taxable. It was the intention that from 1997 the definitive origin system would apply in a true single market, whereby intra-Community supplies would be subject to the standard or reduced VAT rate in the state of dispatch, but this has never been brought about.

Place of supply of goods

3.2   The place at which a supply is deemed to take place is as follows:

(*a*)   if the goods are dispatched or transported, the place of supply is where such transport starts. However, where the place of departure of the consignment or transport of the goods is in a non-EU member state, the place of supply by the importer shall be deemed to be within the member state into which the goods are imported;

(*b*)   if the goods are installed or assembled, with or without a trial run, by or on behalf of the supplier, the place of supply shall be deemed to be the place where the goods are installed or assembled, although under EU simplification rules the sale may be treated as an intra-Community supply meaning the purchaser would account for acquisition VAT;

(*c*)   in the case of goods not dispatched or transported, the place where the goods are located at the time of the supply.

If goods are supplied on board ships, aircraft or trains to passengers during their journey within the EU, the supplies are deemed to take place where the passengers commenced their journey.

[*EC Sixth Directive 77/388, Art 8*].

Place of supply of intra-Community acquisitions of goods

General

3.3   The place of supply of the intra-Community acquisition of goods is the place where the goods are at the time when dispatch or transport to the person acquiring them ends.

[*EC Sixth Directive 77/388, Art 28B(A)(I)*].

Triangulation

3.4   For triangular arrangements special rules normally apply. Triangular transactions are transactions where three purchasers are involved from different member states and the goods are delivered directly from the first vendor to the last purchaser. If the goods are delivered from one EU member state to another, the intra-Community acquisition in principle takes place in the EU member state where the transport ends. However, where all three parties are established or registered in different EU member states, the acquisition is deemed to take place in the EU member states which issued the VAT identification number under which the transaction takes place. The acquisition will not be subject to VAT under the normal rules provided that:

(*a*)   the acquirer in the second member state establishes that he has effected the intra-Community acquisition for the purposes of a subsequent supply effected in the third member state and for which the final purchaser has been designated as the person liable for the VAT; and

(*b*)   the obligations for declaration have been fulfilled by the acquirer.

[*EC Sixth Directive 77/388, Art 28C(E)(3)*].

Place of supply for distance sales

Main rule: taxation in the EU member state of destination

3.5   Distance sales are, in principle, taxable in the EU member state to which the goods are sent.

A sale of goods is a 'distance sale' if the goods are dispatched or transported by or on behalf of the supplier from one EU member state to another and where the purchaser, for whatever reason, is not registered for VAT. Additionally, the above rule regarding the place of supply only applies for the following purchasers:

(*a*) 'flat rate' scheme farmers;

(*b*) 'taxable' persons who are not entitled to deduct VAT and whose intra-Community purchases have not exceeded the minimum threshold of € 10,000 and who have not opted for taxation in the EU member state of arrival of the goods;

(*c*) non-taxable legal entities whose intra-Community purchases have not exceeded the minimum threshold of € 10,000 and who have not opted for taxation in the EU member state of arrival of the goods;

(*d*) any other non-taxable persons (e.g. private individuals).

Exception: taxation in EU member state of departure

3.6 Distance sales are taxable in the EU member state of departure if goods are supplied below a threshold of € 100,000 (excluding VAT) to the same EU member state of arrival. If the threshold is exceeded the main rule applies and registration is required in the country to which the goods are dispatched. If the threshold is exceeded in a certain year, sales will be automatically taxable in that EU member state during the following year.

Note that businesses selling below the threshold may opt for taxation in the country of arrival. This can be of benefit if the VAT rate in the EU member state of arrival is lower than that of the member state of departure.

EU member states may limit the threshold to € 35,000 instead of € 100,000.

[*EC Sixth Directive 77/388, Art 28B(B)(1), (2)*].

Exclusions from distance sales

3.7 The main rule for distance sales does not apply to the supply of new means of transport and goods for assembly or installation.

Place of supply of services

Main rule

3.8 The rules with respect to the supply of services are complicated. The basic rule is that it takes place where the supplier belongs. The place of belonging is usually the fixed establishment most closely connected with the supply or, if there is no such establishment, a permanent address or place of residence.

[*EC Sixth Directive 77/388, Art 9*].

Exceptions

3.9   There are, however, several exceptions:

(*a*)   services associated with immovable property, including the services of estate agents and services of preparing and coordinating construction work such as the services of architects and firms involved with on-site supervision, are supplied where the property is situated;

(*b*)   transport of goods and persons takes place where the actual transport occurs, in proportion to distances covered. For the transport of goods from one EU member state to another special rules apply (see below);

(*c*)   the supply of ancillary transport services such as loading, unloading, handling and similar activities is taxable in the EU member state where they are physically carried out. If these services relate to the intra-Community transport of goods, special provisions apply (see 3.8 below);

(*d*)   services consisting of cultural, artistic, sporting, scientific, educational, entertainment or similar activities, including the service of those organising such activities, are supplied where the activity is physically carried out;

(*e*)   the valuation of movable tangible property and work on movable tangible property is where the work is carried out;

(*f*)   hiring out of means of transport is, in principle, taxable in the country of the supplier. Means of transport excludes items such as pallets and containers;

(*g*)   the following services are supplied in the country where the recipient of the services resides, provided the recipient qualifies as a business or is resident outside the EU:

    (i)   transfer and assignment of copyrights, patents, licences, trademarks and similar rights;

    (ii)   advertising services;

    (iii)   advisory and similar services (e.g. lawyers, accountants), data processing and supply of information;

    (iv)   banking, financial, insurance and reinsurance services, except the hire of safety deposit facilities;

    (v)   secondment of personnel;

(vi) obligation to refrain, partly or fully, from pursuing a professional activity or from a transfer or assignment of copyrights, patents, etc.;

(vii) hiring out of movable tangible property, except all means of transport;

(viii) telecommunication services which are deemed to be the transmission, emission or reception of signals, writing images and sounds or information of any nature, including the right to use capacity for such services;

(ix) the services of agents who act in the name and for the account of another when they obtain for their principal any of the services at (i) to (viii) above.

However, in the case of (*f*) and (*g*) above, if the supplier is established outside the EU, each EU member state may consider this service to be taxable in the EU member state where the effective use and enjoyment of the service takes place.

Furthermore, each EU member state may dictate that, if the supplier is established within the territory of the EU, the service is not taxable in that country if the effective use and enjoyment of the services takes place outside the EU.

In the case of (*a*) to (*e*) above member states now operate derogations which move the place of supply to the customer's member state (see below).

Note that there currently exists a draft e-commerce directive. The intention is that non-EU supplies of e-commerce to private EU individuals will be required to register for VAT and accounts for their supplies within the EU, changing VAT at the rate appropriate to the country of residence of the consumer.

[*EC Sixth Directive 77/388, Art 9(2)*].

Place of supply of intra-Community transport services

Intra-Community transport of goods

3.10   The main rule for intra-Community transport of goods is that it is taxable in the country of departure. Intra-Community transport of goods means transport where both the country of departure and the country of arrival are EU member states. The country of departure means the country where the transport of goods physically starts. The country of arrival means the country where the transport of goods physically ends.

However, provided the customer is registered for VAT purposes in EU member states other than that of the EU member state of departure, the service is taxable in the EU member state of the customer.

[EC Sixth Directive 77/388, Art 28B(C)].

Services ancillary to the intra-Community transport of goods

3.11   The place of supply of services relating to ancillary transport activities such as loading, unloading, handling and similar activities is the place where those services are physically carried out.

However, provided the customer is registered for VAT purposes in another EU member state other than that in which the services are physically performed, the service is taxable in the country of the customer.

[EC Sixth Directive 77/388, Art 28B(D)].

Services relating to transport services rendered by intermediaries

3.12   In certain cases special rules apply to the place of supply for intermediaries (e.g. brokers, agents and other intermediaries) acting in the name and on behalf of other persons. If the intermediary services form part of the supply of intra-Community transport of goods, they are taxable in the country of departure. If the intermediary services form part of a supply of services ancillary to the transport of goods, the service is taxable in the country where the ancillary services are physically carried out.

However, provided the customer is registered for VAT purposes in another EU member state other than that of the place of departure, or in the case of ancillary services the EU member state where the services are physically performed, the service is taxable in the country of the customer.

[EC Sixth Directive 77/388, Art 28B(E)].

Intermediary services other than those relating to transport services

3.13   The place of supply of services provided by intermediaries (e.g. brokers, agents and other intermediaries) acting in the name and on behalf of other persons in so far as these services are not covered already by other rules (e.g. relating to transport), shall be the place where the supply is being carried out.

However, if the intermediary services are rendered to a customer registered for VAT purposes in an EU member state other than that in which the intermediary services are actually carried out, the place of supply of the intermediary service is deemed to be in the EU member state where the customer is registered for VAT purposes.

Services relating to valuation or work on movable tangible property

3.14   The place of supply of services involving valuations or work on tangible movable property provided to a customer registered for VAT purposes in another EU member state other than where the work is carried out, shall be in the customer's member state. This is provided the goods leave the member state where the work was carried out.

[*EC Sixth Directive 77/388, Art 28B(F)*].

Place of supply of software

3.15   In the case of shrink-wrapped software, this is generally treated as a supply of goods, whereas the supply of specific designed software is a supply of services. The service may be considered to be taxable in the country of the customer provided the customer is a taxable business or established outside the EU.

Place of supply of services to public broadcasting organisations

3.16   If a business supplies services to a public broadcasting organisation, e.g. consultancy services, they are taxable in the country where this body is established.

Specific rules in the various EU countries

Austria

Place of supply of goods

3.17   The place of supply of goods is considered to be the place where the goods are located when the right to dispose of them is transferred from the supplier to the buyer.

Transport services

3.18   Where goods are transported outside the EU, that part of the transport which is within Austria is treated as supplied in Austria. Where goods are transported within the EU, a supply of services is considered to have been made at the place where the transport first started.

Services in connection with immovable property

3.19   Services in connection with immovable property are treated as supplied where the immovable property is located. Advisory (or consultancy) contracts with tax advisors or lawyers are generally not considered to be services related to immovable property.

Consulting activity

3.20   The place of consulting or advisory activity is considered to be the place where the client belongs. If advisory services are supplied to non-business clients within the EU the service is deemed to be supplied at the place where the supplier belongs.

Belgium

Place of supply of goods

3.21   Goods are deemed to be supplied at the time and at the place where they are located when they are put at the disposal of the acquirer, with the following exceptions:

(*a*)   if transportation is involved, the place of supply is deemed to be where transportation starts, except in the case of imported goods;

(*b*)   if goods are installed by the supplier, the place of supply is the location of the installation.

A general presumption exists that movable goods are supplied in Belgium if one of the contracting parties is located, or has a fixed place of activity, residence or domicile, in Belgium.

VAT is due at the time of delivery, or at the date the invoice is issued or payment is made if this takes place before the delivery.

Place of supply of services

3.22   Services are supplied at the place at which the supplier has established his place of economic activity or establishment from which the services are rendered, or place of residence or domicile, with the following exceptions:

Services in connection with real estate

3.23   Services which relate to immovable property are deemed to be supplied where the real property is situated. These services include:

(*a*)   any work on buildings;

(*b*)   studies and supervision which are part of the regular activities of architects, land surveyors and construction engineers, carried out in preparing or co-ordinating the activities involved in the construction of the building;

(*c*)   inspection of immovable property;

(*d*)   rental of parking space for cars;

(*e*)   rental of storage space;

(*f*)   supplies of furnished rooms and camping;

(*g*)   leasing of safes, if they are immovable;

(*h*)   leasing of commercial property;

(*i*)   real estate management.

Services which take place where the activities are organised or used

3.24   These include:

(*a*)   transportation services;

(*b*)   cultural, artistic, scientific or sports services;

(*c*)   supplies of food and beverages.

Services which take place where the beneficiary of the services is located

3.25   These include:

(*a*)   author's rights;

(*b*)   sale of goodwill;

(*c*)   advertising;

(*d*)   services of an intellectual nature;

(*e*)   temporary personnel;

(*f*)   rental of movable goods (with the exception of cars) and leasing;

(*g*)   commercial agents and intermediaries (excluding commission agents);

(*h*)   telecommunications.

There is a general presumption that the services are rendered in Belgium if one of the contracting parties is located in, or has a fixed place of activity, residence or domicile, in Belgium.

The VAT is due when the service has been completed, or at the time the invoice is issued or cash received, if this takes place before the service is completed.

Distance sales

3.26   Distance sales by foreign businesses to non-registered entities in Belgium are taxable in Belgium if annual sales exceed € 35,000.

Leasing of means of transport

3.27   The leasing of a means of transport is deemed to take place where the transport is actually used, but only if it is leased:

(*a*)   by a lessor established in Belgium, but only to the extent that it is used outside the EU; or

(*b*)   by a lessor established outside the EU.

Containers are treated as a means of transport for VAT purposes.

Denmark

Place of supply of goods

3.28   Goods are deemed to be supplied in Denmark, as follows:

(*a*)   when the transportation of goods begins in Denmark;

(*b*)   when the transportation of goods starts abroad but the ownership changes in Denmark;

(*c*)   when the goods are not being transported and they are physically in Denmark when ownership changes.

Place of supply of services

3.29   Services are deemed to be supplied in Denmark when the supplier has established his business or has a permanent establishment in Denmark or is domiciled in Denmark and the service is rendered from Denmark.

The following services are deemed to be supplied in Denmark if they are delivered to customers in Denmark:

(*a*)   the sale of patent rights, etc.;

(*b*)   advertising services;

(*c*)   advisory services (provided by lawyers, accountants, etc.);

(*d*)   restrictive covenants;

(*e*)   bank, financial and insurance services;

(*f*)   supplies of staff;

(*g*)   the hiring out of movable property except means of transportation;

(*h*)   telecommunications.

If these services are delivered to customers in Denmark, the place of supply is where the supplier belongs if:

(i)   the service is only utilised outside the EU;

(ii)   the service is supplied from other EU member states to non-taxable persons in Denmark.

If the services mentioned above are supplied from Denmark the place of supply is, however, not deemed to be in Denmark, if:

(*a*)   the service is supplied to VAT taxable persons in other EU member states;

(*b*)   the service is supplied to non-VAT taxable persons in Denmark and the service is only utilised outside the EU;

(*c*)   the service is supplied to businesses and non-taxable persons outside the EU.

Services in connection with real property

3.30   The place of supply is in Denmark if the services are related to immovable property situated in Denmark. If the immovable property is situated abroad, Denmark is not deemed to be the place of supply.

The use of the term 'services' in connection with immovable property is interpreted broadly to include services rendered by estate agents, brokers, etc., as well as services provided by planning and advisory consultants.

Distance sales

3.31   Distance sales by foreign businesses to non-registered entities in Denmark are taxable in Denmark if annual sales exceed DKK 280,000.

Finland

Place of supply of goods

3.32   The place of supply is Finland if the goods are in Finland when delivered to a purchaser. When the supplier imports goods from outside the EU for sale in Finland the place of supply is Finland. The place of supply of installed or assembled goods is the country where the installation or assembly takes place, but this is subject to simplification rules.

Place of supply of intra-Community acquisition of goods

3.33   The place of supply of an intra-Community acquisition is Finland if the transport or dispatch ends in Finland. VAT is not payable on the intra-Community acquisition in Finland in cases of triangulation where three taxable persons supply goods and use VAT numbers from three different member states and the buyer does not have a business establishment in Finland. The customer who is registered for VAT in Finland is liable to pay VAT.

In the case of distance sales, a non-resident business will be required to register in Finland if the amount of sales exceeds € 35,000 in a calendar year. For sales of less than this amount, the vendor may opt for taxation.

Place of supply of services

3.34   The place of supply of services is Finland if the purchaser has a permanent establishment in Finland and the supply is to that establishment, or if the purchaser has his domicile in Finland. If the purchaser has a permanent establishment outside Finland or a domicile outside Finland, no Finnish VAT is due from the supplier, provided the purchaser provides a VAT number. This rule applies to the following services:

(*a*)   transfer and assignment of rights, patents, licences and similar rights;

(*b*)   advertising services;

(*c*)   consultancy services, engineers, consultancy bureaux, lawyers, accountants, data processing, computer programs and systems, and the supply of information;

(*d*)   financial and notary services;

(*e*)   supply of staff;

(*f*)   hiring out of movable tangible property (excluding means of transport);

(*g*)   the obligation to refrain from resuming a business activity;

(*h*)   services of an agent who acts for and on behalf of another person when they provide such services for their principal;

(*i*)   telecommunication services.

However, the supplier of services related to education, scientific services, artistic, cultural and sports services, entertainment and services directly related to their arrangement are taxable in Finland if performed in Finland.

The place of supply of hiring out a means of transport follows the main rule. The hiring out of a means of transport is deemed to be supplied in

Finland if the transport is exclusively used in Finland and the lessor is established outside the EU. If the transport is exclusively used outside the EU the service is deemed to be supplied outside the EU.

Services connected with real property are supplied in Finland if the property is in Finland.

International transport

3.35   If the transport of goods starts in Finland and ends in another EU member state the transport is liable to VAT in Finland, unless the purchaser of the transport provides the supplier with a VAT number from another member state. Transport services from Finland directly to outside the EU and from outside the EU to Finland are exempt. Transport between the Åland islands and the continent of Finland and other member states is zero-rated.

Intermediaries

3.36   Intermediary services, other than those connected with transport and intangible services, are deemed to be supplied in Finland if the goods or services are supplied in Finland. If the purchaser of the intermediary service provides the supplier of the service with a VAT number from another member state, the intermediary service is deemed as supplied in that member state.

Assembly and installation

3.37   See Chapter 2.

France

Place of supply of goods and services

General

3.38   Goods are deemed to be supplied in France in the following cases:

(*a*)   where the place of departure of the goods sent or transported is located in France, whatever the destination;

(*b*)   where the goods are in France at the time of the dispatch by the seller, or the purchaser, or on behalf of either of them, to the purchaser;

(*c*)   when the goods are not transported but are physically situated in France when ownership changes;

(*d*) when the goods are subject to a contract for supply and installation in France;

(*e*) when the goods are imported from a non-EU member state to France or received from an EU member state.

Services are deemed to be supplied in France where the provider of services has in France:

    (i) a registered office; or

    (ii) a fixed place of business; or

    (iii) a domicile or regular residence.

Particular cases

3.39 Intra-Community transport of tangible goods and transparent intermediaries' services are taxable in France:

(*a*) when the place of departure or the place of operations concerning the supplies of services is in France, except if the purchaser provides to the supplier of services, a VAT identification number in another EU member state;

(*b*) when the place of departure or the place of operations concerning the supplies of services is in another EU member state and the purchaser provides to the supplier of services a VAT identification number in France.

Services materially executed in France and taxable in France:

    (i) cultural, sporting, artistic, educational, scientific services and incidental services;

    (ii) supplies of lodging and meals consumed on the premises;

    (iii) incidental services of transport other than intra-Community transport of tangible property.

Expert valuations of tangible property are taxable in France:

(*a*) if they are materially executed in France, except if the purchaser presented to the provider of services a VAT identification number in another EU member state and the goods are sent or transported out of France;

(*b*) if they are materially executed in another EU member state and the purchaser presented a VAT identification number in France, except if the goods are not sent or transported out of this EU member state.

The incidental services of the intra-Community transport of tangible goods and the services of intermediaries connected with these operations are taxable in France:

(i) if they are materially executed in France, except if the purchaser presented to the provider of services his VAT identification number in another EU member state;

(ii) if they are materially executed in another EU member state and the purchaser presented to the provider of services a VAT identification number in France.

Services of transparent intermediaries other than for the transport of tangible property and supplies of services of tangible property are taxable in France:

(*a*) when the place of the operations concerning the supply of services is in France, except if the purchaser presents to the provider of services a VAT identification number in another EU member state;

(*b*) when the place of the operations concerning the supply of services is in another EU member state and the purchaser presents to the provider of services a VAT identification number in France.

Other services

3.40   These services are deemed taxable in France if the provider of services is not established in France and the client who is liable for VAT has his head office or a fixed place of business or his domicile or regular residence in France.

A specified list of these services under French law is as follows:

(*a*) transfers and concession of royalties, patents, licences, trademark and other comparable rights;

(*b*) renting of property other than means of transport;

(*c*) advertising services;

(*d*) banking, financial and insurance operations, except the renting of safes;

(*e*) secondment of staff;

(*f*) services of chartered accountants, consultants, engineers, research department or consultancy engineers;

(*g*) data processing and supplies of information;

(*h*) services of transparent intermediaries related to this list of services;

(*i*) restrictive covenants;

(*j*)   telecommunications services.

Services in connection with real estate

3.41   Services in connection with real estate located in France are deemed to take place in France. These services include:

(*a*)   construction work;

(*b*)   preliminary work performed before the construction of immovable property by, for example, architects, construction engineers, geologists, land surveyors, etc.;

(*c*)   preparation of a building site;

(*d*)   services supplied by real estate developers;

(*e*)   services supplied by building supervisors;

(*f*)   services supplied by intermediaries who assist with the sale and purchase of immovable property or shares in immovable property;

(*g*)   maintenance of immovable property (cleaning, painting, repairs, etc.).

Hiring and leasing of means of transport

3.42   The hiring of means of transport is deemed to be taxable in France when:

  (i) the lessor is established in France, and the vehicle is actually used in France or in another EU member state by the customer;

 (ii) the lessor is established outside the EU and the vehicle is used in France by the customer.

The leasing of means of transport is deemed to be taxable in France when:

(*a*)   the lessor is established in another EU member state where the leasing is equivalent to a delivery; and

(*b*)   the lessee has his registered office or a fixed place of business or his domicile or regular residence in France; and

(*c*)   the vehicle is used in France or in another EU member state.

Distance sales

3.43   Distance sales by foreign businesses to non-registered persons in France are taxable in France if the previous annual sales exceed € 100,000 per year.

Distance sales by a French seller to another EU customer are taxable in the member state of destination if the seller made distance sales to customers of that member state for more than € 35,000 exclusive of VAT for Belgium, Denmark, Finland, Greece, Ireland, Italy, Portugal, Spain and Sweden, or € 100,000 exclusive of VAT for Austria, Germany, Luxembourg, The Netherlands and the United Kingdom, according to the country where the goods are sent.

The value of these distance sales must be recorded in the French VAT returns.

Germany

Place of supply of goods

3.44   A supply of goods is the disposal of tangibles by a business to a recipient. Putting goods to private use is considered to be a supply of goods.

The determination of the place of supply of goods is complex and involves several steps:

(*a*)   in the case of private use it is where the business resides;

(*b*)   special rules apply to the supply of goods during transport by ship, train or plane;

(*c*)   intra-Community acquisitions have their place of supply where the despatch of goods terminates, except where the recipient uses the VAT identification number of another member state;

(*d*)   where an intra-Community acquisition cannot be assumed, and this may be for a number of reasons, e.g. because the recipient is not buying for a business purpose, or the recipient is a business engaged solely in tax-free activities, or a small business, or the business is agricultural and the amount of purchase is neither increased nor is there an option for taxation, the place of supply is where the movement of goods concludes.

If none of the above cases applies, the place of supply of goods may be determined as follows:

(i)   when goods are imported from a non-member state the place of supply is assumed to be Germany, if the supplier is liable to turnover tax;

(ii)   when there is no movement of goods the place of supply of goods is where the goods are located at the time that the transfer of ownership to the customer takes place;

(iii) in the case of movement of goods, the place of supply is where the goods are located when the movement commences.

In the case of a chain supply, where the goods are dispatched from the first business to the final customer, there is only one supply. If the dispatcher and the recipient are the same person, the supply is made by the preceding business (unless the dispatcher proves that he acts in his capacity as selling party, then the supply is by him). The previous supply takes place where the dispatch originates, the subsequent supply takes place where the dispatch terminates. If the dispatcher is the first business, the supply is allocated to his business; if the dispatcher is the last recipient, the supply is allocated to the last delivering business.

Services

3.45   The place of supply for other services is determined as follows:

(*a*)   services related to real estate are supplied where the real estate is located, e.g. the development or purchase of real estate;

(*b*)   for services related to art, science, sports, entertainment or comparable services, the place of supply is where the activity takes place;

(*c*)   the service of an intermediary is considered to take place where the supply which is being arranged takes its place of supply, except where the recipient uses the VAT identification number of another member state;

(*d*)   special services, i.e. advertising, tax or legal consultancy, data processing and leasing, are supplied where the recipient resides, provided the recipient is a business. If the recipient is not a business, and is a resident of another member state, the service is considered to be supplied in the supplier's member state. These rules have been extended to include the supply of telecommunications services.

(*e*)   all other services take place where the business conducts its activities.

Transport services

3.46   For transport services between a location within Germany and a location outside Germany, that part of the transport which is within Germany is considered to be supplied in Germany. The following formulae apply for calculating the part of the consideration which is taxable in Germany:

Taxable consideration = net price of total supply of transport services = km travelled within Germany as a fraction of the total km travelled.

For transport of passengers, the consideration is calculated as the gross price of total supply of transport services = km travelled within Germany as a fraction of the total km travelled.

Note that relatively short distances of domestic transportation will be regarded as foreign transportation and relatively short distances of foreign transportation will be regarded as domestic transportation.

Exchange transactions

3.47 If the consideration for the supply of goods is itself a supply of goods, this is treated as an exchange transaction. If the consideration for services is the supply of goods or other services, it is known as an exchange-like transaction.

Greece

Services in connection with real estate

3.48 Services connected with real estate located in Greece are considered to take place within Greece. These include, inter alia, the services of:

(*a*)   estate agents;

(*b*)   experts in real estate;

(*c*)   architects;

(*d*)   engineers;

(*e*)   supervisory officers.

Leasing of means of transport

3.49 The leasing of a means of transport is deemed to take place where the vehicle is actually used, but only if it is leased:

(*a*)   by a lessor established in Greece, and only to the extent that it is used outside the EU; or

(*b*)   by a lessor established outside the EU.

Supplies of staff

3.50 Supplies of staff are taxable in the country of the recipient, provided the recipient is a taxable person in another EU member state or a person established outside the EU.

Supplies of staff are considered to be disposals of personnel by a business to another business (whether taxable or not) for a fee for the performance of work or services where the staff fall under the responsibility, direction and supervision of the recipient.

Distance sales

3.51   Distance sales by foreign businesses to non-registered persons in Greece are taxable in Greece if annual sales exceed € 24,064.56 (GRD 8,200,000).

Ireland

Place of supply of services

3.52   The general rule is that the place of supply of services is the place where the person making the supply has his establishment, or if there is more than one establishment, the location of the establishment most connected with the supply.

Certain services are deemed to be supplied where they are physically performed such as:

(*a*)   cultural, artistic, sporting, scientific, educational, entertainment or similar services;

(*b*)   valuation of movable goods;

(*c*)   work on movable goods.

The place of supply of services connected with immovable goods, i.e. property, is the place where the property is situated.

For certain services, which are covered in more detail at 9.20, the customer rather than the supplier is liable to account for the VAT due on the transaction.

Leasing of movable tangible goods

3.53   The leasing of movable tangible goods (excluding means of transport) where the lessor is established outside the EU is deemed to be supplied in Ireland if the goods are (or are to be) effectively used there.

Leasing of means of transport

3.54   Such services are liable to VAT in Ireland only where the person supplying the service has an establishment in Ireland and the goods are hired from that establishment.

Distance sales

3.55   Distance sales by foreign businesses to non-registered entities in Ireland are taxable in Ireland if annual sales exceed € 35,000.

Italy

Distance sales

3.56   Distance sales by foreign businesses to non-registered entities in Italy are taxable in Italy if annual sales exceed € 27,889.00.

Leasing of means of transport

3.57   The leasing of means of transport is deemed to take place where the vehicle is actually used, but only if it is leased:

(*a*)   by a lessor established in Italy, but only to the extent that it is used outside the EU; or

(*b*)   by a lessor established outside the EU.

Luxembourg

Supplies of services

3.58   The place of supply of services is generally the place where the supplier of the service belongs or has a fixed establishment from which the services are supplied. If a supplier has his business or fixed establishment in Luxembourg, the place of supply is always deemed to be in Luxembourg unless the business can demonstrate otherwise.

Where certain intangible services are supplied to customers outside Luxembourg then the customer will be required to account for VAT if in business within the EU under the reverse charge procedure, or if established outside the EU.

Services in connection with real estate

3.59   The place of supply of services in connection with immovable property, including services related to the preparation and co-ordination of construction work, is the place where the immovable property is situated. This includes the services supplied by architects and firms providing on-site supervision, etc.

Distance sales

3.60   Distance sales by foreign businesses to non-registered entities in Luxembourg are taxable in Luxembourg if annual sales exceed € 105,000.

The Netherlands

Certain types of service supplied by non-EU businesses

3.61   Operating leases of movable tangible property, consultancy services and the supply of staff to Dutch non-taxable legal entities, provided by businesses having a fixed establishment or who are resident outside the EU, are subject to VAT in the Netherlands, if the effective use and enjoyment of the services take place within the Netherlands.

Leasing of means of transport

3.62   The leasing of a means of transport by businesses outside the EU is considered to be performed in the Netherlands if the customer is a Dutch resident, whether an individual, partnership or corporate body.

Agents

3.63   The services of agents acting on behalf of third persons are, in principle, taxable in the Netherlands if they are performed in the Netherlands. However, if the customer of the intermediary supplier of services is a resident of, or is registered for VAT purposes in, another EU member state, the service is taxable in the other EU member state according to Dutch VAT law.

Services in connection with real estate

3.64   The place of supply of services in connection with immovable property, including the services of estate agents, architects, and other experts, as well as the services of preparing or coordinating construction work, is the place where the property is located.

Distance sales

3.65   Distance sales by foreign businesses to non-registered entities in the Netherlands are taxable in the Netherlands if annual sales exceed € 104,369 (NLG 230,000).

Portugal

Supplies of services

3.66   If a supplier has its headquarters, i.e. a fixed establishment through which the services are supplied, or its domicile, in Portugal, then the services are generally deemed to be supplied in Portugal.

Distance sales

3.67   Distance sales by foreign businesses to non-registered entities in Portugal are taxable in Portugal if annual sales exceed € 31,424.27.

Spain

Supplies of goods

Installed or assembled goods

3.68   The rule stating that the place of supply of installed or assembled goods is the place where the goods are physically installed or assembled, applies only where the value of the installation or assembly exceeds 15% of the value of the goods supplied.

Supplies of services

3.69   Services are taxed when they take place in the Spanish VAT territory. The VAT Act establishes the general rule that the service is rendered in Spain where the company or professional rendering the service has its headquarters within the Spanish VAT territory.

However, certain special rules apply, as follows:

(*a*)   services directly related to immovable property located in Spain are taxable in Spain;

(*b*)   for transport services, that part of the transport which takes place within Spanish territory is taxable in Spain;

(*c*)   the following services are taxable in Spain when they are rendered in Spain:

    (i)   services relating to arts, culture, sports, science;

    (ii)   games of chance;

    (iii)   broadcasting of television programmes;

    (iv)   ancillary services to the transport of goods;

(*d*)   the following services will be taxed in Spain when the recipient is a taxable person with a permanent establishment in Spain:

    (i)   the supply of authors' rights, licences, patents, brands, and other rights of industrial and intellectual property;

    (ii)   the sale of a company's goodwill;

    (iii)   advertising services;

    (iv)   services of assessment, audit, engineering, consulting, etc.;

    (v)   computer data processing;

(vi)   supply of information;

(vii)   translation services;

(viii)   assurance and reinsurance;

(ix)   company management;

(x)   supply of staff;

(xi)   dubbing of movies;

(xii)   renting of movable goods;

(xiii)   refraining from pursuing or exercising any business activity, or any such rights as listed above;

(xiv)   the mediation and management of the services listed above.

(*e*)   works performed on movable goods, and the reports and valuations referring to such goods, are taxed when performed in Spain, or when performed abroad where a Spanish VAT number is applied;

(*f*)   telecommunication services are taxed in Spain provided certain conditions are met.

Foreign businesses without a permanent establishment in Spain

3.70   Where a foreign business does not have a permanent establishment in Spain, the tax liability on supplies of goods and services may be transferred to the Spanish recipient if he is a taxable person.

Distance sales

3.71   Distance sales by foreign businesses to non-registered entities in Spain are taxable in Spain if annual sales exceed € 27,346.05 (ESP 4,550,000).

Sweden

General

3.72   When the place of supply is not deemed to be Sweden and the supply is treated as an export, the seller should not charge Swedish VAT on the invoice to the purchaser.

See also under 3.75 (*c*) regarding changes with effect from 1 July 2002 in certain situations.

Place of supply of goods

3.73   For supplies of goods, the destination principle applies. Deliveries of goods to other EU member states are not subject to Swedish VAT if the customer is a taxable person who is registered for VAT in an EU member state other than Sweden. When goods are sent outside the EU this is treated as an export and Swedish VAT is not levied.

Place of supply of services

3.74   With reference to services, the main rule is that the place of supply is deemed to be the place (country) where the seller has established his business or has a fixed establishment from which the service is supplied.

Exceptions

3.75   The following exceptions apply to the main rule:

(*a*)   *real estate:* the place of supply is the place where the real estate to which the services are connected is situated.

(*b*)   *physical services:* the place of supply is the place where the services are physically carried out. This rule applies to education, cultural activities, creative artists' performances, entertainment, sports, science and equivalents. Services ancillary to the transport of goods within the EU, e.g. loading, are subject to a reverse charge in the customer's member state provided the customer gives his VAT number there. The same applies to work on movable property sent from another EU member state where carried out in Sweden, if the goods are returned to the other EU member state once the work has been completed.

(*c*)   *customer's rule:* applies to a wide range of intangible services, e.g. transfers and assignments of copyrights, patents, licenses, and so forth and consultancy services. The place of supply is Sweden, where both the seller and customer are situated in Sweden or where the seller is situated in Sweden and the customer is a non-taxable person in another EU member state. The supply is otherwise a dispatch or export of services, e.g. when the customer is a taxable person in another EU member state or a person situated outside the EU. If the customer is situated in Sweden and the seller is situated in another EU member state, the customer must apply the reverse charge in Sweden if the customer is a taxable person ('import services'). The same applies when the seller is situated outside the EU. If the customer is a non-taxable person (e.g. a private person), it is mandatory for a seller situated in another EU member state or outside the EU to register in Sweden (a VAT representative may be used) and to levy Swedish VAT in the invoice to the customer.

With effect from 1 July 2002, whereas the reverse charge rule by a Swedish customer (taxable person) is mandatory, a non-resident supplier can instead opt to apply for a registration via a VAT representative in Sweden and then levy Swedish VAT in the invoice to the customer. After such an application all services made by the foreign entrepreneur in

Sweden will be deemed to be supplies within the scope of Swedish VAT. If the Swedish customer is a non-taxable person (e.g. a private person) it remains mandatory also for a supplier from another EU member state to register in Sweden (via a VAT representative) and to levy Swedish VAT in the invoice to the customer.

(*d*)   *letting of means of transport:* the place of supply is deemed to be outside the EU (i.e. an export supply), if the place of effective use and enjoyment is entirely outside the EU.

United Kingdom

Supplies of goods

3.76   Essentially, where the supply of goods does not involve their removal to or from the UK, the place of supply is where the goods are located when allocated to a customer order. However, if they are removed from the UK, the place of supply is the UK whereas if they are removed to the UK, the place of supply is outside the UK.

Supplies of services

3.77   As in all EU member states, the rules for determining the place of supply of services are far more complicated. Services are supplied where the supplier belongs with certain exceptions as follows:

(*a*)   services related to land are supplied where the land is situated;

(*b*)   cultural, scientific etc. services in accordance with the *EC Sixth Directive, Article 9(2) (c)* are supplied where performed;

(*c*)   professional, advertising services etc. in accordance with the *EC Sixth Directive, Article 9(2)(e)* are supplied where received, when they are received by a taxable person in another member state, or any person outside the EU.

The last category of services, when imported into the UK, are subject to the reverse charge accounting procedure whereby the recipient accounts for VAT as if the supply were made by the recipient and to the recipient.

Single Market simplification procedures

3.78   The EU simplification procedures require acquisition VAT to be paid by the final customer only. This applies to triangular transactions and certain other transactions. This avoids multiple VAT registrations throughout the EU.

Distance sales

3.79   Distance sales by foreign businesses to non-registered entities in the UK are taxable in the UK if annual sales exceed GBP 70,000.

Chapter 4

Exemptions

Exemptions: EU rules

Introduction

4.1   Certain activities are exempt from VAT. A distinction should be made between exemptions with and without a right to deduct input tax. Further, in essence, the regime of exemptions separates into three sets of rules:

(*a*)   exemptions within the territory of each EU member state;

(*b*)   exemptions with regard to cross-border transactions (import, export and international movement of goods);

(*c*)   exemptions in relation to intra-Community transactions.

These categories are analysed in detail below.

Exemptions within the territory of each EU country

Exemptions exist in all EU member states for certain activities in the public interest

4.2   The following activities of public interest should, in principle, be exempt from VAT in all EU countries:

(*a*)   the supply by the public postal service of services other than passenger transport and telecommunications services, and the supply of goods incidental thereto. Private postal and telecommunications services are not exempt;

(*b*)   hospital and medical care and closely related activities, undertaken by bodies governed by public law or under social conditions comparable to those applicable to bodies governed by public law, by hospitals, centres for medical treatment or diagnosis and other duly recognised establishments of a similar nature;

(*c*)   the provision of medical care in the exercise of the medical and paramedical professions as defined by the EU member state concerned;

(*d*)   supplies of human organs, blood and milk;

(*e*)   services supplied by dental technicians in their professional capacity and dental prostheses supplied by dentists and dental technicians;

(*f*)   where an independent group of persons whose activities are exempt from or are not subject to VAT, renders services to its members which are directly necessary for the exercise of their activity and the group merely claims from their members exact reimbursement of their share of the joint expenses, provided that such exemption is not likely to produce distortion of competition;

(*g*)   the supply of services and of goods closely linked to welfare and social security work, including those supplied by old people's homes, by bodies governed by public law or by other organisations recognised as charitable by the EU member states concerned;

(*h*)   the supply of services and of goods closely linked to the protection of children and young persons by bodies governed by public law or by other organisations recognised as charitable by the EU member states concerned;

(*i*)   children's or young people's education, school or university education, vocational training or retraining, including the supply of closely related services, and of goods, provided by bodies governed by public law having such as their aim or by other organisations defined by the EU member states concerned as having similar objectives;

(*j*)   tuition given privately by teachers and covering school or university education;

(*k*)   certain supplies of staff by religious or philosophical institutions;

(*l*)   supply of services and goods closely linked to supplies for the benefit of their members in return for a subscription fixed in accordance with their rules by non-profit organisations with aims of a political, trade union, religious, patriotic, philosophical, philanthropic or civic nature, provided that this exemption is not likely to cause distortion of competition;

(*m*)   certain services closely linked to sport or physical education supplied by non-profit making organisations to persons taking part in sport or physical education;

(*n*)   certain cultural services and goods closely linked thereto supplied by bodies governed by public law or by other cultural bodies recognised by the EU member states concerned;

(*o*)   the supply of services and goods by organisations whose activities are exempt under the provisions of sub-paragraphs (*b*) hospital, (*g*) welfare, (*h*) protection of children, (*i*) education, (*l*) members of non-profitable organisations, (*m*) sport and (*n*) cultural services above in connection with fund-raising events organised exclusively for their own benefit provided that exemption is not likely to cause distortion of competition. EU member states may introduce any necessary restrictions, in particular as regards the number of events or the amount of receipts which give entitlement to exemption;

(*p*)   the supply of transport services for sick or injured persons in vehicles specially designed for the purpose by duly authorised bodies;

(*q*)   activities of public radio and television bodies other than those of a commercial nature.

[*EC Sixth Directive 77/388, Art 13(A)(1)*].

Exempt activities of public interest provided by bodies not governed by public law

4.3   Each EU member state may exempt the activities mentioned above in paragraph 4.2, sub-paragraphs (*b*) hospital, (*g*) welfare, (*h*) protection of children, (*i*) education, (*l*) members of non-profitable organisations (*m*) sport and (*n*) cultural services supplied by bodies other than those governed by public law on one or more of the following conditions:

(*a*)   they shall not systematically aim to make a profit, but any profits nevertheless arising shall not be distributed but shall be assigned to the continuance or improvement of the services supplied;

(*b*)   they shall be managed and administered on an essentially voluntary basis by persons who have no direct or indirect interest, either themselves or through intermediaries, in the results of the activities concerned;

(*c*)   they shall charge prices approved by the public authorities or which do not exceed such approved prices or, in respect of those services not subject to approval, prices lower than those charged for similar services by commercial enterprises subject to VAT;

(*d*)   exemption of the services concerned shall not be likely to create distortion of competition such as to place at a disadvantage commercial enterprises liable to VAT.

However, the above services cannot be exempt if:

(i)   they are not essential to the main exempt transactions;

(ii)   their basic purpose is to obtain additional income for the organisations by carrying out transactions which are in direct competition with those of commercial enterprises liable for VAT.

[*EC Sixth Directive 77/388, Art 13(A)(2)*].

Other exemptions justified for reasons of general policy

4.4   Under conditions ensuring the correct and straightforward application of the exemption and preventing any possible evasion, avoidance or abuse, each EU member state should exempt the following activities:

(*a*)   insurance and reinsurance transactions, including related services performed by insurance brokers and agents;

(*b*)   the leasing or letting of immovable property excluding:

   (i)   the provision of accommodation, as defined by each EU member state, in the hotel sector or in sectors with a similar function, including the provision of accommodation in holiday camps or on sites developed for use as camping sites;

   (ii)   the letting of premises and sites for parking vehicles;

   (iii)   lettings of permanently installed equipment and machinery;

   (iv)   the hire of safes;

(*c*)   supplies of goods used wholly for an activity exempt from VAT if these goods have not given rise to the right to deduct;

(*d*)   the following financial activities:

   (i)   the granting and the negotiation of credit and the management of credit by the person granting it;

   (ii)   the negotiation of or any dealings in credit guarantees or any other security for money and the management of credit guarantees by the person who is granting the credit;

   (iii)   transactions, including negotiation, concerning deposit and current accounts, payments, transfers, debts, cheques and other negotiable instruments, but excluding debt collection and factoring;

   (iv)   transactions, including negotiation, concerning currency, bank notes and coins used as legal tender, with the exception of collectors' items;

   (v)   transactions, including negotiation, excluding management and safekeeping, in shares, interest in companies or associations, debentures and other securities, excluding:

   –   documents establishing title to goods and the establishment, assignment, alteration and cessation of certain rights or securities in immovable property;

   (vi)   management of special investment funds as defined by EU member states;

(*e*) the supply at face value of postage stamps valid for use for postal services within the territory of the country, fiscal stamps and other similar stamps;

(*f*) betting, lotteries and other forms of gambling, subject to conditions and limitations laid down by each EU member state;

(*g*) the supply of buildings or parts thereof, and of the land on which they stand, other than the supply before first occupation of buildings or parts of buildings and the land on which they stand. Each EU member state may determine the conditions concerning application of this criterion to work on buildings and the land on which they stand;

(*h*) the supply of land which has not been built on other than building land. 'Building land' shall mean any unimproved or improved land defined as such by each EU member state itself.

[*EC Sixth Directive 77/388, Art 13(B)*].

Options to tax certain activities

4.5   Each EU member state may allow taxpayers to choose taxation instead of exemption in cases of:

(*a*) letting and leasing of immovable property and the supply of buildings or land;

(*b*) financial transactions.

Each EU member state may restrict the scope of this option and shall fix the conditions of its use.

[*EC Sixth Directive 77/388, Art 13(C)*].

Exemptions with regard to cross-border transactions

Exemptions on importation

4.6   Each EU member state shall, in principle, exempt the following:

(*a*) importation of goods from non-EU member states into an EU member state where the domestic supply within that country would in all circumstances be exempt;

(*b*) importation of goods from non-EU member states into an EU member state qualifying for exemption from customs duties other than as provided for in the Common Customs Tariff. This exemption applies to goods which qualify for non-Tariff exemption from customs duties, i.e. under one of the exemptions provided for by the EU member states, subject to their own conditions, in the introductory notes to their national customs tariffs (e.g. removals, wedding gifts);

(c) re-importation, by the person who exported them, of goods into the member state from which they were exported, where they qualify for exemption from customs duties;

(d) importation from a non-EU member state into an EU member state of goods:

(i) under diplomatic and consular arrangements, which qualify for exemption from customs duties;

(ii) by international organisations recognised as such by the public authorities of the host country, and by members of such organisations, within the limits and under the conditions laid down by the international conventions establishing the organisations or by headquarters agreements;

(iii) into the territory of the member state which is party to NATO, by the armed forces of other countries which belong to NATO for the use of such forces or the civilian staff accompanying them or for supplying their messes or canteens where such forces take part in the common defence effort.

(e) import into ports by sea fishing businesses of their catches, unprocessed or after undergoing preservation, for marketing but before being supplied;

(f) the supply of services in connection with the import of goods where the value of such services is included in the taxable amount. The taxable amount for the import of goods normally includes incidental expenses such as commission, packing, transport and insurance costs;

(g) import of gold by central banks.

[*EC Sixth Directive 77/388, Art 14*].

Exemption of exports including transactions and international transport

General

4.7   The destination principle is one of the basic provisions of the VAT system. Therefore, supplies of goods which are to be exported to non-EU member states are exempt from VAT but give rise to a right to deduct input VAT. Thus, they are zero rated.

Export of goods to non-EU member states

4.8   The following supplies are exempt:

(*a*) the supply of goods dispatched or transported to a destination outside the EU by or on behalf of the vendor;

(*b*) the supply of goods dispatched or transported to a destination outside the EU by or on behalf of a purchaser not established within the territory of the country with the exception of goods transported by the purchaser himself for the equipping, fuelling and provisioning of pleasure boats and private aircraft or any other means of transport for private use.

The benefit of the exemption is subject to production of a copy of the invoice or other document in lieu thereof, endorsed by the customs office where the goods left the EU. Evidence of export is usually required.

Further, EU member states may set limits in relation to the application of this exemption and may exclude from the benefit of the exemption supplies to travellers whose domicile or habitual residence is situated in the EU. Domicile or habitual residence means the place entered as such in a passport, identity card or, failing those, other identity documents which the relevant EU member states recognise as valid.

Inward processing

4.9   The supply of services consisting of work on movable property acquired or imported for the purpose of undergoing such work within the EU, and dispatched or transported out of the EU by the person providing the services or by the customer if established in a non-EU member state or on behalf of either of them, is exempt from VAT.

Vessels

4.10   The supply of goods for the fuelling and provisioning of vessels is exempt if:

(*a*) used for navigation on the high seas and carrying passengers for reward or used for the purpose of commercial, industrial or fishing activities;

(*b*) used for rescue or assistance at sea, or for inshore fishing;

(*c*) they are vessels of war.

The supply, modification, repair, maintenance, chartering and hiring of the above vessels are exempt. This also applies to aircraft used by airlines operating for reward chiefly on international routes. The supply of goods for fuelling and provisioning of aircraft is also exempt from VAT. The supply of other services to meet the direct needs of seagoing vessels or aircraft is exempt from VAT.

4.11   Exemptions

Diplomatic and consular exemptions

4.11   The following supplies of goods and services are exempt:

(*a*)   under diplomatic and consular arrangements;

(*b*)   to certain international organisations and their members;

(*c*)   effected within an EU member state which belongs to NATO and intended for the use of the forces of other EU member states which belong to NATO or of the civilian staff accompanying them, or for supplying messes or canteens where such forces take part in the common defence effort;

(*d*)   to another EU member state and intended for the forces of any EU member state which is a member of NATO, other than the EU member state of destination itself, or for the use of those forces or of the civilian staff accompanying them, or for supplying their messes or canteens where such forces take part in the common defence effort.

In cases where the goods are not dispatched or transported out of the EU member state, and in the case of services, the benefit may be implemented by means of a refund of the VAT.

Gold

4.12   The supply of gold to central banks is exempt from VAT.

Exports as part of humanitarian, charitable or teaching activities

4.13   Goods supplied to approved bodies which export them as part of their humanitarian, charitable or teaching activities abroad are exempt from VAT.

Directly linked services

4.14   The supply of services including transport and ancillary transactions, but excluding the supply of services which are exempt without credit, is exempt from VAT, when these are directly linked to:

(*a*)   the export or import of goods which are intended to be placed under private warehousing arrangements not involving Customs;

(*b*)   supplies of goods which are intended to be:

    (i)   produced to Customs and, where applicable, placed in temporary storage;

    (ii)   placed in a free zone or in a free warehouse;

(iii) placed under Customs warehousing arrangements or inward processing arrangements;

(iv) admitted into territorial waters in order to be incorporated into drilling or production platforms, for the purposes of the construction, repair, maintenance, alteration, or fitting-out of such platforms, or to link such drilling or production platforms to the mainland, or for the fuelling and provisioning of drilling or production platforms;

(v) imports of goods placed under the arrangements of temporary importation;

(vi) goods placed under external transit arrangements; or

(vii) goods placed under internal transit arrangements.

Services supplied by brokers and other intermediaries

4.15 Services supplied by brokers and other intermediaries, acting in the name and on behalf of another person, where they form part of transactions of import or export or of transactions executed outside the EU, are exempt from VAT. This exemption does not apply to travel agents who supply in the name and on behalf of the traveller, services which are supplied in other EU member states.

The Portuguese Republic may treat sea and air transport between the Azores and Madeira and mainland Portugal in the same way as international transport.

[*EC Sixth Directive 77/388, Art 15*].

Exemptions in connection with certain Customs arrangements (e.g. warehousing)

4.16 Each EU member state may take special measures to relieve from VAT the following transactions:

(*a*) importation of goods which are intended to be placed under private warehousing arrangements not involving Customs;

(*b*) supplies of goods which are intended to be:

(i) produced to Customs and, where applicable, placed in temporary storage;

(ii) placed in a free zone or in a free warehouse;

(iii) placed under Customs warehousing arrangements or inward processing arrangements;

(iv) admitted into territorial waters in order to be incorporated into drilling or production platforms, for the purposes of the construction, repair, maintenance, alteration or fitting-out of such platforms, or to link such drilling or production platforms to the mainlands, or for the fuelling and provisioning of drilling or production platforms;

(v) placed under warehousing arrangements other than Customs;

(*c*) supplies of services relating to the supplies of goods referred to in (*b*) above;

(*d*) supplies of goods and services carried out in the places listed in (*b*) and still subject to one of the arrangements specified therein;

(*e*) EU member states which take up the option provided for in (*b*) shall also exempt the intra-Community acquisition of such goods;

(*f*) supplies:

(i) of goods still subject to arrangements for temporary importation with total exemption from import duty or goods subject to the external transit arrangements;

(ii) of goods still subject to the internal Community transit procedure;

(iii) of services relating to such supplies of goods.

[*EC Sixth Directive 77/388, Art 16*].

Exemptions in relation to intra-Community transactions

General

4.17 The general rule is that supplies of goods from one EU member state to another should be exempt, provided the supply is carried out by a taxable person. Small undertakings and flat rate farmers are excluded. Exceptions are usually determined by the type of transaction and the status of the acquirer. Special rules also apply to new means of transport.

Intra-Community exemptions

4.18 Within the exemptions linked to intra-Community transactions, distinction can be made between:

(*a*) exempt supplies of goods;

(*b*) exempt intra-Community acquisitions of goods;

(*c*) exempt transport services;

(*d*) exempt importation of goods.

Exempt supplies of goods

4.19   Each EU member state must exempt intra-Community supplies effected for another taxable or non-taxable legal entity. For the supply of new means of transport this applies to any purchaser, regardless of status.

For excise goods, this rule applies under certain conditions. An intra-Community supply is considered to be a supply where the goods are dispatched or transported by, or on behalf of, the vendor or the person acquiring the goods from one EU member state to another. Supplies to Monaco and the Isle of Man are treated as supplies to France and the UK, respectively.

The supply under a contract to make something from the customer's materials is included under the exempt intra-Community rules.

Intra-Community acquisitions of goods are not subject to VAT if effected by flat rate scheme farmers, taxable persons who are not entitled to deduction and non-taxable legal entities, provided the acquisitions in the current year and the previous calendar year are below the threshold of € 10,000 and they have not opted for the general scheme. The exemption does not apply to intra-Community supplies of goods effected for such taxable or non-taxable persons.

As the intra-Community acquisition of new means of transport by anyone is subject to VAT, the corresponding intra-Community supply is exempt. This also applies to the person who occasionally supplies a new means of transport from one EU member state to another.

[*EC Sixth Directive 77/388, Art 28C(A)*].

Exempt intra-Community acquisitions of goods

4.20   In the following three situations, intra-Community supplies are exempt from VAT:

(*a*)   if the supply of goods would be exempt within the relevant EU member state;

(*b*)   if the importation of the goods would be exempt;

(*c*)   if the person acquiring the goods would be entitled to full reimbursement of the VAT.

[*EC Sixth Directive 77/388, Art 28C(B)*].

Exempt transport services

4.21   The intra-Community transport of goods between the Azores and Madeira and mainland Portugal is exempt from VAT.

4.22 *Exemptions*

[*EC Sixth Directive 77/388, Art 28C(C)*].

Exempt importation of goods

4.22 Each EU member state must exempt imports where goods dispatched or transported from a non-EU member state are imported into an EU member state other than that of the arrival of the dispatch or transport, provided the supply by the importer is considered to be an intra-Community supply. This means that the exemption applies if, upon importation of the goods, the final destination is known and if the import is followed by an intra-Community transaction.

This also implies that the importer must be registered for VAT in the country of import. However, some countries apply a postponed accounting system for the levying of VAT on import of goods. The system directs that the VAT due on importation is not paid immediately to the customs authorities, but rather on the next periodical VAT return. The same VAT is then deducted as input VAT on the same return according to the importer's taxable status.

[*EC Sixth Directive 77/388, Art 28C(D)*].

Specific rules in the various EU countries

Austria

Exemptions without credit

Real property

4.23 The supply of real property is generally exempt from VAT. However, the supplier may opt for taxation.

The leasing and renting of residential buildings is subject to a reduced tax rate.

Financial transactions

4.24 Financial transactions are generally not taxable. These include:

(*a*)   credit transactions;

(*b*)   dealings in shares, dividends and securities;

(*c*)   insurance transactions;

(*d*)   dealings in foreign currency and bank notes.

Other exemptions

4.25   Several other transactions are exempt from VAT. The main ones are:

(*a*)   certain supplies in the course of education;

(*b*)   health services (especially services provided by hospitals, physicians and dentists);

(*c*)   insurance transactions;

(*d*)   dealings in foreign currency and bank notes;

(*e*)   lotteries and gambling.

Exemptions with credit

4.26   The following transactions are exempt from VAT, with credit:

(*a*)   exports;

(*b*)   cross-border commission processing;

(*c*)   international passenger transportation by ship or air transport;

(*d*)   purchases and sales in intra-Community triangular arrangements.

Belgium

Exemptions without credit

Leasing and rental

4.27   The leasing and renting of real property is generally exempt from VAT except in the case of leasing of real property for industrial or commercial purposes by a business which specialises in the financing and leasing of property.

Financial transactions

4.28   The following financial services are normally exempt from VAT:

(*a*)   deposits and acceptance of funds;

(*b*)   credit operations;

(*c*)   transactions involving the payment and acceptance of funds on another person's account.

Other exemptions

4.29   Certain other transactions are exempt from VAT, for example:

(a) the services of notaries and lawyers registered in Belgian courts;

(b) services supplied by physicians, dentists, midwives, nurses, other medical attendants, masseurs and physiotherapists;

(c) services supplied by veterinary surgeons;

(d) services supplied by hospitals, psychiatric institutions, clinics and dispensaries in the course of normal business activities, family assistance services, transportation of sick and injured persons by special means of transport;

(e) services supplied to members of independent non-profit making groups of individuals who conduct exempt activities, if the services supplied are directly required for the performance of those activities and if such institutions only claim a refund of costs;

(f) services supplied by homes for the aged, by nurseries and children's homes and by institutions whose main purpose according to their objects is the supervision, support and education of young people;

(g) services supplied by institutions for sports or physical education;

(h) instruction by educational institutions and by individual teachers;

(i) services supplied by those providing educational or family guidance;

(j) lending of books or publications, gramophone records, and tapes;

(k) entrance to museums, monuments, etc.;

(l) organisation of theatrical, choreographed, or cinematographic performances, exhibitions, concerts or conferences by listed non-profit making bodies;

(m) the services provided by religious institutions;

(n) contracts by authors or composers for the publication of their work.

Exemptions with credit

4.30 A certain number of transactions will be VAT exempt but nevertheless allow the deduction of VAT charged. These transactions include:

(a) supplies of gold to central banks;

(b) supplies of newspapers appearing at least 50 times per year which provide general information to the public;

(c) supplies to recognised international organisations, embassies, etc.;

(d) export of goods outside the EU;

(e) intra-EU deliveries of goods;

(*f*)   services provided to EU businesses;

(*g*)   services provided to clients outside the EU for business purposes;

(*h*)   certain operations relating to immovable goods where the VAT must be declared by the client (e.g. activities in the building sector);

(*i*)   transfer of business to a VAT-registered transferee (e.g. sale or contribution to capital).

Denmark

Exemptions without credit

Real property

4.31   The supply, leasing and hiring out of real estate is usually exempt from VAT.

The exemption does not include hiring out hotel rooms, etc., hiring out serviced business accommodation for a short period of time (less than one month), or hiring out camping sites, parking space and advertising sites.

Businesses which rent out commercial property may opt for taxation in the following circumstances:

(*a*)   letting of existing buildings with sitting tenants or where binding agreements for tenancies exist;

(*b*)   acquisition of property for rental purposes where no tenancies exist on the date of purchase;

(*c*)   for the purpose of renting out planned or existing property where no tenancy agreements exist prior to the construction, modernisation or repair of the property.

The option to tax relating to existing tenancies is only allowed provided the tenant agrees.

Financial transactions

4.32   Financial activities are generally exempt. However, the deposit and management of shares and bonds, the management of credits and credit guarantees by a person other than the person granting them, as well as the renting out of safe deposit boxes, are taxable.

Other exemptions without credit

4.33   The following transactions are also exempt from VAT without credit for input VAT:

(*a*) sales of works of art by the artist;

(*b*) gas, water and electricity in certain cases;

(*c*) health services (dental instruments manufactured and used by dentists are included);

(*d*) social services;

(*e*) education unless provided on a commercial basis;

(*f*) cultural activities, with the exception of theatre and cinema performances, concerts, radio and television (sales of catalogues by museums qualify if the price does not exceed the cost of production);

(*g*) sports activities unless professionals participate;

(*h*) passenger transport;

(*i*) lotteries and gambling;

(*j*) information services of travel agencies and tourist offices;

(*k*) postal services;

(*l*) funeral services.

Exemptions with credit

4.34 The following transactions are exempt from VAT with credit, i.e. they are zero-rated:

(*a*) sales of newspapers which are published at least on a monthly basis;

(*b*) supply of goods to a VAT registered company in another EU member state;

(*c*) supply of new means of transport to a buyer in another EU member state;

(*d*) supply of goods, on which excise duty must be paid in another EU member state;

(*e*) supply of goods to countries outside the EU;

(*f*) work on goods, for subsequent transportation to countries outside the EU;

(*g*) necessary equipment for ships;

(*h*) sale and hiring out of aircraft and ships over five gross register tons (sports planes and pleasure crafts are excluded).

Finland

Exemptions within Finland

4.35   Small businesses with turnover of less than € 8,500 are not required to register, but may opt for taxation.

Finland can exempt from VAT the sale, lease, repair and maintenance of vessels for international trade provided the vessel is at least 10 metres in length and is not used for pleasure. Also exempt are subscribed news-papers and periodicals and the printing of membership publications distributed to corporations organised for public benefit. Services supplied by authors, artists and performers are exempt. Agents for such persons are also exempt provided the individual is not an independent legal entity. The sale of goods and related services by blind persons are exempt, provided the only help given is by the blind person's family, as are interpretation services for deaf persons.

Other exemptions include hospital and medical care, social welfare services, educational, financial and insurance services, lotteries, transactions in bank notes and coins used as legal tender and rental property including building land.

Exemptions at importation

4.36   Exemptions at importation apply if the goods would have been exempt if sold in Finland. This includes subscribed newspapers and periodicals and certain types of vessels and aircraft.

Exemptions from intra-Community supplies

4.37   Intra-Community supplies are zero-rated provided that the supplier is registered for VAT and retains proof of the transport of the goods to another member state and receives the VAT number of the purchaser.

When goods are transferred by a business in Finland to a branch of the same business in another member state, there is deemed to be an intra-Community supply in Finland and an intra-Community acquisition in the other member state.

International traffic

4.38   The domestic leg of international goods transport is exempt if it is part of the transport to or from Finland and a non-EU country. The same applies to ancillary transport services.

France

Exemptions without credit

Real property

4.39   The following rules apply:

(*a*)   leasing of residential immovable property is always VAT exempt unless hotel services are included;

(*b*)   leasing of commercial immovable property is subject to VAT if it is furnished. For other properties the lessor has an express option to tax, provided this is disclosed in the leasing agreement if the lessor is not registered for VAT;

(*c*)   the first sale of new buildings which occurs within five years of construction is subject to VAT.

Financial activities

4.40   Most banking activities are VAT exempt, but certain persons may opt to tax certain supplies, e.g.:

(*a*)   credit transactions regarding receipts other than interest;

(*b*)   transactions involving commercial paper and covering receipts other than discounts and similar commission fees;

(*c*)   dealing in securities;

(*d*)   administration of investment funds;

(*e*)   factoring operations.

Other exemptions

4.41   The following transactions are also exempt without credit:

(*a*)   certain fishing products;

(*b*)   goods sold by associations for disabled persons;

(*c*)   new waste material and recycled material under certain conditions;

(*d*)   certain used goods;

(*e*)   dental prostheses supplied by dentists and dental surgeons;

(*f*)   transactions in human organs, blood and milk (delivery, commissions, etc.) and other human products on condition that they are used for medical purposes;

(*g*)   medical services by public and private hospitals (but the exemption does not apply to additional services which are not part of the medical treatment nor to veterinary services);

(*h*)   education (private language institutes, driving schools, and sports schools are usually taxable);

(*i*)   services rendered by authors, composers and sculptors unless they opt for taxation;

(*j*)   betting, lotteries and casinos;

(*k*)   leasing or letting out of furnished immovable property for dwelling purposes;

(*l*)   insurance transactions;

(*m*)   transactions by non-profit making organisations;

(*n*)   stamp duty, postage stamps.

Exemptions with credit

4.42   The main exemption with credit supplies in France are exports and intra-Community supplies.

An export supply by a taxable person is in principle taxable since the place of the supply will usually be in France. However, export transactions and services are exempt from VAT and the exporter is allowed to deduct VAT previously paid in relation to these exports. This exemption is subject to formal conditions checked by the French Tax Authorities.

Germany

Exemptions without credit

General

4.43   German VAT law contains no significant differences from the general exemptions under EU law, but there are some minor differences.

Exempt with the option to tax

4.44   Provisions in German law allow the option to tax certain supplies, as follows:

(*a*)   financial activities – the turnover from the management of special investment funds is excluded.

(*b*)   supplies of real estate – the sale of real estate is subject to a special transfer tax in Germany (*Grunderwerbsteuer*). If the business opts to tax, the VAT basis is influenced by this. An option requires that the acquiring party is a business which uses the property for the purpose of its business.

(c)   letting of real estate – the option only applies where the tenant can claim input tax relief.

Only the supplier of any of the above has the right to opt to tax.

Exemptions with credit

4.45   Certain transactions are exempt from VAT with credit, for example:

(a)   both purchases and sales in intra-Community triangular arrangements, where three different VAT registered parties are involved and the goods move from the first EU member state to the last. The exemption also applies to non-EU businesses registered for VAT in an EU member state;

(b)   contract work, in which case it is not necessary for the finished work to be returned to the business dispatching the materials;

(c)   export of goods to EU member states and non-EU countries.

Greece

Exemptions without credit

Real property

4.46   The supply and leasing of real estate is usually exempt from VAT, but a supply prior to first occupation of the building is taxable.

Financial activities

4.47   The following financial activities are exempt from VAT:

(a)   insurance and reinsurance transactions, including related services performed by insurance brokers and agents;

(b)   dealings in foreign currency, bank notes and coins used as legal tender with the exception of collectors' items;

(c)   transactions in shares, dividends, bonds, debentures and other securities;

(d)   management of mutual funds;

(e)   granting and negotiation of credit, as well as the management of such credit;

(*f*)   deposits, current accounts, payments, transfers of deposits, remittances, claims, credit notes, cheques, excluding collection of claims on behalf of third parties.

Other exemptions

4.48   Certain other transactions are exempt from VAT, for example:

(i)   supplies of public postal services;

(ii)   activities of the national radio and television company;

(iii)   supplies of non-bottled water;

(iv)   supplies of services by lawyers and public notaries;

(v)   supplies of services by dental technicians including dental prostheses;

(vi)   supplies of services by veterinary surgeons;

(vii)   supplies of services by authors, artists and critics of works of art, except those provided directly to the general public;

(viii) educational services provided by public or private institutions;

(ix)   state lotteries, soccer coupons and the national horse racing lotteries;

(x)   supplies and distribution of newspapers and periodicals by agencies, news-stands and other retailers, provided these are circulated through distribution agencies.

Exemptions with credit

4.49   Certain transactions are exempt from VAT with credit, for example:

(*a*)   purchases and sales in intra-Community triangular arrangements where three different VAT registered parties are involved and the goods move from the first EU member state to the last;

(*b*)   contract work is also exempt where more than two parties and/or more than two EU member states are involved.

Ireland

Exemptions without credit

Real property

4.50   The supply of property is exempt from VAT, except for the supply of property which has been developed since 31 October 1972 and where certain other conditions are met. The short-term letting of property, i.e. for a period of less than ten years, is exempt from VAT, excluding:

(*a*) letting of machinery or business installations when let separately from any other real property of which such machinery or installations form a part;

(*b*) parking accommodation for vehicles;

(*c*) hire of safes.

Financial activities

4.51 The following financial activities are exempt from VAT:

(*a*) issue, transfer or receipt of, any dealing in, stocks, shares, debentures and other securities, other than documents establishing title to goods;

(*b*) operation of any current, deposit or savings account and the negotiation of or dealings in, payments, transfers, debts, cheques and other negotiable instruments, excluding debt collection and factoring;

(*c*) issue, transfer, receipt of, or any dealing in currency, bank notes and metal coins, in use as legal tender in any country, excluding such bank notes and coins when supplied as investment goods or as collectors' items;

(*d*) lending money or affording credit;

(*e*) management of an undertaking which is:

  (i) a collective investment fund;

  (ii) administered by the holder of an authority granted pursuant to the EU;

  (iii) a unit trust scheme established solely for the purpose of superannuation fund schemes or charities; or

  (iv) determined by the Minister of Finance to be a collective investment undertaking;

(*f*) services providing for the reimbursement of a person in respect of the supply by him of goods or services in accordance with a credit card, charge card or similar card scheme.

Other exemptions

4.52 Certain other transactions are exempt from VAT, for example:

(*a*)   school or university education, and vocational training or retraining, provided by recognised educational establishments, and education, training or retraining of a similar kind;

(*b*)   professional services of a medical nature, excluding such services supplied in the course of carrying on a business which consists wholly or partly of selling goods;

(*c*)   supplies by dental technicians of services of a dental nature and of dentures or other prostheses;

(*d*)   professional services of a dental or optical nature;

(*e*)   hospital and medical care or treatment provided by a hospital, nursing home, clinic or similar establishment;

(*f*)   services for the protection or care of children and young persons;

(*g*)   supplies of goods and services closely related to welfare and social security by non-profit making organisations;

(*h*)   promotion of and admissions to live or theatrical musical performances, including circuses, but excluding dances;

(*i*)   agency services with regard to:

    (i)   arrangement of passenger transport or accommodation for persons;

    (ii)   collection of insurance premiums and financial activities noted above;

(*j*)   insurance services, including the collection and sale of premiums and claims handling and settlement services;

(*k*)   public postal services;

(*l*)   national broadcasting and television services, excluding advertising;

(*m*)   transport of passengers and their accompanying luggage;

(*n*)   betting;

(*o*)   issue of tickets or coupons for the purpose of a lottery;

(*p*)   promotion of, and admission of spectators to, sporting events.

Exemptions with credit

4.53   Exemptions with credit are known as zero-rated supplies in Ireland. Certain transactions are exempt from VAT with credit; for example, intra-Community supplies, provided:

  (i)   the customer is registered for VAT in another EU member state;

  (ii)   the customer's VAT number is obtained and retained in the supplier's records;

(iii) both the VAT number of the supplier and the customer are shown on the invoice;

(iv) goods are dispatched to another EU member state; and

(v) evidence that the goods have left Ireland is retained (e.g. delivery dockets, bills of lading, proof of payment from customer, etc.).

In addition, there are special exemptions linked to bonded warehouses, free zones and other areas. Ireland has two free zones, Shannon Customs Free Airport and Ringaskiddy Free Port.

Italy

Exemptions without credit

Real property

4.54   The supply of unimproved land is not subject to VAT.

The letting of real property and any movable goods intended for the permanent use or furnishing of that real property, excluding properties used exclusively to carry on commercial activities, is exempt from VAT.

Financial activities

4.55   The following financial activities are exempt from VAT:

(*a*)   credit transactions and related services of banks and other credit institutions including credits secured by warrants and similarly secured transactions;

(*b*)   management services of banks and credit institutions with respect to mutual investment funds;

(*c*)   activities related to foreign exchange and credit transactions in foreign currency;

(*d*)   insurance, life insurance and reinsurance activities and the services of intermediaries;

(*e*)   activities related to shares, bonds, and other securities not representing merchandise.

Other exemptions

4.56   Certain other transactions are exempt from VAT, for example:

(*a*)   public transportation of individuals between towns less than 50km apart;

(*b*)   services of the national post;

(*c*) services supplied by hospitals, clinics and other authorised health institutions;

(*d*) supplies of medicines by hospitals and similar establishments;

(*e*) ambulance services;

(*f*) funeral services;

(*g*) services by homes for abandoned children, orphanages, asylums, rest homes for old people etc.;

(*h*) social welfare and assistance services to employees;

(*i*) supplies of human organs, blood and milk;

(*j*) services rendered by persons in medical professions, except services by veterinary surgeons;

(*k*) instruction provided by recognised schools or education institutions;

(*l*) services supplied by libraries, museums, monuments, galleries, castles, etc.;

(*m*) supplies of goods purchased or imported without deducting VAT;

(*n*) supplies of investment gold (ingots and coins) having determined purity;

(*o*) free supplies of certain assets to public administration agencies and not profit companies.

Exemptions with credit

4.57 Certain transactions are exempt from VAT with credit, for example:

(*a*) both purchases and sales in intra-Community triangular arrangements, where three different VAT registered parties are involved and the goods move from the first EU member state to the last;

(*b*) services on movable goods (e.g. work, repair) under the following conditions:

   (i) services must be carried out on national or EU goods;

   (ii) goods must be transported or forwarded from another EU member state by, or on behalf of, the resident company rendering the service, or by the customer who must be registered for VAT in another EU member state.

Luxembourg

Exemptions without credit

Real property

4.58   The supply of real estate is generally exempt, with the exception of supplies pursuant to a building contract. However, a business may opt for taxation, provided the purchaser agrees and uses it for taxable activities.

The letting of real estate is exempt from VAT, except:

(*a*)   letting of temporary accommodation to non-permanent guests;

(*b*)   letting of camping sites;

(*c*)   letting of parking spaces, other than those beside public roads;

(*d*)   leasing of machines and business installations of any kind;

(*e*)   letting of safe deposit facilities by banks.

The option to tax exists for all the above supplies under the same provisions as for the sale of real property.

Financial activities

4.59   The following financial activities are exempt from VAT:

(*a*)   granting, negotiation and management of credit;

(*b*)   entry into and the negotiation and administration of credit guarantees or any other security for credit;

(*c*)   transactions in respect of debts (except debt collection) and the negotiation of such operations;

(*d*)   transactions involving cheques and other commercial paper;

(*e*)   transactions involving deposits and current accounts;

(*f*)   payments and bank transfers;

(*g*)   transactions involving foreign currency, bank notes and coins (except gold coins);

(*h*)   supplies (other than those to the Central Bank of Luxembourg) regarding gold bars, plaquettes or gold coins which are legal means of payment;

(*i*)   transactions involving shares and company bonds;

(*j*)   services connected with issuing transactions;

(*k*)   services concerning the administration of undertakings for collective investment;

(*l*)   supplies of stamps valid for use in postal services;

(*m*)   insurance and reinsurance transactions, including related services performed by insurance brokers and insurance agents, except supplies by experts who evaluate insurance indemnities.

Other exemptions

4.60   Certain other transactions are exempt from VAT, for example:

(*a*)   supplies of water by public bodies;

(*b*)   supplies of goods and services (e.g. supplies of water, electricity, gas, heating, cooling) supplied to the joint owners of apartments, buildings, condominiums, etc. by a union of joint owners;

(*c*)   betting and gambling at sporting events or in games of chance;

(*d*)   certain medical services;

(*e*)   certain social sector supplies;

(*f*)   educational supplies.

Exemptions with credit

4.61   The transfer of a business is not subject to VAT but the transferor may still recover input VAT relating to the transaction. Also, exports and intra-Community supplies are exempt with credit if certain conditions are met.

The Netherlands

Exemptions without credit

Real property

4.62   The supply of immovable property is a taxable supply from the time of construction until two years after it has been put into use for the first time. Other supplies of immovable property are exempt unless both seller and buyer opt for taxation.

In the Netherlands, the letting of immovable property is taxable if both the supplier and the customer opt for taxation, provided the property is not for residential purposes.

Financial activities

4.63   The following financial transactions are exempt from VAT:

4.64 *Exemptions*

(*a*)   all transactions in respect of Dutch or foreign coins and bank notes which have the status of legal tender in any country;

(*b*)   all transactions involving securities which do not represent goods, except administration and safe keeping;

(*c*)   management of funds for collective investment raised by investment funds and investment companies;

(*d*)   the provision of credit and the establishment of credit transactions;

(*e*)   all transactions involving the operating of current accounts, deposits, payments, transfers, debt claims, cheques and other such documents, with the exception of the collection of debts;

(*f*)   guarantee transactions;

(*g*)   insurance transactions and services of insurance agents.

The option to tax is not available for the above activities.

Other exemptions without credit

4.64   Certain other exemptions apply in the Netherlands, for example:

(*a*)   non-commercial activities of public radio and television broadcasting organisations;

(*b*)   supplies of food and medicine by a hospital or nursing home, provided there is no intention to make a profit;

(*c*)   supplies of goods by dentists and dental technicians;

(*d*)   certain supplies of goods of a social or cultural nature (specified by general government administrative orders), provided the business does not aim to make a profit and that its activities do not distort competition with profit making businesses;

(*e*)   nursing care by hospitals or nursing homes, provided there is no intention to make a profit;

(*f*)   services by officially recognised youth organisations;

(*g*)   services supplied by physicians, psychologists, nurses, speech therapists, midwives, physiotherapists, dentists and dental technicians, with the exception of those supplied by veterinary surgeons;

(*h*)   transportation by ambulance;

(*i*)   certain supplies of services of a social or cultural nature;

(*j*)   officially recognised institutions providing education;

(*k*)   services supplied by composers, writers and journalists;

(*l*)   services supplied (including supplies of related goods) by employees' and employers' organisations or organisations with a political, religious, patriotic, ideological, or charitable character, to their members for a consideration according to the articles of association. The exemption may be waived if serious distortion of competition is expected. Employers' organisations may also elect to be treated as taxable persons;

(*m*) services supplied by certain non-profit making organisations in such fields as health care, nursing home care and the building of houses for low income groups, provided there is no serious distortion of competition;

(*n*) certain fund-raising activities of organisations which supply exempt services, e.g. services in the social or cultural fields;

(*o*) management of collective investment funds.

Exemptions with credit

4.65 Certain transactions are exempt with credit for VAT, for example:

(*a*) supplies of goods by Dutch businesses to businesses in other EU countries. If a customer returns goods to his supplier in the Netherlands, no intra-Community supply occurs, provided the supplier sends a credit invoice to the customer. If goods are stored in the Netherlands, before they are delivered by the supplier to another EU member state, no intra-Community supply occurs. The supplier should charge the local Dutch VAT rate to the customer unless the purchaser gives a VAT identification number to the supplier, in which case the supplier may assume that the customer will pay VAT on the acquisition of the goods in the EU member state of destination. However, the supplier should keep documentary evidence that the goods have left the Netherlands, although there are no clear guidelines as to how much evidence is required. Dutch VAT must be charged if the EU customer cannot supply a VAT identification number;

(*b*) services regarding tangible goods and domestic transport of goods, ancillary services such as loading etc. connected with the intra-Community transport of goods. The above services are zero-rated provided the customer is registered for VAT purposes in another EU member state;

(*c*) transfer of all or part of a business as a going concern.

Portugal

Exemptions without credit

Real property

4.66   The supply of real estate is exempt from VAT, unless the supplier opts for taxation and the purchaser uses the real estate for taxable purposes.

In Portugal, the leasing and renting of immovable property is usually exempt unless the lessor opts for taxation and provided both the lessor and the lessee are businesses. However, the exemption does not apply to the following transactions which are always subject to VAT:

(*a*)   the letting of facilities in the course of carrying on a hotel business;

(*b*)   the letting of facilities for camping in tents and caravans and for collective parking of vehicles;

(*c*)   the letting of safes;

(*d*)   the letting of facilities designated for exhibition and advertising purposes;

(*e*)   the letting of permanently installed machinery and equipment separately from any other immovable goods;

(*f*)   the leasing of immovable property resulting in a transfer for consideration of the right to exploit a business or industry.

Financial activities

4.67   Banking and insurance, including reinsurance and the services of insurance brokers and agents, are generally exempt from VAT.

Other exemptions without credit

4.68   Certain exemptions apply in Portugal, for example:

(*a*)   copyrights supplied by authors;

(*b*)   literary, scientific, technical or artistic original works edited and supplied by the author;

(*c*)   stamps;

(*d*)   human organs, blood and milk;

(*e*)   services of veterinary surgeons, translators, interpreters, guides and private couriers, unless they opt for taxation;

(*f*)   physicians, dentists and paramedic services;

(*g*)   hospital and medical care or treatment at hospitals, clinics, health resorts and similar establishments;

(*h*)   services provided without a profit motive for the protection and care of children or young people;

(*i*)   welfare and social security services;

(*j*)   education services by institutions and individual teachers;

(*k*)   services supplied by public bodies or non-profit making bodies in connection with meetings, seminars, lectures, courses and similar events of a scientific, cultural, educational or technical nature;

(*l*)   services supplied by lecturers to conferences;

(*m*)   services rendered to the organisers of theatrical productions and concerts, to producers of records and other sound producing devices, to producers of movies and other picture producing devices and to organisers of sporting events and other artists and by athletes and bullfighters;

(*n*)   gaming and lottery transactions and any game of chance.

Exemptions with credit

4.69   Certain transactions are exempt with credit for VAT, for example:

(*a*)   both purchases and sales in intra-Community triangular arrangements, where three different VAT registered parties are involved and the goods move from the first EU member state to the last;

(*b*)   imports of goods from a non-EU member state into Portugal followed by an intra-Community supply to another EU member state provided the following conditions are met:

   (i)   the import is by a taxable person;

   (ii)   goods are transported to another EU member state within 30 days of import;

   (iii)   the taxable person is able to prove the dispatch of the goods to another EU member state; and

   (iv)   a bank guarantee is provided if requested.

Spain

Exemptions without credit

Real property

4.70   The leasing of residential immovable property is exempt from VAT except for services supplied by hotels as covered in the EU

Directive. The leasing of land including agricultural buildings is also exempt but this does not apply to parking spaces, warehouses or leasing of land (or housing) with a purchase option where the purchase itself would be taxable.

Exemptions in the public interest

4.71   The remaining exemptions in Spanish legislation are broadly in line with EU legislation although there are minor differences in respect of certain activities in the public interest.

The election to waive exemption

4.72   Spanish legislation allows an election to waive exemption on the following otherwise exempt supplies:

(*a*)   purchase of rural land which is not available for development;

(*b*)   the contribution of land to private bodies (*Juntas de Compensación*) for development;

(*c*)   the purchase of buildings including the land on which they stand provided they are not new, i.e. they must have been put to use in the two years prior to purchase.

Other conditions also apply as follows:

(i) the purchaser must be VAT registered;

(ii) the purchaser must be entitled to 100% input tax deduction.

Other exemptions

4.73   Professional services comprising authors' rights rendered by artists, writers, photographers, composers and similar are exempt.

Supplies of works of art and similar goods that are not normally used for industrial purposes when supplied directly by the artist or his agent are taxable at the 7% reduced rate.

Sweden

Transfer of a going concern

4.74   In the case of a transfer of all or part of a business including assets, exemption applies to the supply of stock, equipment and other assets. Exemption also applies to the supply of equipment for which the supplier had no right to deduct input tax at the time of the acquisition by him. Otherwise, the transfer of assets is subject to VAT at 25%.

Real estate

4.75   The transfer and letting of all real estate is exempt. Exemption also applies to gas, water, heating and network for radio and television connected with the letting of real estate. However, the transfer or letting of permanently installed equipment and machinery is subject to VAT at the 25% standard rate.

The main rule concerning real estate is that the transfer and letting of real estate is exempt from VAT. However, for the letting of real estate used for business purposes, the owner may apply to opt for taxation at the standard VAT rate of 25% provided that the tenant is at least partly liable to VAT. This option applies under the same conditions for both the owners of the real estate and, in the case of sub-letting, to the first tenant and also to the second tenant when there is further subletting.

Health and welfare

4.76   Exemption applies to the following activities:

(*a*)   health, dental and social services;

(*b*)   transportation of patients by specially equipped vehicles;

(*c*)   medical chiropody;

(*d*)   supply of human organs, blood and milk.

Education

4.77   Education is exempted when comprising compulsory, upper secondary or university education, as is education provided by schools which are recognised by the government or where the student is entitled to study grants. Exemption also applies to a teacher who is hired by an exempted school and to adult education where this is subsidised by government or municipal departments. However, certain education supplies are subject to VAT at the standard VAT rate of 25%, as are certain books/manuals used for individual studies and certain types of education which cannot be exempted under the above provisions.

Banking, finance and insurance

4.78   Bank and financing activities including the transfer or dealing in shares and services of intermediaries and similar activities are exempt, as are the activities of insurance agents' intermediaries and the administration of securities and investment gold. Taxable persons may opt for taxation of investment gold where the purchaser is subject to a reverse charge for a supply taking place within Sweden. Insurance and financial services and investment gold are zero-rated when supplied to customers outside the EU.

Cultural activities

4.79   Library and museum activities are exempted when subsidised by government or municipality, otherwise the reduced VAT rate of 6% applies.

A creative artist's works of literature, music, etc. are exempt where the work performed is protected by Swedish copyright, although the transfer or letting of rights to audio or visual recordings of such works or performances are subject to the reduced VAT rate of 6%.

Entrance fees to sports grounds or centres for both participants and the audience are exempt when the services are supplied by government, municipality or non-profit making organisations. Otherwise the reduced VAT rate of 6% applies.

Other exemptions

4.80   Exemption applies to radio and television production where these are subsidised by the government. Exemption also applies to periodical magazines of sports clubs, churches, etc. and to advertising in such papers. The production of such periodicals, including printing services, is zero-rated.

Coins and notes valid as means of payment in general circulation are exempt, as are churchyard services, lotteries, betting and gambling.

United Kingdom

Exemptions without credit

Real property

4.81   There are numerous exclusions applying to the exemption of the leasing or letting of immovable property, including the following selection:

(*a*)   the grant of facilities for playing sport;

(*b*)   the grant of a right to occupy a seat at a sports ground, theatre or concert hall;

(*c*)   the grant of the right to take game or fish;

(*d*)   the grant of any right to fell or take standing timber;

(*e*)   the provision of hotel, caravan pitches, or camping facilities.

Financial activities

4.82   Most financial activities in the UK are exempt without credit and there is no facility for the option to tax.

Certain other exemptions apply in the UK, for example:

(*a*)   postal services;

(*b*)   betting, gaming and lotteries;

(*c*)   education;

(*d*)   health and welfare services;

(*e*)   burial and cremation;

(*f*)   services by trade unions and professional bodies in return for subscriptions;

(*g*)   sport, sports competitions and physical education;

(*h*)   works of art;

(*i*)   certain fund-raising events by charities;

(*j*)   cultural services;

(*k*)   supplies of goods where VAT on acquisition cannot be recovered.

Exemptions with credit (zero rate)

4.83   Supplies eligible for zero rating have been covered elsewhere in this book and include exports and intra-Community supplies. Simplified arrangements apply to EU triangular transactions in that all supplies are zero-rated and the final consumer accounts for acquisition VAT. Supply and installation contracts are also treated as intra-Community supplies subject to simplification rules.

Chapter 5

Basis of Taxation

Basis of taxation: EU rules

General

5.1   The basis of taxation for any transaction is the total sum paid for the goods or services by the customer or third party. The basis of taxation on importation is the amount payable or the value for customs purposes.

The consideration for supplies of goods and services must, in principle, be capable of being expressed as an amount in money excluding any reference to estimated values and based on objective criteria, such as open market value. However, EU member states may be authorised by the EU Council to apply different criteria provided they are under strict control. There must be a direct link between the goods or services supplied and the consideration received.

Supplies of goods and services

Expenses included in the taxable amount for the supply of goods and services

5.2   The following expenses are included in the taxable amount:

(*a*)   subsidies directly linked to the price;

(*b*)   taxes, duties, levies and charges;

(*c*)   incidental expenses, such as commission, packing, transport and insurance costs;

(*d*)   expenses covered by separate agreement if considered incidental by the EU member state;

(*e*)   returnable packing costs, based on each EU member state's option;

(*f*)   price reductions in case of partial or total non-payment under conditions allowed by member states.

[*EC Sixth Directive 77/388, Arts 11(A)(2), (C) and 28E*].

Expenses excluded from the taxable amount for the supply of goods and services

5.3   The following expenses are excluded from the taxable amount:

(*a*)   VAT itself;

(*b*)   price reductions by way of discount for early payment;

(*c*)   price discounts and rebates accounted for at the time of supply;

(*d*)   suspense account items for expenses paid out by a taxable person in the name of the customer and recovered from the customer;

(*e*)   returnable packing costs based on each EU member state's option;

(*f*)   price reductions for cancellation;

(*g*)   price reductions in case of partial or total non-payment under conditions allowed by member states.

[*EC Sixth Directive 77/388, Art 11(A)(3), (C)*].

Values expressed in a foreign currency

5.4   If the taxable amount is expressed in a foreign currency, it is calculated using the exchange rate applicable at the latest selling rate recorded, at the time the VAT is due.

Furthermore, it should be the exchange rate on the most representative exchange market or markets of the EU member state concerned, in accordance with the procedures laid down by that EU member state.

[*EC Sixth Directive 77/388, Art 11(C)(2)*].

Private use and self-supplies of goods and services

5.5   The above general rules do not apply if no consideration is received. In the case of private use and self-supplies of goods, the purchase price of the goods or similar goods or, if there is no purchase price, the cost price, determined at the time of supply, is considered to be the taxable amount.

For private use of services, the full cost to the taxable person providing the services is the taxable amount. For self-supplies of services, the open market value is the taxable amount. 'Open market value' shall mean the amount which a customer at the marketing stage would have to pay to a supplier at arm's length within the territory of the country at the time of supply under the conditions of fair competition to obtain the services in question.

[*EC Sixth Directive 77/388, Art 11(A)(1)*].

Second-hand goods and works of art

5.6   For second-hand goods, rules provide for the taxable basis to be reduced to the difference between the purchase and selling price. This rule applies if the supplier buys the goods from non-taxable persons such as private individuals.

Leasing

5.7   Leasing is not dealt with separately and the taxable amount provisions.

Subsidies

5.8   In the case of subsidies paid by public authorities, it is important to identify whether there is a connection between the subsidy given and the supply made. Much will depend on the circumstances whether this applies.

Import of goods

General

5.9   The taxable amount for the import of goods shall be the value for customs purposes, determined in accordance with the Community provisions. The value for customs purposes usually means the transaction price.

Expenses included in the taxable amount

5.10   The taxable amount shall include the following expenses:

(*a*)   taxes, duties, levies and other charges due outside the member state of import and those due by reason of import, excluding the VAT to be levied;

(*b*)   incidental expenses, such as commission, packing, transport and insurance costs, incurred up to the first destination within the EU member state of importation. First destination means the place shown on the consignment note or any other transport document used to clear the goods in the country of importation.

In the absence of such evidence, the first destination shall be taken to be the place of the first transfer of cargo in that member state. Each EU member state may include in the taxable amount the incidental expenses referred to above where they result from transport to another destination, if the latter is known at the time when the chargeable event occurs.

[*EC Sixth Directive 77/388, Art 11(B)*].

Expenses not included in the taxable amount

5.11   The taxable amount shall not include:

(*a*)   price reductions by way of discount for early payment;

(*b*)   price discounts and rebates allowed to the customer and accounted for at the time of import.

[*EC Sixth Directive 77/388, Art 11(B)(4)*].

Temporary exports of goods followed by re-import

5.12   If goods have been temporarily exported outside the EU and are reimported after having undergone repair, processing or adaption abroad or having been made up or reworked abroad, and are then reimported, each EU member state shall take steps to ensure that the treatment of the goods for VAT purposes is the same as that which would have applied to the goods in question had the above operations been carried out within an EU member state.

[*EC Sixth Directive 77/388, Art 11(B)(5)*].

Imports where values are expressed in a foreign currency

5.13   If the taxable amount on importation is expressed in a foreign currency, the exchange rate shall be determined in accordance with the Community provisions governing the calculation of the value for customs purposes.

[*EC Sixth Directive 77/388, Art 11(C)(2)*].

Intra-Community acquisitions of goods

5.14   The taxable amount for intra-Community acquisitions is the same as for domestic supplies of goods in the relevant EU member state. For so-called fictitious acquisitions (e.g. transfers of own assets from one EU member state to another) the purchase price of similar goods or cost price is the taxable amount.

Specific rules in the various EU countries

Austria

General

5.15   The basis of taxation in Austria comprises all payments by the customer to the supplier in consideration for a supply of goods or services, excluding the VAT itself.

For imports, the taxable basis is the same as the value for customs purposes.

There are special rules for business transactions between related parties. Open market value is usually used to establish the value of the supply.

Discounts

5.16   If a discount is already shown on the invoice it is excluded from the taxable basis where the buyer is entitled to rely on it immediately. If the discount is granted after the supply, it reduces the buyer's debt and the subsequent basis of taxation.

Transactions between connected parties

5.17   There are special rules for business transactions between related parties. Open market value is normally used to establish the value of the supply.

Goods traded in

5.18   The value of trade in goods is taken into account as part of the basis of taxation.

Part exchange of goods

5.19   The taxable basis for the buyer is the open market value of the goods supplied by the seller and vice versa.

Bad debts

5.20   VAT may be adjusted at the time when bad debts are written off.

Returned goods

5.21   Returned goods reduce the basis of taxation of the initial transaction. If the goods are returned, the transaction is treated as a supply of goods by the initial buyer.

Second-hand goods

5.22   There are special provisions in Austrian VAT law regarding supplies of used cars and antiques. Only the margin between the purchase and the selling price is subject to taxation, provided the goods have not been purchased from another VAT registered business.

Works of art

5.23   For VAT purposes works of art are treated in the same way as antiques. VAT is charged on the difference between the purchase and selling prices.

Self-supplies

5.24   The basis of taxation for self-supplied goods or services is the cost price of the goods or services to the supplier.

Private use

5.25   The taxable basis of goods appropriated for private use is the purchase price. Where there is no purchase price the basis of taxation is the cost price of the goods.

Belgium

General

5.26   The taxable basis is the aggregate of the price, charges, and other consideration levied by the supplier of goods or services on the contracting party. It includes, inter alia, any insurance and transportation costs charged by the supplier, regardless of whether or not those costs are part of a separate agreement between the parties.

Open market value

5.27   Open market value is the price which would be charged in Belgium at the time the VAT is due under conditions of free competition in an arm's length transaction between a supplier and a purchaser on the same commercial level.

Discounts

5.28   Discounts given by a supplier for early payment are excluded from the taxable basis. Once a discount for early payment is stated in a contract between the supplier and the customer, it is excluded from the taxable basis even if the customer does not pay in time to actually receive the discount.

Exchange transactions

5.29   An exchange of goods between two businesses constitutes two distinct supplies and VAT is due at the appropriate rate on both transactions. The value of the goods is the open market value.

If goods are exchanged between a business and a private individual or other non-taxable person, VAT is due on the open market value of the supply made by the business.

The same rules apply for services.

Goods traded in

5.30 If payment for goods is made partly in cash and partly with goods traded in, VAT is due on the total value of the consideration. The value of the traded-in goods is their open market value.

Bad debts

5.31 The supplier is entitled to a refund if the bad debt is totally or partially written-off, provided the loss of the debt is definite. This will depend on the circumstances.

In the case of a client's bankruptcy, a statement should be obtained from the liquidator or administrator of the business.

Returned goods

5.32 The supplier is entitled to a refund of VAT if a contract is dissolved by agreement or by court decision. VAT is also refunded where goods supplied are returned within six months.

Second-hand goods

5.33 Businesses which regularly purchase second-hand goods from non-businesses for resale may, with the permission of the Minister of Finance, compute the VAT due according to the margin between the purchase and selling prices.

Self-supplies of goods and services

5.34 The taxable basis for self-supplied goods is the purchase price of comparable goods. If there is no comparable price, the taxable basis is the cost of supplying such goods.

Private use

5.35 The taxable basis for private use of services is the open market value. The taxable basis for the private use of goods is the purchase price, or if the goods are self-produced and there is no comparable price, the cost price.

Buildings

5.36   If buildings and the land on which they stand are supplied for a single price, the taxable basis is obtained by deducting from the price the open market value of the land at the date of transfer. (The sale of land is subject to a 12.5% registration duty.)

Vehicles

5.37   The government has the power to determine a minimum taxable basis for supplies of vehicles for land, sea and air transportation.

Denmark

General

5.38   The taxable basis is the total amount of consideration payable for goods delivered and services rendered, excluding VAT itself.

In the case of transactions which are not conducted at arm's length, the taxable value may be determined as the normal selling price of the goods or services concerned. If that price is not available, the consideration comprises all costs plus the profit margin usually included in the taxable basis of such goods and services.

Discounts

5.39   Discounts which are subject to conditions that have not been satisfied at the time of supply are included in the taxable basis. Discounts may be excluded provided the following conditions are met:

(*a*)   the discount is granted to a registered business which is fully entitled to deduct VAT as input tax; and

(*b*)   a credit invoice is issued showing the amount of the discount and the corresponding amount of VAT.

Discounts subject to conditions that have been satisfied at the time of delivery may be deducted immediately in computing the taxable basis.

Part exchange transactions

5.40   If goods are traded in on the purchase of new goods, the taxable basis of the new goods is not affected. Part exchange is treated in the same way as barter transactions. The taxable basis of the new goods is equal to the normal price charged for such goods.

Barter trading

5.41 Barter trades are subject to taxation and VAT is computed on the normal selling price of the goods or services. Where both the seller and the buyer in a barter transaction have the full right to deduct the purchase VAT, it may be calculated on the basis of the difference between the respective values of the barter goods.

Bad debts

5.42 Businesses may deduct from their taxable sales 80% of the loss (the amount lost net of VAT) sustained due to bad debts which arise from goods and services supplied. If such debts are subsequently paid, whether in full or in part, 80% of the amount recovered is added to taxable turnover.

Returned goods

5.43 If a customer returns goods to a supplier and the supplier, accepting the returned goods, credits the customer for them, the supplier can deduct 80% of the credited amount from taxable turnover.

Second-hand cars

5.44 As a general rule, second-hand goods are taxable on their full selling price.

Special rules apply to car dealers when calculating VAT in connection with the purchase or sale of certain second-hand cars, e.g. private cars and small lorries. The rules state that the dealer is only required to account for VAT on any value that has been actually added, ie. the margin.

Self-supplies

5.45 The taxable price for self-supplied goods and services is the value of the transaction to a third party.

Private use

5.46 If the owner of a business uses goods or services of the business for private purposes, the taxable basis of those goods or services is their purchase or production price. The same applies for supplies to employees, shareholders, etc.

Finland

5.47 The taxable amount is the consideration excluding VAT itself. The taxable amount at importation includes taxes, duties, levies and other charges due, plus packing, transport and insurance incurred up to the point the goods reach their destination in Finland. It is possible to exclude from the taxable base discounts, rebates and returns. However, if granted after the supply, a credit note should be issued.

VAT on bad debts may be recovered if it is clear that the customer will not pay. A debt may be considered bad in accordance with the Accounting Act.

In the case of a self-supply of goods or services, the tax base is the total of the direct and indirect expenses incurred in order to produce the goods or services. Otherwise, it is the purchase price or market price, whichever is the lower. There is a de minimis limit of € 840 per year for private entrepreneurs.

France

General

5.48   The taxable basis for supplies of goods and services is generally the amount received by the supplier. In certain cases only the profit element is subject to VAT, e.g. real estate (taxation on the margin).

Interest charged to a customer, including interest for late payment, if it is identified on the same invoice of supply, is included in the taxable basis.

Transparent intermediaries

5.49   Intermediaries are subject to VAT on their commission fee if the following conditions are met:

(*a*)   they receive an express order before the transaction was carried out;

(*b*)   title to the property is not transferred to them;

(*c*)   they gave an account to their principal with respect to the details of the transaction and any additional expenses; and

(*d*)   their remuneration is fixed before the transactions take place in terms of a percentage of the purchase or selling price of the goods or services concerned.

Goods traded in

5.50   Where goods are traded in, VAT is due on the full consideration.

Part exchange of goods

5.51   Part exchange of goods between two businesses involves two transactions both of which are usually taxable. VAT is due on the value of the goods supplied, increased by the balance of any cash paid. If goods are exchanged between a business and a non-business, VAT will be due on the normal value of the supply made by the business.

Bad debts

5.52   The taxable basis is not reduced in the case of bad debts. However, the business is entitled to a credit for input VAT if the price charged cannot, or can only partly, be collected. This input VAT will be either deducted or refunded. Formal conditions must be observed in order to claim the relevant VAT credit.

Returned goods

5.53   If a contract is cancelled and the goods are returned then the same provisions as for bad debts are applicable.

Second-hand goods

5.54   Businesses which sell business assets must usually charge. VAT on such sales under the normal rules. However, no VAT is due if input VAT was not recovered on the acquisition or import of the assets.

Businesses which trade in second-hand goods may opt to be taxed on either the difference between the purchase price paid and the selling price charged to their customers, or on the full selling price.

Sometimes second-hand goods may be purchased in a job lot. In such cases it will be impossible to determine the margin for individual items and the trader may compute VAT on 50% of the total selling price.

Works of art – VAT on the margin

5.55   Traders selling works of art must charge VAT on the difference between the purchase and selling price, provided the goods have not been purchased from another business. This does not apply to works of art which were exempt from VAT at import, when VAT is due on the full selling price.

If the purchase price cannot be exactly determined, 30% of the selling price may form the basis.

Self-supplies

5.56   The taxable basis for self-supplied goods is the purchase price of the goods concerned or of similar goods. If it is not possible to determine the purchase price (e.g. when the goods have been manufactured by the taxable person himself) then the cost price is used.

Private use

5.57   The private use of goods, i.e. the use of business assets for non-business purposes, is a taxable transaction. The taxable basis for the private use of goods is the same as for the self-supply of goods. For private use of services, cost price is used.

Buildings

5.58   The taxable basis for the supply of buildings is the selling price or open market value, whichever is higher.

Cost price is used as the basis for self-supplies of immovable property. This includes the value of the land acquired together with financial and administrative costs. The value of the work by the main contractor in order to complete the property is not part of the taxable basis.

Germany

General

5.59   The basis of taxation is everything paid by a customer to a supplier in order to receive goods or services, excluding the VAT itself. For imports, the value for customs purposes is used.

All incidental payments and charges except intermediary fees are included in the taxable basis, e.g. tips, premiums, disbursements, expenses, transport and insurance costs. Default interest, interest for late payment, interest upon a judgment and similar charges are treated as non-taxable compensation for damages.

There are special rules in Germany for business transactions between related parties if values are below open market value. The purchase price of the goods sold is used, or the costs in relation to the respective goods and/or services.

'Related parties' are defined as relatives or other persons and companies with close legal, economic or personal ties.

Discounts

5.60   If a discount is allowed to a customer and is shown separately on the invoice, it is excluded from the taxable basis. If it is granted after the supply, the liability may be reduced provided that the customer makes a corresponding reduction in the amount of previously paid VAT which may be deducted.

Calculation

5.61 In general, VAT is accounted for on the basis of invoices issued. However, it may be calculated on a cash basis in the following cases:

(*a*) businesses with an annual turnover of less than € 125,000 (€ 500,000 for businesses in the Eastern Part of Germany) in the previous year;

(*b*) businesses which have special permission from the tax authorities;

(*c*) self-employed professionals such as doctors, dentists, lawyers, tax advisors and auditors.

Goods traded in

5.62 No special rules apply for goods traded in.

Part exchange of goods

5.63 Where goods are given in part exchange for new goods, there are two independent transactions. VAT is due on the total open market value of both supplies. The same rules apply to services.

Bad debts

5.64 If a supplier is not able to collect debts due, the amount of VAT due may be adjusted.

Returned goods

5.65 If goods are returned to a supplier, the taxable basis must be adjusted and the supplier may claim a refund of VAT accordingly.

Second-hand goods

Margin scheme

5.66 Margin scheme rules apply on the supply of movable tangibles, if:

(*a*) the business buys and sells goods;

(*b*) the supply to the business took place within the EU and this acquisition was not subject to VAT or was taxed as a margin scheme supply; and

(*c*) the goods are neither precious stones nor rare metals.

The business may opt for the margin scheme for the supply of works of art and antiques imported by it, if the supply to it was taxable. The option is binding for two years.

The tax base is the difference between purchase price and sales price, excluding VAT. For goods with a purchase price not exceeding € 500, the tax base for the margin scheme may be the total difference of all sales within one year.

Margin scheme rules do not apply on the supply of intra-Community acquired goods, if the supply to the business was tax-free in the other member state or in the case of the intra-Community acquisition of new cars.

Private use of goods

5.67   If a taxable person takes goods out of the business for private use, the taxable basis is the purchase price plus ancillary expenses. If there is no purchase price, the taxable basis is the aggregate of production and acquisition costs.

If a taxable person performs a service for purposes outside the scope of his business, the value of the supply is based on the expenses attributable to the service provided.

The taxable basis for supplies of goods and services by a business to the following is the same as for private use:

(*a*)   employees and their relatives;

(*b*)   shareholders, members or persons related to them;

(*c*)   associated persons;

Self-supplies

5.68   The taxable basis for self-supplies of goods is the same as for private use.

Transport of persons by foreign businesses

5.69   The taxable basis for foreign businesses involved in the occasional transport of passengers within Germany is an average transportation fee per passenger per kilometre for the domestic leg of the journey.

Greece

General

5.70   The following items are included in the taxable basis:

(*a*)   interest on credit sales and interest as a result of delayed payments;

(*b*)   incidental expenses such as commissions, brokers fees, packing, insurance, transport, loading and unloading costs.

The following items are not included in the taxable basis:

(i)   price discounts granted to the purchaser, provided that they are duly documented according to the applicable legal provisions;

(ii)   price refunds in the event of total or partial cancellation of the supply of goods or services.

Newspapers and periodicals

5.71   The taxable basis for newspapers and periodicals for sales made by publishing and import companies, is their delivery price, without VAT, and after deducting commission payable to distribution agencies.

Part exchange of goods

5.72   For the part exchange of goods, the taxable basis is the open market value.

Self-supplies of goods and services

5.73   The taxable basis for the self-supply of goods is the purchase price of the goods themselves, or of similar goods, or in the absence of such a price, their cost at the time of supply.

For self-supplies of services, the taxable basis is the full overhead cost of providing such services.

Private use

5.74   The same rules apply to private use of goods and services as for self-supplies.

Ireland

General

5.75   The taxable basis is normally the total consideration which the supplier receives including all taxes, commission, costs and charges, excluding the VAT itself. The basis of taxation of imports of goods is the value of the goods for customs purposes, plus any taxes, duties or other charges levied outside the Republic and import duties levied in Ireland.

If the goods or services are supplied other than for monetary consideration, the open market value is the taxable basis.

If no separate charge is made for the packing of goods, the rate appropriate to the goods is applied. If containers are separately charged, each separate supply is chargeable at the appropriate rate. If, in connection with the supply of services, reasonable amounts are separately charged for postage or insurance paid on behalf of the customers, the supplier may treat such charges as not being liable to VAT.

Part exchange of goods

5.76   For exchanges of goods, the taxable basis is their open market value.

Calculations

5.77   Instead of calculating the VAT due on the basis of the invoice issued by a trader in any taxable period, it is possible for certain businesses to calculate VAT due on the basis of cash received during the particular taxable period. The following businesses may opt for the cash basis of accounting for VAT:

(*a*)   businesses whose turnover does not exceed € 635,000 per annum;

(*b*)   businesses where not less than 90% of turnover is derived from sales to persons who are not registered for VAT.

The cash basis provides automatic bad debt relief. If the rate of VAT changes between the date of the supply and the date of payment, VAT is payable at the rate in force when the supply was made.

Self-supplied goods and services

5.78   The taxable basis for self-supplied goods is the cost price of the goods to the supplier. The self-supply of a canteen service is considered to be a taxable service, and the taxable amount is the total cost of providing the service.

Second-hand goods

5.79   If second-hand movable goods are given in exchange or part exchange for goods of the same kind, only the actual amount of money paid is taxable.

Leasing

5.80   There is no distinction in relation to the taxable amount between finance and operating leases.

Italy

General

5.81   Normally, the taxable basis is the amount recorded on invoices issued by a supplier. If a business is not required to issue invoices, the taxable basis is the actual rather than the accrued revenue.

Incidental charges are included in the taxable basis, e.g. premiums, disbursements, expenses, transport and insurance costs.

If the price does not wholly consist of a sum of money, the taxable basis is the open market value.

The following items are excluded from the taxable basis:

(*a*)   interest for late payment or incorrect fulfilment of obligations;

(*b*)   normal value of goods supplied free of charge as a reduction or premium to conform with the original conditions of the contract;

(*c*)   any sum paid as reimbursement of advance payments made in the name of and charged to the other party to the contract;

(*d*)   the cost for packaging materials when the reimbursement upon surrender is expressly agreed upon.

Discounts

5.82   If a discount is shown separately on an invoice, it does not form part of the taxable basis.

If, however, the discount is not shown separately on an invoice, but is allowed at a later date, the VAT liability may be reduced provided the purchaser makes a corresponding reduction in the amount of previously paid VAT.

Goods traded in

5.83   The trade-in value of second-hand goods forms part of the consideration and is included in the taxable basis. For cars, the Minister of Finance accepts that if a new car is bought in exchange for money and a traded-in car, the purchaser of the car traded-in may be considered to be an agent who is entitled to sell the traded-in car on behalf of the former owner. Thus, the sale of the traded-in car by the former owner to the purchaser is not taxable.

Part exchange of goods

5.84   The taxable basis for each transaction is the open market value of the goods.

Bad debts

5.85   There is no relief for bad debts in Italy.

Returned goods

5.86   A supplier is entitled to reclaim VAT paid on goods and services supplied when the contract for such a supply is dissolved or nullified by agreement or by judgment. VAT is also refunded if the supplied goods are entirely or partially returned. If the return is agreed between the parties, the claim for a refund must be submitted within a year of the supply.

Second-hand goods

5.87   Suppliers of second-hand goods, fine arts and antiquities are subject to a special VAT regime. The taxable amount is equal to the difference between the selling price, inclusive of VAT, and the purchase price increased by any repair expense incurred. Suppliers of second-hand goods may not deduct input VAT paid on goods and services purchased. Input VAT related to general expenses is allowed.

Self-supplies of goods and services

5.88   The taxable basis for self-supplies of goods is their open market value. Self-supplies of services are not subject to VAT.

Private use

5.89   The taxable basis of goods appropriated for private use is the open market value of those goods. The same applies for supplies to the employees of a business and to the shareholders, members and other related persons of a legal entity.

Luxembourg

General

5.90   The taxable basis for supplies is either the price payable or, in the absence of such a price, the open market value.

The price includes any duties or taxes (other than VAT), any charges for commissions, packaging, transport, insurance and public subsidies.

The following items are excluded from the taxable basis:

(*a*) amounts received by a supplier from a purchaser as reimbursement for expenses paid out by the supplier in the name of and on behalf of the purchaser and entered into the records of the supplier in a suspense account;

(*b*) in the case of customs agents and other forwarding agents, customs duties and taxes paid on import in their own name.

The open market value is the price which a customer buying in the open market would have to pay for the supplies in question, had he dealt:

(i) with an independent trader;

(ii) within Luxembourg;

(iii) at the time of supply; and

(iv) under conditions of fair competition.

Goods traded in

5.91 The taxable basis for goods traded in is as follows:

(*a*) for a supplier who is entitled to an additional payment, the open market value of the goods traded in plus the amount of the additional payment;

(*b*) for a supplier who is required to pay an additional payment, the open market value of the traded-in goods less the amount of the additional payment made by him.

Part exchanges of goods

5.92 If goods are exchanged, there are two taxable transactions. The taxable basis for both transactions is open market value.

Bad debts

5.93 If it is expected that a customer will not pay all or part of a debt, an adjustment may be made provided a debt is up to two years old. If the unpaid amount is paid at a later stage, an adjustment must be made to reflect the payment. The adjustment must be made by both the supplier and the customer.

Returned goods

5.94 If a customer returns goods to a business and receives a refund or a credit for their value, an adjustment to the taxable basis must be made using the same procedure as for bad debts.

Self-supplies of goods and services

5.95   The taxable basis for self-supplies of goods is their open market value.

There are no provisions for the self-supply of services.

Private use

5.96   The taxable basis for private use of goods is their open market value. For the private use of services, the value is based on the expenses incurred by the supplier. The above also applies to supplies to employees, shareholders, etc.

The Netherlands

General

5.97   The taxable basis is the total sum or value charged for the goods or services supplied, excluding the VAT itself. All incidental charges (e.g. bonuses, fixed charges and packing charges) are included in the taxable basis.

The following items are excluded from the taxable basis:

(*a*)   interest charges for late payments;

(*b*)   certain incidental charges such as insurance costs and certain amounts collected and expended by the business in the name of and on behalf of a third party.

Discounts

5.98   If a discount is granted for immediate payment, the taxable amount is the cost of the goods and services less the discount, provided it is separately shown on the invoice.

If the discount is not separately shown, a VAT refund can be obtained by submitting a credit invoice.

Goods traded in

5.99   When a new item is supplied and the supplier takes a used item of the same kind in part exchange, the taxable amount is reduced by the value of the used item.

Part exchange of goods

5.100   If a business supplies goods in exchange for goods not of the same nature, the taxable basis for VAT is the open market value of the goods.

Bad debts

5.101   If a customer does not pay all or part of a debt, the supplier is allowed a refund of VAT on the amount outstanding. There must be certainty that the customer has not paid.

Returned goods

5.102   If goods are returned, the supplier may reclaim the VAT paid to the authorities.

Second-hand goods

5.103   The taxable basis for sales of second-hand goods by a business is, in general, the total price paid by the customer. However, special rules apply for certain categories of goods sold at auctions, and for antiques, works of art, coins, stamps and used cars.

Calculations

5.104   The supplier must, in principle, calculate VAT due to the authorities on the basis of invoices issued within a return period. In certain cases, VAT may be calculated on a cash received basis. Calculation on a cash basis applies to the following:

(*a*)   businesses (hairdressers and shopkeepers, etc.) which generally supply goods or services to persons who receive those goods or services for non-business purposes;

(*b*)   certain businesses which are listed for this purpose in the VAT legislation, e.g. hotels and petrol stations;

(*c*)   businesses which have special permission from the tax authorities.

Finance and operating leases

5.105   In accordance with a resolution of the Dutch Ministry of Finance, finance leases are treated as supplies of goods. The interest is excluded from the taxable amount for VAT purposes. Operating leases are treated as supplies of services. For operating leases, interest is included within the taxable amount.

Portugal

General

5.106   The taxable basis of a supply for monetary consideration is the total consideration received by the supplier, including incidental expenses such as commissions, packing, transport and advertising costs.

The taxable basis of a supply for consideration not wholly in money is the amount of money received plus the open market value of any goods and services received as payment.

Open market value is the price that a purchaser would have to pay to a supplier at arm's length at the place and time the supply takes place, under conditions of fair competition.

The following items are excluded from the taxable basis:

(*a*)   interest on late payments, and the amount of any indemnity imposed by a court decision, for non-fulfilment of obligations;

(*b*)   the amount of any discount;

(*c*)   repayment of any sums paid by a supplier on behalf of and on account of a purchaser;

(*d*)   packing expenses and the cost of containers provided they are separately shown on the invoice.

Goods traded in

5.107   The value of goods traded in forms part of the consideration.

Exchange of goods

5.108   An exchange of goods constitutes two supplies taxable in the normal way.

Bad debts

5.109   A supplier may take credit for VAT in the case of the bankruptcy or insolvency of the customer and, subject to certain conditions, in the case of credits of up to € 4,987.98 (VAT included), subsequent to a court decision recognising the credit.

Returned goods

5.110   If a contract is revoked or goods are returned, the supplier may credit the VAT.

If goods are returned, the supplier is required to issue a voucher or credit note in duplicate and record it within five business days of the date of return.

Second-hand goods, works of art, antiques

5.111   If a business buys and sells second-hand goods, artefacts, works of art and antiques, the taxable basis is the margin between the purchase and selling prices, unless the business elects to be taxed under the normal rules.

Self-supplies of goods and services

5.112   The taxable price for self-supplies of goods is the purchase price of the goods in question or like goods or, in the absence of such a price, the historic cost price determined at the time of the self-supply.

Private use

5.113   The same rules apply for the private use of goods and services as for self-supplies.

Spain

General

5.114   Where the consideration is in money, the value is the amount which, when VAT is added, equals the consideration. Where the consideration is not in money or not wholly in money, or concerning gold other than investment gold, the value is such amount in money as equals the consideration when tax is chargeable.

The taxable amount also includes the amount of any debts assumed by the purchaser.

However, excluded from the consideration is any sum receivable as a result of the postponement of payment beyond the date when the goods or services are supplied.

Also excluded is any indemnity received by way of compensation.

Imports

5.115   The value of imports is the price of the goods plus any duties, taxes, commissions, packaging, transport, and any other charges due.

Discounts

5.116 Discounts applied after a transaction has been made do not alter the taxable base of the original transaction. The Spanish system requires alteration of the taxable base by the issue of a credit note. This rule also applies to any transaction that has been cancelled for whatever reason and to packing returned to a supplier since they must also be included in the taxable base.

Transactions between connected parties

5.117 Special rules apply in order to establish the taxable base for transactions between connected parties. Where actual values used are below open market value, the taxable base must be at least equal to the original purchase price paid by the selling party and, usually, any additional expenditure incurred in arranging the supply. If the actual price set for the transactions between related parties is higher than the amount calculated according to the above rules, then the higher amount should be used as the taxable base.

The following qualify as related parties:

(*a*) businesses and individuals connected either by reason of employment, by administrative relationship or by close family relationship;

(*b*) companies and their shareholders when they hold more than 5% of the capital or 1% if the company is listed on the Stock Exchange;

(*c*) a company and its board members;

(*d*) a company and the close family members of shareholders and board members;

(*e*) companies constituting part of a group of companies according to Spanish legislation;

(*f*) a company and the shareholders and board members of another company, or their close family members, when both companies are part of a group of companies according to Spanish legislation;

(*g*) a company with investment in another company amounting to 25% or more of that company's capital;

(*h*) a Spanish resident company and its permanent establishments abroad;

(*i*) a non-resident company and its permanent establishment in Spain;

(*j*) two companies, where one exercises a degree of control over the other.

Sweden

General

5.118 The price of goods and services supplied should, in the case of goods, at least equal the purchase cost or manufacturing value, and, in the case of services, the cost of supplying the service.

The valuation basis for the import of goods is to include carriage insurance and freight.

In the case of discounts, no deduction is allowed for VAT previously accounted for, when the discount is given under any sort of condition.

Builders and contractors

5.119 A building contractor may either:

(*a*)   build a house for the purpose of a later sale, using his own land; or

(*b*)   carry out building services.

A builder is not liable for VAT when supplying services under category (*a*) and has no right to deduct input tax. A builder supplying services under both categories above is subject to a tax charge for the construction of a house in the case of (*a*). The charge should be accounted for, at the latest, in the VAT return for the accounting period two months after the building becomes ready for use. Building services within (*b*) above are subject to taxation in the usual way with VAT charged on the invoice to the customer on completion. If a final invoice has not been issued by such time, then VAT on the payments on account received should be accounted for in the VAT return for the accounting period two months after the final examination. If the builder has issued invoices on account with VAT before that time, he should account for VAT on payments on account in the VAT return for the accounting period in which they were received. When a tax charge arises under (*a*), the taxable amount corresponds to the costs, interest on equity and value of the builder's own work performed. The tax rate is 25% on the value calculated excluding VAT.

United Kingdom

General

5.120 Where the consideration is in money, the value is the amount to which, when VAT is added, equals the consideration. Where the consideration is not in money or not wholly in money, the value is such amount in money as makes up the consideration when tax is chargeable.

Imports

5.121   The value of imports is the price of the goods plus any duties, taxes, commissions, packaging, transport, and any other charges due.

Discounts

5.122   Where discounts are offered for prompt payment, the value is the discounted amount whether or not the offer is accepted.

Transactions between connected parties

5.123   Where supplies are made between connected parties for a consideration below open market value, the UK authorities may substitute open market value if the customer's input tax would normally be restricted. 'Open market value' is defined as the consideration that would be payable if there were no relationship between the parties involved.

Vouchers

5.124   Where a right to receive goods or services for an amount stated on a voucher is granted for a consideration, the consideration is ignored for VAT purposes except to the extent, if any, that it exceeds the face value.

Accommodation

5.125   After a continuous stay in excess of four weeks, VAT is only payable on the supply of facilities provided other than the right to occupy the accommodation. The facilities element must not be less than 20% of the total supply.

Catering and accommodation supplies to employees

5.126   There is no value unless the supplies are paid for.

Margin scheme

5.127   If certain conditions are met, VAT is payable on the margin between the purchase and selling price for certain types of second-hand goods. This applies to:

(*a*)   motor vehicles;

(*b*)   works of art, antiques or collector's items;

(*c*)   second-hand goods.

Cash accounting

5.128   Businesses with a turnover not exceeding GBP 600,000 may account for VAT on a cash basis. Output tax is only payable when payment is received, thus automatically avoiding bad debts, but input tax cannot be claimed until creditors are paid.

Chapter 6

Tax Rates

Tax rates: EU rules

General

6.1   Most EU member states apply more than one VAT rate. The standard rate of VAT is fixed by each EU member state as a percentage of the taxable amount and is the same for the supply of goods and for the supply of services.

The EU member states are required to implement a standard rate with a minimum of 15%. Currently the standard VAT rate in the EU member states varies from 15% to 25%. In certain cases, the supply of goods or services may be made subject to reduced rates which must be at least 5%. The rate applicable on the importation of goods will be the same as for domestic supplies of the same goods.

The rate applicable to taxable transactions shall, in principle, be that in force at the time of the chargeable event.

[*EC Sixth Directive 77/388, Art 12*].

Reduced rates

Reduced rates with a minimum of 5%

6.2   Each EU member state has the option of applying, apart from the standard rate, one or two reduced rates not lower than 5%. These reduced rates may only apply to the following goods and services:

(*a*)   foodstuffs (including beverages but excluding alcoholic beverages) for human and animal consumption; live animals, seeds, plants and ingredients normally intended for use in preparation of foodstuffs, and products normally intended to be used to supplement or substitute foodstuffs;

(*b*)   water supplies;

(*c*)   pharmaceutical products of a kind normally used for health care, prevention of diseases and treatment for medical and veterinary

145

purposes, including products used for contraception and sanitary protection;

(*d*) medical equipment, aids and other appliances normally intended to alleviate or treat disability, for the exclusive personal use of the disabled, including the repair of such goods, and children's car seats;

(*e*) transport of passengers and their accompanying luggage;

(*f*) supplies of books including library loans (including brochures, leaflets and similar printed matter, children's pictures, drawing or colouring books, music printed or in manuscript, maps and hydrographic or similar charts), newspapers and periodicals, other than material wholly or substantially devoted to advertising matter;

(*g*) admissions to shows, theatres, circuses, fairs, amusement parks, concerts, museums, zoos, cinemas, exhibitions and similar cultural events and facilities;

(*h*) reception of broadcasting services;

(*i*) services supplied by, or royalties due to, writers, composers and performing artists;

(*j*) supplies, construction, renovation and alteration of housing provided as part of a social policy;

(*k*) supplies of goods and services of a kind normally intended for use in agricultural production but excluding capital goods such as machinery or buildings;

(*l*) accommodation provided by hotels and similar establishments including the provision of holiday accommodation and the letting of camping sites and caravan parks;

(*m*) admission to sporting events;

(*n*) use of sporting facilities;

(*o*) supplies of goods and services by organisations recognised as charities by EU member states and engaged in welfare or social security work, to the extent that these supplies are not exempt from VAT;

(*p*) services supplied by undertakers and cremation services, together with the supply of related goods;

(*q*) provision of medical and dental care as well as thermal treatment to the extent that these services are not exempt;

(*r*) services supplied in connection with street cleaning, refuse collection and waste treatment, other than the supply of such services by government bodies;

(*s*) supplies of natural gas and electricity provided that no risk of distortion of competition exists.

For works of art, antiques and collectors' items, a reduced rate of at least 5% may be applied.

[*EC Sixth Directive 77/388, Art 12(3)*].

On the basis of a report by the Commission, the Council shall review the scope of the reduced rates every two years. The Council may decide to alter the list of goods and services identified at (*a*) to (*s*) above.

Restaurant services, children's clothing, children's footwear and housing

6.3　　EU member states which applied a reduced rate to restaurant services, children's clothing, children's footwear and housing, may continue to apply it.

Specific rules in the various EU countries

Austria

6.4　　Austria has the following rates: zero, 10% and 20%.

The 10% rate applies mainly to the following goods and services:

(*a*)　　food (meat, fish, milk, eggs, fruit, coffee, tea);

(*b*)　　medical goods;

(*c*)　　gas, electricity and heat;

(*d*)　　artists' turnover;

(*e*)　　petrol, crude oil and timber;

(*f*)　　letting and leasing of residential buildings;

(*g*)　　museums, theatrical and musical performances;

(*h*)　　all kinds of passenger transportation.

The zero rate applies mainly to exports.

The standard 20% rate applies to all other goods and services.

Belgium

6.5　　In Belgium the following rates apply: zero, 1%, 6%, 12% and 21%.

These categories may vary from time to time by Royal Decree, and rates should therefore be checked in specific cases.

The zero rate applies to exports and a limited number of other items (e.g. newspapers), provided certain conditions are met.

The 1% reduced rate applies to the supply of gold used for investment purposes.

The 6% reduced rate applies mainly to basic goods and services, for example, certain livestock, food, agriculture, etc.

The 12% reduced rate applies to the delivery and importation of specified goods and services, such as:

(*a*)   coal;

(*b*)   coke;

(*c*)   social housing;

(*d*)   pharmaceutical supplies;

(*e*)   pay-television;

(*f*)   margarine;

(*g*)   tyres.

The 21% standard VAT rate applies to taxable supplies of goods or services not listed elsewhere.

Denmark

6.6   Denmark operates two rates of VAT for taxable goods and services, zero and 25%.

The zero rate applies to exports and a few other items. The standard 25% rate applies to all supplies of non-exempt goods and services.

Finland

Standard rate

6.7   The standard rate of VAT is 22%.

Reduced rates

6.8   Lower tax rates are applied to the supply of the following services and the sale, intra-Community acquisition or importation of the following goods, as well as to the removal of goods from certain warehouse regimes.

A reduced rate of 17% applies to the following:

(*a*)   foodstuffs, groceries, drinks and other human nutritive substances, ingredients, spices, preservatives, colour and other additives used in their manufacture;

(*b*)   fodder and fodder mixtures, ingredients and additives used in their manufacture, industrial waste used as animal fodder and fodder fish.

A reduced rate of 8% applies to the following:

(i)   sporting facilities;

(ii)   books;

(iii)   medicines and certain pharmaceuticals;

(iv)   entrance fees for cultural and entertainment events (theatre, circus, music and dance performances, cinemas, exhibitions, sports events, amusement parks, zoos, museums, etc.);

(v)   passenger transport;

(vi)   accommodation;

(vii)   certain compensation from the State television and radio fund to the Finnish Broadcasting Company (*Yleisradio Oy*).

Zero rate sales include:

(*a*)   subscription (at least one month) to newspapers and periodicals;

(*b*)   printing services for membership publications (newsletters) of non-profit organisations for issues published at least four times a year;

(*c*)   vessels' (excluding those constructed primarily for sport or leisure or with a maximum hull length of less than 10 metres) sale, hire, charter, repair and maintenance;

(*d*)   aircraft and spare parts if the buyer is involved in commercial international traffic;

(*e*)   supply of gold to the Central Bank;

(*f*)   export of goods.

France

6.9   The standard VAT rate in France is 19.6%, which applies to all taxable supplies not subject to a reduced rate. There is no zero rating as such, but exemption with credit for exports, intra-Community supplies and similar transactions. There are two reduced rates.

5.5% applies to the following basic necessities:

(*a*) from 15 September 1999 to 31 December 2002, maintenance, improvement, refurbishment and fittings in dwellings over two years old;

(*b*) supplies of domestic assistance services by a registered firm;

(*c*) water, including mineral water and non-alcoholic beverages. Excluded are beverages sold for consumption on the premises from which they were bought (e.g. cafes, restaurants, etc.);

(*d*) food for human consumption. Excluded is catering supplied in, for example, cafes and restaurants;

(*e*) medicine for human use which is not covered by the social security legislation;

(*f*) produce for agricultural use;

(*g*) certain equipment for disabled people;

(*h*) firewood for household use;

(*i*) feeding stuffs (pet foods);

(*j*) books and most periodicals;

(*k*) public transport of passengers with a travel agreement;

(*l*) treatment in registered water cure establishments;

(*m*) legal services supplied under a legal aid programme;

(*n*) supplies of accommodation in hotels, camp sites and old people's homes;

(*o*) supplies of food in office canteens and hospitals;

(*p*) electricity and gas subscriptions;

(*q*) waste collection;

(*r*) certain transactions made by news agencies;

(*s*) subscriptions to receive private or cable television;

(*t*) entrance fees to monuments, museums, parks, gardens, cinemas, theatres, concert halls, etc.;

(*u*) copyright transfers;

(*v*) brokerage and commissions on these transactions.

2.1% applies to the following supplies:

(i) medicine for human use which is covered by the Social Security legislation (otherwise the 5.5% VAT rate applies);

(ii) sales of qualifying newspaper publications;

(iii) the first 140 performances of new or classical plays, musicals, concerts, ballets etc., if the work is original;

(iv) sales of animals to non-taxable persons for slaughter;

(v) television and radio licence fees.

In Corsica, the same rates apply as in mainland France, although certain supplies are subject to reduced rates.

In the French overseas regions of Martinique, Guadeloupe, Réunion and Guyane, tax rates are different:

(*a*) the standard VAT rate is 8.5%;

(*b*) the reduced rate is 2.1%;

(*c*) certain specific rates apply for certain services.

Germany

6.10 Germany has a standard VAT rate of 16% and a reduced rate of 7%. There is no zero rate as such, but exemption with credit exists for exports, intra-Community supplies and similar transactions.

The reduced rate of 7% applies to specifically listed supplies, including:

(*a*) food (meat, fish, milk, eggs, fruit, coffee, tea, margarine, etc.). Supplies of food and drink for consumption on the premises from which they are sold are standard rated;

(*b*) books and newspapers;

(*c*) medical goods;

(*d*) certain cultural goods and services;

(*e*) copyrights;

(*f*) transport of passengers.

Greece

6.11 Greece has two VAT rates: 8% and 18%.

The 8% reduced VAT rate applies mainly to basic or essential goods and services, for example:

(*a*) foodstuffs;

(*b*) pharmaceutical products;

(*c*) certain essential services;

(*d*) utilities.

6.12   *Tax Rates*

The 18% standard rate applies to all other goods and services.

For the islands of Lesbos, Chios, Samos, the area of the Dodecanese, the Cyclades Islands and the Islands of Thasos, Samothraki, North Sporades and Skyros, the above rates are reduced to 6% and 13%. These rates do not apply to means of transport and tobacco products. For agricultural goods and services there are also special rates.

Ireland

6.12   Ireland has the following rates: zero, 4.3%, 12.5% and 21%.

The zero rate applies, for example, to:

(*a*)   exports, intra-Community supplies and similar transactions;

(*b*)   animal feed;

(*c*)   gold supplied to the Central Bank of Ireland;

(*d*)   food and drink for human consumption (excluding alcoholic beverages);

(*e*)   medicines;

(*f*)   medical equipment;

(*g*)   printed books and booklets;

(*h*)   children's footwear.

The 4.3% reduced rate applies to supplies made by unregistered farmers to VAT registered persons and to supplies of live cattle.

The 12.5% reduced rate applies, for example, to:

(i)   agricultural and veterinary services;

(ii)   domestic fuels (coal, electricity, etc.);

(iii)   food and drink in restaurants etc.;

(iv)   entertainment;

(v)   newspapers and periodicals;

(vi)   tour guide services and short-term hire of certain vehicles, boats and caravans;

(vii)   works of art.

The 21% standard rate applies to all other supplies which are not subject to the above reduced rates.

Italy

6.13   The following VAT rates are currently in force in Italy: 4%, 10% and 20%.

The 4% special reduced rate has a limited scope and includes:

(*a*)   certain supplies of food and drink;

(*b*)   periodicals and books;

(*c*)   certain real estate transactions;

(*d*)   devices for disabled people.

The reduced rate of 10% is applicable to the following items:

(i)   supplies of most foodstuffs such as meat, chocolate, fish, coffee and bread;

(ii)   medicines;

(iii)   telecommunications and cinemas;

(iv)   hotel accommodation (excluding luxury hotels) and restaurants;

(v)   construction and maintenance of non-luxury houses (with certain restrictions).

The standard VAT rate of 20% is applicable to all goods and services which are not specified in the reduced rate tables.

Luxembourg

6.14   Luxembourg has four different rates: 3%, 6%, 12% and 15%.

The 3% special reduced rate applies to certain goods considered as essential, for example:

(*a*)   certain foods and drinks;

(*b*)   pharmaceutical products;

(*c*)   water;

(*d*)   transportation of passengers;

(*e*)   books, daily newspapers.

The 6% reduced rate also has limited scope, for example:

(i)   gas and fuels for domestic use;

(ii)   electricity;

(iii) newspapers (except daily newspapers);

(iv) certain art objects.

The 12% rate is an intermediate rate which applies to certain supplies, for example:

(*a*) wine;

(*b*) wood for heating systems;

(*c*) unleaded fuels for transport vehicles;

(*d*) laundry products;

(*e*) tobacco;

(*f*) advertising services;

(*g*) services supplied by travel agents and tour operators.

The 15% standard rate applies to all other taxable supplies, unless they are specifically subject to one of the above reduced rates.

The Netherlands

6.15 In the Netherlands, intra-Community supplies and similar transactions are exempt with credit for input tax.

Two positive rates apply: 6% and 19%.

The 6% reduced rate applies to basic necessities, for example:

(*a*) food and drink excluding alcoholic beverages;

(*b*) medical goods;

(*c*) cultural goods;

(*d*) hotel accommodation;

(*e*) books, daily and weekly newspapers, periodicals;

(*f*) gold bars;

(*g*) transport of passengers;

(*h*) labour-intensive services (e.g. hairdressing, shoe repairs).

The 19% standard rate applies to all other taxable supplies not subject to the reduced rate described above.

Portugal

6.16   Portugal applies exemption with credit for exports, intra-Community supplies and similar transactions, and has three positive rates of VAT: 5%, 12% and 17%.

The 5% reduced rate applies to basic necessities, including:

(*a*)   certain foodstuffs and supplies of unprepared food for human consumption;

(*b*)   water;

(*c*)   electricity;

(*d*)   medicines;

(*e*)   newspapers, magazines and periodicals;

(*f*)   books;

(*g*)   hotel accommodation;

(*h*)   transport of passengers;

(*i*)   entertainment (e.g. cinema, sports, etc.);

(*j*)   goods for agro pastoral activities etc.

The 12% VAT rate applies to specific supplies, including:

 (i)   certain foodstuffs;

 (ii)   coffee and similar products;

(iii)   flowers and plants;

(iv)   fuel;

 (v)   food and beverages supplied by restaurants and similar businesses;

(vi)   wine;

(vii)   agricultural equipment.

The 17% standard rate applies to all taxable supplies not specified in law as subject to the above mentioned 5% and 12% rates.

For the autonomous regions of the Azores and Madeira, VAT rates are 4% (reduced rate), 8% and 12% (standard rate).

Spain

6.17   Spain has three different VAT rates: 4%, 7% and 16%.

A special 4% reduced rate applies to the following:

(*a*)   basic foodstuffs (bread, flour, eggs, milk, etc.);

(*b*)   cars for disabled persons and wheelchairs, as well as repair services carried out to them;

(*c*)   books and newspapers;

(*d*)   pharmaceutical products (excluding beauty and hygiene products);

(*e*)   certain protected buildings;

(*f*)   prosthesis and other operations or articles for disabled persons.

The 7% reduced rate applies to supplies including:

(*a*)   basic foodstuffs for human consumption (excluding alcoholic beverages, and tobacco);

(*b*)   goods for agricultural, forestry and cattle use;

(*c*)   water;

(*d*)   medicines for animal use;

(*e*)   sanitary items;

(*f*)   housing and attached garages;

(*g*)   motorcycles;

(*h*)   flowers and live plants;

(*i*)   liquid gas;

(*j*)   transport of passengers;

(*k*)   camping supplies;

(*l*)   restaurant services;

(*m*)   showing of films, theatre and musical shows etc.;

(*n*)   agricultural, forestry and cattle activities;

(*o*)   artistic supplies;

(*p*)   urban cleaning;

(*q*)   collection and treatment of waste;

(*r*)   cultural and recreational activities;

(*s*)   services related to sports;

(*t*)   social assistance;

(*u*)   funeral services;

(*v*)   sanitary assistance;

(*w*)   sports events;

(*x*)   fairs and commercial exhibitions;

(*y*)   hairdressing services;

(*z*)   building services;

(*aa*)   letting of real estate (time-share).

The 16% standard rate applies to all taxable supplies not listed as subject to one of the above reduced rates.

Sweden

General

6.18   Sweden applies the following rates of VAT:

(*a*)   standard rate, currently 25%;

(*b*)   reduced rate of 12%;

(c)   reduced rate of 6%;

(*d*)   zero rate.

Standard rate, 25%

6.19   Supplies of goods or services which are neither exempt nor subject to reduced rates, zero rate or exemptions are subject to VAT at the standard rate of 25%.

Reduced rate, 12%

6.20   The following are subject to the reduced VAT rate of 12%:

(*a*)   accommodation in hotels and inns as well as camping grounds;

(*b*)   an artist's supply of own works of art and imports from outside the EU of works of art, collectors' items and antiques;

(c)   passenger transport and ski lift services;

(*d*)   foodstuffs.

Reduced rate, 6%

6.21   The following are subject to the reduced VAT rate of 6%:

(*a*)   library and museum activities, as well as archives, where these are not exempt by virtue of subsidy from the government or municipality;

(*b*)   cinema, theatre, opera, ballet performances, as well as the transfer or letting of rights to works of literature and music;

(*c*)   the transfer or letting of rights to audio or visual recording of the works or performances of an artist's works of literature, music, etc.;

(*d*)   entrance fees to sports grounds or centres for both participants and audience, where these are not exempt by virtue of a grant by the government, municipality or a non-profit making organisation;

(*e*)   newspapers, books and periodicals.

6.22   The following are zero-rated for VAT purposes:

(*a*)   human organs, blood and milk, insurance and financial services and investment gold are zero-rated when supplied to customers outside the EU;

(*b*)   the production (including printing services) of periodical magazines for sports clubs, churches, etc.

Exemption from VAT

Other supplies of goods or services may be exempted from VAT (see Chapter 4), and such supplies lead neither to a liability to charge VAT nor – unlike zero-rated supplies – to a right to deduct input tax.

The renting of real estate is usually exempt from VAT, but the owner may register for VAT voluntarily and taxable persons may opt for the taxation of investment gold under the provisions mentioned in Chapter 4, where the option, having been made, gives the right to deduct input tax (see also Chapter 7).

United Kingdom

6.23   The UK has two main rates: the standard rate, currently 17.5% and the zero rate. The standard rate applies to all supplies of goods and services within the scope of the tax which are not specifically listed in VATA 1994 as exempt or zero rated.

There is also a reduced rate of 5%. The number of items falling into the reduced rate category have been expanded considerably in recent years and now includes;

(*a*)   children's car seats;

(*b*)   domestic fuel or power;

(*c*)   energy saving materials and installation services;

(*d*)   heating equipment, security goods and gas supplies, and grant funded installation or connection services;

(*e*)   renovation and alteration of certain dwellings;

(*f*)   conversion of certain properties to dwellings;

(*g*)   women's sanitary products.

The following categories are zero-rated:

(*a*)   foodstuffs;

(*b*)   sewerage services and water;

(*c*)   books;

(*d*)   certain types of equipment for the blind;

(*e*)   construction of dwellings;

(*f*)   work to protected buildings;

(*g*)   certain international services;

(*h*)   transport of passengers;

(*i*)   caravans and houseboats;

(*j*)   gold;

(*k*)   bank notes;

(*l*)   drugs, medicines and aids for the handicapped;

(*m*)   imports, exports;

(*n*)   certain supplies by or to charities;

(*o*)   children's clothing and footwear.

Chapter 7

Credit for Input Tax

Credit for input tax: EU rules

General

7.1   A taxable person is, in principle, entitled to recover VAT on goods and services to the extent that they are used for the purposes of his taxable activities.

This includes:

(*a*)   VAT due or paid in respect of goods or services supplied or to be supplied to him by another taxable person;

(*b*)   VAT due or paid in respect of imported goods;

(*c*)   VAT due in respect of intra-Community acquisitions of goods.

Furthermore, every taxable person is also entitled to deduct VAT in so far as the goods and services are used for the purposes of economic activities in another country, provided they would be eligible for deduction of VAT if the activities had occurred in their own country.

[*EC Sixth Directive 77/388, Art 17(2), (3)*].

Foreign businesses

7.2   Non-resident taxable persons can also claim a refund of VAT. The basic rule for taxable persons established in another EU member state or in a country outside the EU is that the business claiming a refund must not have any business establishment in that member state or carry out any business activities there which would render him liable to register for VAT.

If it is an EU business, it must be registered for VAT in its own EU member state. If it is a non-EU business it must be registered for tax in its own country or prove that it is a business. The basic rule for businesses established outside the EU is that the claiming business must not have any business establishment within the EU member state concerned or carry out any business activities there which would render it liable to register for VAT in that particular EU member state.

Note that the businesses registered in the EU under the proposed e-commerce Directive with effect from 1 July 2003, will be required to use these above procedures to reclaim VAT on costs incurred.

[*EC Sixth Directive 77/388, Art 17(4)*].

No credit

7.3   No credit is allowed where VAT has been paid on goods and services which are subsequently used by the taxable person in connection with exempt without credit transactions (see Chapter 4). However, an exception exists for certain financial and insurance transactions, when the customer is established outside the EU.

Partial credit

General

7.4   VAT incurred on goods and services to be used by a taxable person both for taxable and exempt or non-business activities may be deducted to the extent that it is attributable to taxable activities.

However, EU member states may:

(*a*)   authorise the taxable person to determine a proportion for each sector of his business, provided that separate accounts are kept for each sector;

(*b*)   compel the taxable person to determine a proportion for each sector of his business and to keep separate accounts for each sector;

(*c*)   authorise or compel the taxable person to make the deduction on the basis of the use of all or part of the goods and services;

(*d*)   authorise or compel the taxable person to make the deduction in accordance with the rule laid down in (*a*) above, in respect of all goods and services used for all transactions referred to therein;

(*e*)   provide that where non-deductible VAT is insignificant, it shall be treated as fully recoverable.

[*EC Sixth Directive 77/388, Art 17(5)*].

Calculation of the deductible proportion

7.5   The proportion deductible shall be made up of a fraction having:

(*a*) as numerator, the total amount, exclusive of VAT, of turnover per year attributable to transactions in respect of which VAT is deductible;

(*b*) as denominator, the total amount, exclusive of VAT, of turnover per year attributable to all transactions. The EU member states may also include any subsidies in the denominator.

The proportion shall be determined on an annual basis, fixed as a percentage and rounded up to a figure not exceeding the next unit.

[*EC Sixth Directive 77/388, Art 19(1)*].

Turnover attributable to the supplies of capital goods shall be excluded from the calculation of the deductible proportion. The provisional proportion for a year shall be calculated on the basis of the previous year's transactions. In the absence of any such transactions to refer to, or where they were insignificant, the deductible proportion shall be estimated provisionally, under the supervision of the tax authorities, by the taxable person from his forecasts. However, each EU member state may retain their current rules.

Adjustments made on the basis of provisional proportions shall be adjusted when the actual proportion is fixed during the next year.

[*EC Sixth Directive 77/388, Art 19(2), (3)*].

Adjustments of deductions

7.6 The initial deduction shall be adjusted according to the provisions laid down by the EU member states, in particular:

(*a*) where the deduction was higher or lower than that to which the taxable person was entitled;

(*b*) where, after the return is made, some change occurs in factors used to determine the amount to be deducted, in particular where purchases are cancelled or price reductions are obtained. However, adjustments shall not be made in cases of transactions remaining totally or partially unpaid or where destruction, loss or theft of property is duly proved or confirmed, in the case of use for the purpose of making gifts of small value and producing samples, but member states may insist on adjustment in cases of theft or where transactions are totally or partially unpaid.

In the case of capital goods, adjustments shall be spread over five years, including that in which the goods were acquired or manufactured. The annual adjustment shall be made only in respect of one fifth of the VAT charged for the goods.

The adjustment shall be made on the basis of variations of taxable status in subsequent years in relation to that for the year in which the goods were acquired or manufactured. Each EU member state is allowed to base the adjustment on a period of five full years starting from the time at which the goods are first used. The adjustment period may be up to ten years for immovable property acquired as a capital asset.

If capital goods are sold during the period of adjustment, they shall be deemed used for business purposes by the taxable person until the end of the period of adjustment. Such business activities are presumed to be fully taxable where the supply of the said goods is taxable, but exempt where the supply is exempt, e.g. the sale of immovable property.

The adjustment for the remaining intervals shall be made only once for the whole period of adjustment still to be covered. However, EU member states are entitled to waive the requirement for adjustment to the extent that the purchaser is a taxable person using the capital goods in question solely for transactions in respect of which VAT is deductible.

EU member states may, for the purpose of the above adjustments:

  (i)   define the concept of capital goods;

 (ii)   indicate the amount of VAT which is to be taken into consideration for adjustment;

(iii)   adopt any suitable measures with a view to ensuring that adjustment does not involve any unjustified advantage;

 (iv)   permit administrative simplifications.

If the practical effect of applying the above provisions would be insignificant, any EU member state may, subject to the consultation procedure with the European VAT Committee, elect not to apply them.

In that case, the need to avoid distortion of competition, the overall tax effect in the EU member state concerned and the need for due economy of administration must be considered. Where a taxable person changes from normal accounting procedures to use of a special scheme or vice versa, EU member states may take all necessary measures to ensure that the taxable person neither benefits nor is prejudiced unjustifiably.

[*EC Sixth Directive 77/388, Art 20*].

Expenditure on luxuries, amusements and entertainment

7.7   VAT which is not strictly business expenditure, such as that on luxuries, amusements or entertainment, is not deductible.

No reclaim for certain capital goods

7.8   Each EU member state may, for economic reasons, totally or partly exclude all or some capital goods or other goods from the system of deductions.

To maintain identical conditions of competition, each EU member state may, instead of refusing deduction, tax the goods manufactured by the taxable person himself, or which he has purchased in the country or imported, in such a way that the amount does not exceed the VAT which would have been charged on the acquisition of similar goods.

[*EC Sixth Directive 77/388, Art 17(7)*].

Rules on exercising the right to credit

7.9   The right to deduct shall arise at the time when the deductible tax becomes chargeable. A credit for input tax can normally be claimed on the VAT return for the period during which the supplier made his supply, as shown on the invoice. For reclaiming VAT on imported goods, the taxable person must hold an import document, specifying him as consignee or importer, and showing calculation of the amount of VAT due.

If the VAT liability for a particular period is less than the VAT credit, each EU member state may either make a refund or carry the excess forward to the following period according to conditions they shall determine. However, each EU member state may refuse to refund or carry forward if the amount of the excess is insignificant. A dated invoice in the correct format must be kept in order to claim a credit.

[*EC Sixth Directive 77/388, Art 18*].

Specific rules in the various EU countries

Austria

General

7.10   In Austria, VAT is deductible as input tax when goods or services are supplied to a registered business. Evidence must be kept in the form of tax invoices received where the consideration exceeds € 150.

Input VAT restrictions

7.11   Credit is not allowed if expenditure relates to exempt or non-business activities. Expenditure relating partly to exempt or non-business activities must be distinguished. If the non-deductible part is more than 50% no VAT is deductible.

VAT cannot be recovered on the purchase and running costs associated with passenger cars where they are used for business or private purposes.

Refunds for non-resident businesses

7.12   Foreign companies may apply for a refund of any VAT paid on goods or services purchased in Austria, if the amount of credit for input tax exceeds € 36.34.

Foreign businesses with no taxable turnover in their own countries are not permitted to make claims for a refund of VAT on business expenses in Austria. Evidence of taxable turnover must be provided by confirmation from the foreign tax authorities.

Belgium

General

7.13   VAT is only deductible on the basis of a complete and dated invoice showing the full name, address and VAT registration of both the supplier of the goods and services and of the client, as well as all other relevant information, including the nature of the goods and services and the VAT rate applicable.

If an invoice does not contain the full information, the VAT charged may be disallowed.

VAT on suppliers' invoices for goods and services is deductible in the period in which the invoice has been received. The same rules apply for VAT on overheads and on construction.

A VAT credit may be repaid at the end of each quarter provided the amount exceeds € 1,485 (or € 615 for small businesses), or at the end of each year if exceeding € 245.

Input VAT restrictions

7.14   Input VAT is disallowed on the following supplies:

(*a*)   tobacco products;

(*b*)   alcoholic beverages, unless they are for resale or to be supplied as part of a supply of services, e.g. by cafes, hotels and restaurants;

(*c*)   the cost of lodgings, meals and beverages supplied by hotels, restaurants and cafes, unless the costs were incurred by:

    (i)   personnel responsible for supplies of goods or services to third parties;

(ii)   travel agencies and tourist organisations on behalf of their customers;

(*d*)   entertainment expenses;

(*e*)   car related expenses (only 50% of the VAT paid will be deductible).

Adjustment of credit

7.15   Input VAT on certain movable goods and immovable property may be reclaimed over five or ten years (fifteen years for real estate and related improvements) with adjustments to allow for changes in taxable status.

Refunds for non-resident businesses

7.16   A non-resident business without a permanent establishment in Belgium may request a refund for VAT charged on goods and services.

Claims must be for periods of at least three months but no more than one calendar year. The amount of refund may not be less than € 200. Claims must be made on a specified form.

Applications must be sent at the latest within the six months following the end of the year concerned, in triplicate, together with a certificate issued by the taxpayer's own authorities indicating that it is VAT registered, if from an EU member state, or that it is a registered business, if from outside the EU.

The original invoices or import documents must be sent together with the claim, to the central VAT office for non-resident taxpayers in Brussels.

Payments are usually made no later than six months after receipt of an accurate claim.

Appeals must be made within five years of notification of a rejected claim.

Denmark

General

7.17   Businesses may claim VAT as input tax provided the expenditure relates solely to their business of selling taxable goods and services. Businesses are not entitled to reclaim VAT on expenditure relating to exempt services or private use.

Input VAT restrictions

7.18   VAT on the following purchases is non-deductible:

(*a*)   private consumption, e.g. when an owner takes out for private use goods which are normally sold or produced by the company;

(*b*)   food or other provisions for staff;

(*c*)   construction, repair and maintenance of residential property for the owner's use or an employee of the company;

(*d*)   setting-up and running of day nurseries, kindergartens, youth centres, holiday camps, summer homes, etc. for staff;

(*e*)   land for sale and ready for development;

(*f*)   maintenance of roads used solely as access to residential property;

(*g*)   hotel accommodation (25% of the VAT may be deducted if the hotel accommodation and dining in restaurants are strictly for business purposes);

(*h*)   prizes (e.g. cups) given to sports clubs etc. for commercial purposes;

(*i*)   entertainment and gifts, e.g. dining in restaurants, tobacco, chocolate, wine, liquor and flowers. (25% of the VAT may be deducted for dining in restaurants where this is strictly for business purposes);

(*j*)   VAT on the purchase and operation of passenger cars is non-deductible whether the cars are used for business or private purposes. In respect of commercial vehicles of a permitted total weight of up to and including three tonnes used wholly in connection with taxable business activities, VAT may be deducted in full.

Special deduction provisions come into force if commercial vehicles are not wholly used for taxable business activities.

VAT on the purchase and operation of commercial vehicles may be deducted in full if total weight exceeds three tonnes and if they are exclusively used for taxable activities. However, where they are only used partly for taxable activities, only the VAT relating to taxable activities is deductible.

Adjustments of credit

7.19   Input VAT on certain assets must be adjusted to allow for changes in taxable status, including:

(*a*)   machinery, fixtures and fittings and other operating equipment purchased at a price exceeding DKK 75,000 exclusive of VAT;

(*b*)   real estate;

(*c*)   extension, reconstruction, modernisation, repair and maintenance work on real estate with a total taxable value of more than DKK 75,000 per year.

Where input VAT is fully or partly recovered on the purchase of these assets, annual adjustments are required. The adjustment period with respect to (*a*) and (*c*) above is five years, and ten years for item (*b*).

Refunds for non-resident businesses

7.20 Foreign companies, not registered in Denmark for VAT purposes, may apply for a refund of any VAT paid on goods or services purchased in Denmark.

Refunds may be made to companies which would have been liable to register if they had a fixed establishment in Denmark. Moreover, a refund may only be granted to the same extent that Danish companies may deduct input VAT.

Applications are submitted on a specific form and must cover a period of at least three months and not more than a calendar year. The minimum amount is DKK 1,500 for annual claims and DKK 200 for any remaining months of a year.

Original invoices must be filed with the claim.

First applications must always include documentation certified by a competent public authority in the country of domicile of the applicant confirming that the applicant carries on a business and giving the VAT registration number where applicable.

The application form must be filed with the Customs and Tax Region Soenderborg (*Told & Skatteregion Soenderborg*) by 30 June following the year covered by the claim.

The refund will be made within six months of receipt of an accurate claim.

Finland

General

7.21 A taxable person may deduct the VAT included in the price of goods or services charged by another person, provided the goods or services are used for a taxable activity. Similarly, the tax paid on imports and accounted for on intra-Community acquisitions may be deducted. Businesses entitled to regular refunds may make monthly claims.

Foreign businesses

7.22 Taxable persons who do not have a permanent establishment in Finland or who have not voluntarily registered for VAT in Finland can recover VAT by applying for a refund. The refund is restricted to VAT incurred on goods on which a Finnish business would be able to claim a refund, and must relate to supplies made abroad or subject to the reverse charge and for which a Finnish business would account for VAT (if carried out in Finland).

Applications must cover at least three months but no longer than one year. Applications for the remainder of a year may be for less than three months.

Claims must be accompanied by the original invoices and a certificate from the claimant's own tax authorities confirming the claimant's status. If a claim is made by a representative, the representative must have the power of attorney.

Claims must be made within six months of the end of the calendar year. Claims must be for a minimum of € 201.83 or, if for the whole year, the minimum of € 25.23.

Without credit

7.23   Suppliers of the following services are unable to recover VAT:

(a)   hospital, medical care, research and laboratory services and certain associated services;

(b)   social welfare;

(c)   education;

(d)   lotteries and money games;

(e)   transactions concerning bank notes and coins used as legal tender, and other exempt financial services;

(f)   insurance;

(g)   remuneration for athletic and other public performances;

(h)   certain copyrights;

(i)   works of art if sold by the artist;

(j)   leasing and the supply of real property including building land (unless the lessor has opted for taxation on lease of property to a taxable lessee);

(k)   certain transactions carried out by blind persons and interpretation services for the deaf.

Partial credit

7.24   When businesses make both taxable and exempt supplies, VAT is recoverable on costs incurred on a pro rata basis.

Limitations on deductions

7.25   The following are excluded from the general right to deduction:

(*a*)   commodities related to housing provided by employers and to recreational facilities;

(*b*)   expenses for travel to and from work;

(*c*)   business entertainment expenses;

(*d*)   postage or similar if no tax is paid (i.e. for mail to outside the EU no deduction is allowed);

(*e*)   passenger cars, motorcycles, caravans and certain vessels and aircraft including expenses related to these and to the use of them. However, tax may be deducted on vehicles and vessels bought for resale or rental or for commercial passenger transport or driver training or on passenger cars which have been acquired solely for a tax-deductible purpose.

Note that the handing out of gifts and samples by a taxable business is considered as a taxable supply unless the gifts and samples are low in value.

Capital goods

7.26   Finland has not introduced a capital goods scheme and therefore VAT may be recovered in full or pro rata on taxable and exempt supplies.

On disposal VAT is chargeable in the same ratio to which it was recovered. There is no time limit in respect of movable tangible property, but in respect of immovable property only VAT which was deducted during the current year or five previous calendar years is chargeable.

Local authorities

7.27   Municipalities are entitled to a refund on purchases for non-taxable purposes.

France

General

7.28   An invoice indicating the amount of VAT is required to claim input VAT. In the case of imported goods, the entry customs documents must be available.

Further, VAT must have been paid in accordance with the law. However, if an error is made in good faith as to the rate to be applied, this may be revised. A credit is not allowed for input VAT paid in connection with goods and services made which are not within the scope of VAT.

Input VAT can be claimed in the same month as it is incurred. For goods, the relevant date is the date of receipt. For services, the relevant date is the date of payment, except if the provider of services has opted for a particular regime called '*option pour les débits*'.

7.29   Input VAT is not deductible on the following business expenses:

(*a*)   passenger cars and related expenses;

(*b*)   goods supplied free and related expenses, except small gifts with a value less than € 30.49;

(*c*)   hotel, restaurant and entertainment expenses and related expenses;

(*d*)   certain advertising (alcoholic drinks);

(*e*)   certain rented goods.

Adjustments of credit

7.30   Input VAT on movable goods and immovable property is adjusted annually over five and ten years respectively to allow for fluctuations in taxable status.

Refunds for non-resident businesses

7.31   There are different rules for EU and non-EU businesses (except for certain non-EU countries which grant a reciprocal benefit to French businesses and are treated as EU businesses). The main features are as follows:

(*a*)   VAT is refunded to EU businesses provided they are taxable persons and provided French businesses would be entitled to recovery;

(*b*)   for non-EU business, VAT is refunded provided the expense has been incurred in order to supply goods or services in the country and is allowable in France;

(*c*)   refunds may be made on a yearly or quarterly basis and must not be filed later than six months after year end.

Germany

General

7.32   In Germany, VAT is normally deductible as input tax whenever goods are delivered or services are rendered to a business.

This general rule is also applicable if the goods are not exclusively used for business purposes. In this case, the business must account for VAT on the supplies or service put to private use.

Input VAT may be deducted in the period (normally monthly) in which the goods were delivered or the services were rendered if a valid tax invoice is obtained from the supplier.

Input VAT restrictions

7.33   Credit is not allowed if expenditure relates to exempt or non-business activities.

No VAT may be deducted for certain expenses which are also non-deductible for income tax purposes (e.g. gifts, meals and drinks in restaurants), where they exceed certain sums. If a business vehicle is also used for private purposes then VAT may only be deducted (at 50%) if the business use is at least 10%. Special subsistence expenses including food and drink, bed and breakfast and travelling costs are excluded from VAT deduction, as well as relocation costs. The regulations for travel expenses and for cars are currently under discussion.

Credit for input tax

7.34   If a business makes exempt or non-business supplies, it must separate input tax into deductible and non-deductible categories. Where supplies are used for both taxable and non-taxable transactions, the deductible part of the input tax must be calculated according to special rules. Apportionment, using the ratio between the taxable and total supplies value, is generally not allowed. Exemptions are possible.

Adjustments of credit

7.35   Input VAT on movable goods and immovable property must be adjusted over five and ten years respectively to allow for changes in taxable status.

Refunds for non-resident businesses

7.36   A non-resident business is allowed to claim a refund of German VAT under the following conditions:

(*a*)   no taxable supplies are made in Germany;

(*b*)   only supplies of services are made where the liability is transferred from the foreign supplier to the German recipient (see Chapter 9);

(*c*)   goods and services purchased are for the business;

(*d*) proof of business status is available including VAT registration particulars for EC businesses.

Greece

General

7.37 Credit for input VAT is allowed on the condition that goods or services received are used for making taxable supplies.

Input VAT restrictions

7.38 Input VAT is not deductible on the following:

(*a*) purchase or import of manufactured tobacco products;

(*b*) purchase or import of alcoholic beverages not used in taxable activities;

(*c*) reception, entertainment and hospitality in general;

(*d*) accommodation, food, drink, transport and entertainment for the staff or representatives of the business;

(*e*) purchase or importation for private use of passenger cars with up to nine seats, of motorcycles and motorised bicycles, of boats and aircraft intended for private recreation or sport, as well as related maintenance and operating expenses;

(*f*) purchase or importation of packaging materials where delivery is covered by a guarantee.

Adjustments of credit

7.39 Input VAT on certain assets must be adjusted over a period of five years to allow for changes in taxable status.

Refunds for non-resident EU businesses

7.40 Taxable persons established in another EU member state are entitled to reclaim tax charged on goods or services supplied to them by other taxable persons or on importation of goods into Greece, to the extent to which such goods or services are used for:

(*a*) taxable activities where the place of taxation is abroad and for which the business would have a right of deduction had such activities been carried out within Greece;

(*b*) transport services which are carried out in Greece and are exempt from tax as follows:

(i) international air and sea transport of persons;

(ii)   transport of goods destined for export;

(iii) transport of goods given temporary exemption status under special schemes;

(iv)   transport of imported goods to their first place of destination within the country, provided that the value of these services is included in the taxable base on importation;

(*c*)   certain other taxable activities.

The conditions required in order to reclaim are as follows:

(*a*)   the taxable person must not be operating through a permanent establishment in Greece, nor have his residence or abode in Greece; and

(*b*)   no activities, other than those mentioned above, may be carried out in Greece during the period covered.

The claim may not cover a period of less than three months or more than one year and should be made to the competent tax authority.

Claims are usually paid within six months from the date of submission of the relevant request.

Refunds for non-resident non-EU businesses

7.41   The same provisions also apply to businesses established outside the EU provided that their country of origin would grant to a business established in Greece a reciprocal entitlement to a refund of VAT or similar taxes.

Ireland

General

7.42   Generally, VAT incurred on goods and services purchased or acquired within Ireland by a taxable person which are used by him for the purpose of his taxable supplies may be recovered as input tax.

Input VAT restrictions

7.43   Input VAT is not deductible on any of the following supplies of goods or services:

(*a*)   the provision of food or drink, accommodation or other personal services, to a taxable person, his agent or employees, except to the extent that such provision constitutes a supply of services in respect of which the taxable person is accountable for VAT;

(*b*)   entertainment expenses incurred by a taxable person, his agent, or employees;

(*c*)   the acquisition, whether by hiring or outright purchase, of motor vehicles by business persons other than car dealers, car rental companies, and driving schools.

Cars include all vehicles used for the carriage of persons by road other than vehicles having a capacity for 16 persons or more and invalid carriages of any kind. All cars, station wagons, motor cycles, mopeds, and the like, are covered if bought by a business and used by its employees for the purpose of its business unless that business consists of selling, hiring, or giving driving instruction. The credit is disallowed even if the vehicles are used by employees of the undertaking exclusively for business purposes;

(*d*)   the purchase of petrol other than as stock-in-trade.

Adjustments of credit

7.44   Adjustments are not required in Ireland in respect of the VAT incurred on the purchase of capital goods.

Refunds for non-resident businesses

7.45   VAT paid by a non-resident business that does not carry on a business in Ireland, on supplies of goods or services made to it and on imports by it, is generally refundable provided certain conditions are fulfilled, as follows:

(*a*)   the claimant must establish that he does not supply goods or services in Ireland;

(*b*)   the claimant must prove that he carries on a business outside Ireland. If business is carried out in an EU member state he must produce a certificate proving he is registered for VAT there;

(*c*)   the tax charged must be of the kind which would be deductible by Irish businesses; and

(*d*)   the goods included in the claim must not have been purchased for sale or hiring out in Ireland.

Claims should be filed within six months of the end of the calendar year to which they relate but will normally be processed going back six years. They should be made on the appropriate forms and should be accompanied by original invoices or import documents.

Italy

General

7.46   Credit for input tax is allowed to VAT registered businesses where expenditure relates to their taxable activities. The VAT must be recorded on a proper tax invoice.

Credit for VAT on importation is only granted if the business keeps the relevant customs entry documents. If exempt without credit goods or services are exported, they remain exempt and the associated input VAT is not recoverable.

Input VAT restrictions

7.47   Input VAT is not allowed on the following supplies:

(*a*)   goods and services purchased in order to supply exempt goods and services. Exports and related services, intra-Community transactions, transactions made outside the Italian territory and transfers following a merger, even if not actually subject to VAT, give the right to deduct input VAT;

(*b*)   motor vehicles, bikes, aircraft and vessels used for transportation of both persons and goods (with limited exclusions);

(*c*)   fuel, oil, maintenance, garaging, relating to the means of transport described above;

(*d*)   restaurants and hotels;

(*e*)   certain real estate;

(*f*)   goods and services for entertainment purposes;

(*g*)   foodstuffs;

(*h*)   cellular phones and related bills (50% allowable).

Adjustments of credit

7.48   Input VAT adjustments are made for assets used for both exempt and taxable transactions. Such assets include intellectual property adjusted over four years.

Refunds for non-resident businesses

7.49   Non-resident businesses from other EU member states or outside the EU may claim, under certain circumstances, a refund of Italian VAT on goods and services supplied to them in Italy or on goods imported into Italy, provided that they do not have a permanent establishment for VAT purposes in Italy. The minimum claim is € 200.

If the amount in a particular quarter is less than € 200, but the sum of this amount plus the amount refundable in the next quarter is € 200 or more, a refund may be claimed.

At the end of the year, claims may be submitted for a minimum of € 25. Claims must be accompanied by original invoices and import documents and a certificate issued by the official authority of the claimant's country. The certificate must state that the business is VAT registered (EU member states) or a registered business (non-EU member states). The certificate remains valid for one year.

Luxembourg

General

7.50   Credit for input tax is allowed for VAT charged to a business on supplies made to it and on imports by it. Tax invoices should be kept to support claims.

Input VAT restrictions

7.51   Input VAT is not deductible on expenditure exclusively incurred in generating exempt without credit transactions and supplies outside the scope of VAT.

Adjustments of credit

7.52   Input VAT on movable goods and immovable property must be adjusted over five and ten years respectively to allow for fluctuations in taxable status.

Refunds for non-resident EU businesses

7.53   Under certain conditions, a refund of input VAT is granted to foreign businesses without a permanent establishment in Luxembourg. To obtain a refund, the appropriate official application form must be accompanied by original invoices and a certificate confirming the status as a taxable person issued by the relevant tax authorities. Additional information may be requested in specific cases.

Applications must be filed with the tax administration within six months of the end of the calendar year to which the claim relates. They must cover at least three months, but not more than one calendar year. An application for a shorter period of time is only considered if it covers the remainder of a calendar year.

Applications may also include invoices or import documents not covered by previous applications, provided the transactions were completed during the calendar year in question.

The refund is granted only if it exceeds € 225, for a three-month claim, but € 30, for the period to the end of the calendar year.

Accurate claims must be paid within six months from the date the application was filed and payments may be made either in Luxembourg or, at its own cost, in the country where the claimant is established. The normal rules apply to appeals against refused claims.

Refunds to non-resident non-EU businesses

7.54   Refunds may be made to non-EU businesses, provided that Luxembourg businesses are granted reciprocal benefits. The conditions are almost the same as for EU businesses, although for non-EU businesses the claim must relate to a full year and may not be for less than € 125.

The Netherlands

General

7.55   A business may apply for input VAT credit provided the business uses goods or services purchased, or goods imported, in the course of the business, unless they are connected with exempt supplies.

Input VAT restrictions

7.56   VAT is not recoverable on the following:

(*a*)   costs incurred in promoting business status or prestige;

(*b*)   gifts;

(*c*)   supplies for personal or private purposes;

(*d*)   housing, private transportation (except organised home-to-work travel), remuneration in kind or facilities for sport or entertainment, or for other private purposes;

(*e*)   food and drink in restaurants etc.

If the total purchase, production or cost price (excluding VAT) incurred for the above categories of expenditure does not exceed € 226 (NLG 500) in one financial year, the disallowance of the input VAT credit can be ignored.

There are special provisions in relation to cars used for both private and business purposes. VAT on the purchase and operation of cars is normally deductible. However, an annual VAT charge must be paid for private use, normally 12% to 25% of the catalogue price.

When an employee uses his own car for business purposes and his expenses are reimbursed, 12% of the reimbursed amount is allowed to the employer as input VAT.

However, following a recent ECJ decision, this rule whereby an employer may recover VAT on supplies to employees is subject to review.

Adjustments of credit

7.57   Input VAT on certain movable goods and immovable property must be adjusted over five and ten years respectively to allow for fluctuations in taxable status.

Refunds for non-resident businesses

7.58   A non-resident business without a permanent establishment in the Netherlands may claim a refund for VAT charged on goods and services supplied to it and on imports made by it. A refund is allowed if its activities would have been taxable had they been performed in the Netherlands.

The claim must not be for less than three months or more than a calendar year. The amount of the refund must be at least € 213 (NLG 470) for a quarterly claim and € 27 (NLG 60) for a claim covering a year.

The claim must be made on a special form. It must be sent together with a certificate from the tax authorities in the applicant's country of origin stating that the business is subject to VAT. If the business is resident in a non-EU country, it must prove the existence of the business activity and provide the original invoices showing the amount of VAT claimed within six months after the end of the relevant calendar year.

In practice, the tax authorities allow claims going back five years. All documents should be sent to the VAT office in Heerlen.

Partial exemption

7.59   Businesses making both taxable and exempt supplies are entitled to recover only input tax relating to their taxable supplies. VAT on goods and services which are used in both taxable and exempt transactions is deductible based on the ratio between taxable and total transactions. When the actual use of the goods gives a fairer split this ratio is used instead.

Portugal

General

7.60   Businesses may claim credit for input tax on purchases of goods and services and on imports in the course of business or professional activities. They may only reclaim VAT provided that the relevant invoices and customs documents are kept.

Input VAT attributable to exempt activities cannot be recovered.

Input VAT restrictions

7.61   VAT cannot be recovered on the following:

(*a*)   sums paid on behalf of a purchaser or customer;

(*b*)   sums paid in relation to the purchase, manufacture, importation, hire, utilisation, alteration and repair of private cars, motorcycles, pleasure boats and aircraft unless they constitute stock-in-trade of the business. Private cars include any motor vehicle which is not specifically designed for the transportation of goods or of no more than eight passengers excluding the driver, or for farming, business or industrial activities;

(*c*)   purchase of any fuel, other than diesel fuel normally used by motor vehicles, unless as stock-in-trade of the business; 50% of VAT paid on automobile gas oil is treated as input tax;

(*d*)   travel and entertainment costs incurred by a business or its staff. However, VAT incurred by a business on the provision of accommodation to its personnel where the premises belong to the business is treated as input tax;

(*e*)   purchase of second-hand goods and works of art for resale, where the taxable value has been treated as the margin between the purchase and sale price.

Adjustments of credit

7.62   Input tax on movable goods and immovable property must be adjusted over five and ten years respectively to allow for changes in taxable status.

Refunds for non-resident EU businesses

7.63   Businesses established in other EU member states may claim, under certain conditions, a refund of Portuguese VAT paid by them on qualifying purchases or importation of goods and services, provided that the business is not established in Portugal.

Claims should cover the immediately preceding calendar year or quarter where the amount of the claim exceeds € 19,951.92 or €159,615.32 respectively.

An application for refund must be filed, in duplicate, at the latest on the last business day of June in the following year, using the required form and must be accompanied by the following supporting documents:

(*a*)   originals of the relevant tax invoices or similar documents;

(*b*)   an official certificate issued by the EU state in which the claimant is established, proving he is registered for VAT purposes there; this certificate is valid for refund claims made within a twelve-month period of the date of issue;

(*c*)   any other information required in support of the claim by the VAT office in Lisbon.

The application, together with the supporting documents, must be filed with the tax authorities in Lisbon.

Refunds must be paid within a six-month period from the date on which an accurate claim is received.

Refunds for non-resident non-EU businesses

7.64   The VAT refund rules and procedure for EU businesses have been extended to include businesses established in non-EU member states with reciprocal agreements for businesses established in Portugal. Non-EU claimants are required to produce an official certificate issued by the relevant authorities in their own country proving that they are subject to their own turnover tax.

Spain

General

7.65   Businesses may recover input VAT on purchases of goods and services and on imports in the course of their business or professional activities.

VAT returns are completed quarterly and VAT may not be deducted until the following quarter.

Input VAT restrictions

7.66   VAT may not be recovered on the following:

(*a*)   50% of the VAT on the cost of the import, leasing, modification, repair, maintenance and utilisation of private cars, motorcycles and accessories, spare parts and fuel is deductible. However, this does not apply to the following means of transport where VAT is fully deductible:

    (i)   passenger transport for consideration;

    (ii)   cars for driving schools;

    (iii)   cars for exhibition, test or sales promotion by the manufacturers;

    (iv)   vehicles for exclusive use in the business travel of independent commercial agents;

    (v)   vehicles for exclusive use in security and surveillance work;

(*b*)   travel expenses incurred by a business and its staff;

(*c*)   purchases, imports and intra-Community acquisitions of food and drink and hotel, restaurant and entertainment expenses, except where they are for the use of or consumption by staff or by third persons for consideration;

(*d*)   purchases, imports and leasing of other luxury items and manufactured tobacco;

(*e*)   goods and services used as gifts for customers, staff or other third parties.

Adjustments of credit

7.67   Input VAT on movable goods and immovable property must be adjusted over four and ten years respectively to allow for fluctuations in taxable status.

Refunds for non-resident businesses

7.68   Non-resident businesses without a permanent establishment in Spain are entitled to reclaim VAT on business expenses. This refund is granted to businesses which carry on business or professional activities subject to VAT in other EU member states including the Canaries, Ceuta or Melilia. It is also granted to non-EU businesses, provided they are resident in a country which also allows similar refunds.

The application for a refund must relate to goods and services purchased, acquired or imported into Spain during the period for which the claim is made. The refundable amount is calculated according to the actual use of the goods and services purchased or imported by the business for its taxable activities, with regards to the legislation of the country where the business is resident and also with regards to the special pro-rata recovery rule.

The refund may only be claimed for quarterly periods or the immediately preceding calendar year, but in certain cases, an application may be made for a period shorter than one quarter. The amount of the refund must be at least € 201.34 (ESP 33,500) for shorter periods. Where the application relates to the entire calendar year, the claim must exceed € 25.24 (ESP 4,200). The claim must be lodged within six months after the end of the calendar year when the operations took place and must be accompanied by the following documents:

(*a*)   a certificate from the relevant tax authorities stating that the business is a taxable person in its own country;

(*b*)   a declaration signed by the applicant stating that he has not made taxable supplies in Spain;

(*c*)   a formal commitment signed by the applicant to reimburse any amount of refund unduly obtained;

(*d*)   the original invoices and any other supporting documents;

(*e*)   taxpayers who are non EU residents must present a certificate of reciprocity accorded to businesses or professionals resident in Spain, issued by the competent authority in the applicant's country of residence.

Sweden

General

7.69   Only taxable persons ('entrepreneurs') have a right to credit for input tax (i.e. right to deduction) on the acquisition of goods or services (or on imports). Private persons and non-profit making organisations who do not engage in business are unable to deduct input tax. 'Entrepreneurs' making supplies, which are subject to any of the four tax rates of 25%, 12%, 6% or zero rate, have the right to deduct input tax on costs, acquisitions or imports incurred by the business. However, they may not deduct input tax on costs, acquisitions or imports incurred in respect of an exempt supply.

Partial credit

7.70   An 'entrepreneur' who supplies goods or services which are exempt from VAT as well as goods or services which are taxable engages in a mixed business activity. Costs which may be directly attributed to taxable activities enable a full right to deduct input tax on costs, while costs which may be directly attributed to exempt activities do not enable any right to deduct input tax. When costs may be incurred in respect of both kinds of supplies, input tax may be deducted on a pro rata basis. If such 95% on costs can be pro-rated to activities with a right to full deduction, then import tax may be fully deducted on all supplies. The same rules apply if input tax on a single acquisition does not exceed SEK 1,000 and more than 95% of the sales are taxable.

Capital goods

7.71　Capital goods comprise:

(*a*)　machinery, equipment and equivalent depreciatory assets where the cost of acquisition exceeds SEK 200,000 excluding VAT;

(*b*)　real estate where the cost of acquisition exceeds SEK 400,000 excluding VAT (including purchase of new, additional buildings or construction services).

Over a period of ten years for real estate and five years for other capital goods, an adjustment of the initial deduction must be made based on the variations in deduction entitlement. This applies mainly to partly exempt businesses (i.e. where the taxable person may only partially deduct input tax on supplies which are exempt) and may result in an additional tax payment, or a further deduction of input tax. An adjustment does not arise when capital goods are transferred as part of a transfer of a going concern.

Imports

7.72　VAT on the importation of goods from outside the EU (imports), on the intra-Community acquisition of goods and on certain imported services (see above) is deductible under the same provisions and to the same extent as described above.

7.73　A special limitation on the right to deduct input tax applies to 'entrepreneurs' engaged in concerts and the circus, cinema, theatre, opera and ballet shows and their equivalent. In these cases a deduction cannot be made to the extent that the income of the enterprise comes from a government or municipal subsidy.

When goods or services are supplied or removed from the enterprise for no consideration or for a price below the purchase price (goods) or the cost of production (goods/services), VAT must be accounted for on the difference. However, a lower price etc. is accepted where the price is due to the current market situation. The same rules apply where goods in an enterprise with partial credit are fully transferred from the taxable part to the non-taxable part of the enterprise. In such cases there will not be any requirement for adjustment of the initial deduction.

Prohibitions to deduct input tax apply in the following cases:

(*a*)   where it is not possible to obtain an income tax deduction for entertaining customers;

(*b*)   purchase or lease of a permanent dwelling;

(*c*)   acquisition of passenger cars (or motorcycles), except in certain cases (e.g. passenger cars purchased by taxi companies and driving schools).

In addition, a restriction in the case of the margin scheme applies (see 12.52).

Passenger cars, motorcycles

7.74   Special rules for the right to deduct input tax and for private use apply to passenger cars and motorcycles. Vans and buses, if the total weight does not exceed 3,500 kilograms, are treated in the same way as cars. However, this does not apply to lorries where the driver's cab is distinct from storage space.

United Kingdom

General

7.75   Input tax is claimable on supplies of goods and services purchased by registered businesses for making taxable supplies. Tax invoices must be retained for inspection by visiting officers.

VAT may also be recovered on imports and EU acquisitions to the extent that they are used to make taxable supplies. No input tax directly attributable to exempt or non-business supplies may be recovered.

Input tax that cannot be attributed directly to taxable, exempt or non-business activities must be apportioned by using a fair and reasonable method. The standard method expresses the value of taxable supplies as a percentage of the value of total supplies and applies that percentage to non-attributable input tax.

Taxpayers may submit a written request to use an alternative special apportionment method. If this produces a fair result, written approval will be given by the authorities. The most common special methods are as follows:

(*a*)   taxable cost centres as a percentage of total cost centres;

(*b*)   number of taxable transactions as a percentage of total transactions;

(*c*) numbers of staff used full time in taxable activities as a percentage of total staff.

Input VAT restrictions

7.76 Listed below are the main areas where input tax is irrecoverable in the UK:

(*a*) purchase of new cars including fitted accessories;

(*b*) purchases under the tour operators' margin scheme;

(*c*) business entertainment expenses;

(*d*) purchases under the margin schemes;

(*e*) certain articles installed by builders in the course of new constructions;

(*f*) goods purchased for private use.

Note that following a European Court case, steps are being taken by the EU to insist that the UK should not allow businesses to recover VAT on supplies made to employees, e.g. VAT on petrol costs.

Adjustments of credit

7.77 Known as the 'capital goods scheme', this applies to certain computer equipment costing more than GBP 50,000 (excluding VAT) and property (including extensions, refurbishments, etc.) costing more than GBP 250,000 (excluding VAT). The input tax recoverable is adjusted over five years and ten years respectively to allow for changes in business use which may improve or reduce the input tax recovery rate.

Refunds for non-resident businesses

7.78 Refunds of tax are available to overseas businesses under the *EU Eighth and Thirteenth Directives* with certain conditions. Refunds will not be allowed in the following circumstances:

(*a*) where goods are used or are to be used in making a UK supply;

(*b*) on purchases of cars (unless hired or leased);

(*c*) on purchases of margin scheme goods;

(*d*) on business entertainment costs;

(*e*) on goods or services for resale for the benefit of travellers as part of a package holiday.

A standard form for EU and non-EU businesses must be completed and submitted with a certificate of taxable status or equivalent from the country of origin along with original tax invoices to support the claim. The form must be completed in English.

There are strict deadlines for the claims.

Chapter 8

Administrative Obligations

Administrative obligations: EU rules

Registration

General

8.1   Every taxable person should inform the authorities when his activities commence, change or cease, or when national legislation states notification is due. Also, every business which, for whatever reason, is not required to register because of the nature of its supplies (e.g. flat-rate scheme farmers or wholly exempt businesses), must register when its intra-Community acquisitions of goods exceed € 10,000 in a calendar year or any higher threshold determined by the member state in question. They may also register voluntarily.

Under voluntary registration, de-registration is generally permissible only after two years from the effective date of registration.

Where registration is compulsory, it must usually remain in force at least for the following year. At the end of that year, de-registration is permissible, provided the threshold was not exceeded during that year.

Under a proposed e-commerce Directive, non-EU businesses making supplies to EU private persons will be obliged to register in an EU member state with effect from 1 July 2003.

[*EC Sixth Directive 77/388, Art 22(1)*].

VAT identification numbers

8.2   VAT registration or identification numbers are essential for the mutual exchange of information between tax authorities.

Registered persons in a particular EU member state must report the total intra-Community acquisitions of goods under their identification number during a particular reporting period. Suppliers established in other EU member states must list the total value of their intra-Community supplies and the VAT identification number of each acquirer. The tax authorities may then use this information to aggregate the total intra-Community supplies to a particular taxable person and match this with the total intra-Community acquisitions of goods he has reported.

The following persons are required to register for VAT and obtain an identification number:

(*a*)   every taxable person who makes taxable supplies of goods or services with the exception of:

    (i)   any person who from time to time supplies new means of transport to another EU member state;

    (ii)   any person who provides services to which the reverse charge applies;

    (iii)   any person who makes only certain occasional supplies;

(*b*)   every 'flat rate scheme' farmer, and every taxable person who is not entitled to deduct VAT and any non-taxable legal entity which must be registered for VAT because intra-Community acquisitions of goods have exceeded the registration threshold;

(*c*)   every taxable person who makes intra-Community acquisitions of goods for the purposes of his economic activities in general.

Taxable persons do not receive a VAT identification number which is valid throughout the EU. They must obtain a separate number for each EU member state in which they make taxable supplies above the registration threshold.

If legally independent persons form a group registration, they will normally have one registration number for the whole group. In some countries, separate registrations are possible for divisions of a company.

[*EC Sixth Directive 77/388, Art 22(1)*].

Records

8.3   Every taxable person is obliged to keep their books and records to a standard that will facilitate inspection by the tax authorities.

Furthermore, every taxable person must keep a register of the goods transferred from his place of business to another EU member state in cases where the transfer is not treated as a 'fictitious' supply. He must also keep a register of goods dispatched to him from other EU member states by or on behalf of his customers which are taxable persons and identified as such in their own country.

[*EC Sixth Directive 77/388, Art 22(2)*].

Invoices

General

8.4   Invoices, or other documents qualifying as invoices, must be issued by every taxable person in respect of all goods and services supplied by him to another taxable person and in some cases to non-taxable legal entities including those belonging to another member state under the distance selling provisions.

If a new means of transport is supplied, an invoice must be issued in all cases. Furthermore, every taxable person must issue an invoice in respect of payments on account received from another person before the supply of goods or services is made or performed, and a copy must be retained for further inspection.

Currently the EU is debating the terms and conditions under which electronic invoicing may be permitted.

[*EC Sixth Directive 77/388, Art 22(3)*].

Invoice details

8.5   The invoice shall state clearly the VAT-exclusive price and the corresponding VAT charged at each rate as well as any exempt supplies involved. Each individual member state may determine the exact detail required on the tax invoice, although the standardisation of invoice requirements throughout the EU is being considered. However, the following information must be included:

(*a*)   the VAT identification number of the supplier and recipient of intra-Community transport of goods; ancillary services to intra-Community transport of goods or services rendered by intermediaries;

(*b*)   the VAT identification number of the taxable person who supplies the goods to another EU member state and that of the person acquiring the goods; in cases of occasional intra-Community supplies of new means of transport, the invoice must indicate the size, weight or capacity, the period after the date of first service, and the distance covered or the time it has been used.

Under triangular contracts, unnecessary registrations are avoided if the final purchaser treats the transaction as one single acquisition. The taxable person in the intermediate country would be required to treat his sale as an EU supply but his invoice must state that his customer will be accounting for acquisition VAT in the member state of destination. The reference should be to *Article 28C(E)(3)* and the two relevant VAT numbers should also be included.

8.6 *Administrative Obligations*

[EC Sixth Directive 77/388, Art 22(3)].

VAT returns

8.6 Every taxable person must submit a VAT return by the date determined by the tax authorities within each member state.

Tax periods normally cover one month, two months or a quarter although national authorities have the power to fix different periods provided that these do not exceed one year.

The return must include details of all VAT charged on outputs in the period and all input tax deductions to be made including, where appropriate, and insofar as it seems necessary for the establishment of the tax basis, the values for each rate of tax including exemptions. Furthermore, it must also show, although not necessarily as a separate figure:

(*a*)   the total value of exempt intra-Community supplies;

(*b*)   the total value excluding VAT of goods installed or assembled or supplied by distance selling; and

(*c*)   the total amount excluding VAT of supplies of goods under triangular arrangements.

Every taxable person shall pay any net amount shown as due when the return is submitted, although EU member states may fix a different due date or even demand an interim payment.

[EC Sixth Directive 77/388, Art 22(4), (5)].

Statements

Yearly statements

8.7 EU member states may require a taxable person to submit a statement, including the information specified under 8.6 above and covering all transactions performed during the previous year. This statement must provide all information necessary for any adjustments.

[EC Sixth Directive 77/388, Art 22(6)(a)].

Recapitulative statements (EU listings)

8.8 Every taxable person with a VAT registration number must submit regular statements showing total intra-Community supplies to each person identified for VAT purposes as acquiring the goods.

This obligation was introduced because of the regulation on administrative co-operation between EU member states which provides for the exchange of information between them.

Tax authorities in each EU member state can cross-check their own EU sales listings to VAT returns in the state of acquisition to ensure international trade is correctly reported.

The EU listings must set out:

(*a*)   the VAT identification number of the supplier;

(*b*)   the VAT identification number of the customer; and

(*c*)   the total value of supplies of goods to each acquirer in other EU member states for each calendar quarter in which the tax became payable.

They must be completed for each calendar quarter or on a monthly basis although national authorities may also permit different periods provided that they do not exceed one year.

Annual EU listings showing only the VAT identification numbers of customers are permissible if the following conditions are met:

(i)   the total annual value excluding VAT of supplies of goods and/or services does not exceed € 35,000;

(ii)   the total annual value excluding VAT of supplies of goods to other EU member states does not exceed € 15,000;

(iii) no new means of transport are supplied to other EU member states.

[*EC Sixth Directive 77/388, Art 22(6), (12)*].

Compliance

8.9   Where goods or services are acquired from overseas by a business and VAT is payable by the recipient, the tax authorities in the country of destination shall adopt the necessary measures to ensure obligations are fulfilled.

Release of taxable persons from obligations

8.10   EU member states may release taxable persons:

(*a*)   from certain obligations;

(*b*)   from all obligations where those taxable persons cease making taxable supplies;

(*c*)   from the payment of VAT due where the amount is insignificant.

[EC Sixth Directive 77/388, Art 22(9)].

Obligations in respect of imports

8.11   Where goods are imported into an EU member state from outside the EU, there are specific rules laid down for the making of declarations and payments. In particular, member states may provide that the VAT payable on importation of goods by taxable persons need not be paid at the time of importation but deferred to a later date so long as it is declared on the corresponding VAT return.

Specific rules in the various EU countries

Austria

Registration

8.12   Generally, businesses must register with the tax authorities located nearest to the business headquarters. If a business does not have a permanent establishment in Austria it must register with the *Finanzamt Graz-Stadt*.

VAT identification numbers are issued on written application to the local tax authorities. There is no standard application form, but application must include the applicant's name, address and tax number. Austrian VAT identification numbers comprise eight digits with the international prefix 'ATU'.

Records

8.13   Businesses in Austria are required to keep all relevant documents for a period of seven years. During this period, the records must be made available to the tax authorities upon request.

Invoices

8.14   VAT registered businesses must issue tax invoices on which the VAT is separately itemised. Tax invoices must include the following information:

(*a*)   the name and address of the supplier and his customer;

(*b*)   the quantity and clear description of the goods or services supplied;

(*c*)   the date of supply of the goods or services;

(*d*)   the value for VAT purposes;

(*e*)   the amount of VAT; and

(*f*)   the supplier's VAT registration number.

Where the total consideration does not exceed € 150, tax invoices require less detail.

VAT returns

8.15 All taxable persons in Austria must file monthly tax returns on special forms stating the amount of VAT due to or claimed from the tax authorities.

Since the beginning of 1994, periodical returns are not required where turnover in the previous year does not exceed € 22,000; where this is the case, no VAT is due, nor may VAT be recovered.

If turnover exceeds € 25,300 (i.e. 15% higher than the € 22,000 limit) once in a five-year period, the 'exemption' may still apply, but small businesses in this category may then opt for a minimum period of three years during which they must file quarterly VAT returns.

Returns must be filed along with any VAT payment due by the fifteenth day of the second month after the period end. Civil penalties may be applied for late submission.

As well as the requirement to submit monthly or quarterly returns, businesses must also file an annual return. This must be filed within 15 days of the calendar year end.

Belgium

Registration

8.16 Persons liable to register for VAT must inform the local VAT office before they commence taxable activities. There are specific forms for this purpose which are obtained from the tax authorities.

This also applies to a foreign business with a permanent establishment or branch office.

If a foreign business has no permanent establishment or branch office in Belgium, it must apply to the VAT central office for foreign taxable persons and may appoint a responsible representative established in Belgium. The procedure can be protracted and should be started well in advance.

If a fiscal representative is appointed, the representative must fulfil the following conditions, in order to be approved:

(*a*) they must be established or domiciled in Belgium;

(*b*) they must be in a position to be party to contracts;

(c)   they must be solvent and in a position to pay the sums for which they are jointly and severally liable with the person they represent; and

(d)   they must have agreed to represent the foreign taxable person.

A bank guarantee must also be provided.

In Belgium, a VAT identification number has nine digits and the international prefix is BE.

Records

8.17   Each business must keep records in sufficient detail to permit the tax authorities to check the records.

The records must include at least incoming and outgoing invoice ledgers, a financial ledger, copies of outgoing invoices and all original incoming invoices.

Invoices

8.18   Invoices must include the following:

(a)   date of issue and serial number;

(b)   name, address and VAT registration number of both the supplier and his customer;

(c)   date of supply of the goods or services;

(d)   a clear description of the goods or services supplied;

(e)   information needed for determining the applicable rate;

(f)   the quantity of the goods supplied;

(g)   the price;

(h)   the applicable VAT rate and the amount of tax;

(i)   where no VAT is due, the legal provision under which the transaction is exempted (export, EU delivery, etc.).

An invoice must be issued not later than the fifth working day of the month following that in which VAT becomes payable on all or part of the price. For intra-Community supplies of goods, it must be issued not later than the fifth working day of the month following that in which any payment is made.

VAT returns

8.19   Businesses with an annual turnover of more than € 500,000 must file a monthly tax return and pay the VAT due by the twentieth day of the month following the period concerned.

Businesses with an annual turnover of less than € 500,000 may file quarterly VAT returns and payments. In this case however, instalments must be paid each month in the quarter and are based on the VAT due for the preceding quarter.

Small businesses with an annual turnover not exceeding € 5,580 and which are subject to exemption arrangements must report their total annual turnover by 31 March of the following year. The return must be accompanied by a list of those taxable persons to whom the business has supplied goods or services.

Quarterly EU sales statements must be filed for EU deliveries and an annual client listing must be filed for all Belgian transactions.

As from 1 January 2002, VAT payers may opt for electronic filing of their monthly or quarterly VAT returns.

Currency

8.20   As from 1 January 2002, invoices and VAT returns must be completed in euros. If a foreign currency is used, the translation rate should be noted on the invoice. This should normally be the exchange rate at the date at which the invoice is established.

Denmark

Registration

8.21   Applications for VAT registration must be submitted no later than eight days before taxable activities in Denmark commence. A specific registration form which is obtainable from the tax authorities must be presented to the regional customs and tax office responsible for the area where the business is established and will be registered. The trader is then sent a certificate of registration, which includes the VAT identification number.

In Denmark, a VAT identification number has eight digits with the international prefix DK.

Foreign businesses making supplies in Denmark, which are registrable and have a permanent establishment in Denmark are, like Danish businesses, required to register with the regional customs and tax office responsible for the area where the business is established.

If the foreign business does not have an establishment in Denmark, it may appoint a representative who is a person whose permanent address is in Denmark or a business with a fixed establishment in Denmark. The Danish representative must then submit VAT returns and statements on behalf of the foreign business.

The minimum period in cases of voluntary registration for acquisitions by VAT exempt businesses, distance selling traders and VAT exempt services for which a business must remain registered is two years.

Records

8.22 Purchases and sales of goods and taxable services made by a taxable business must be recorded in a manner adequate for calculating the tax liability for each taxation period, as well as for compliance purposes.

Invoices

8.23 An invoice must be issued for each supply of goods and services liable to VAT.

Invoices must include the following items:

(*a*) date of supply of the goods or services;

(*b*) name, address and registration number of the supplier;

(*c*) name and address of the recipient;

(*d*) a clear description of the goods and services;

(*e*) the quantity of the supply;

(*f*) the consideration; and

(*g*) the amount of VAT.

VAT may either be shown separately on the invoice or expressed as 20% of the VAT inclusive price.

An invoice must be issued in respect of intra-Community transactions.

Foreign businesses registered in Denmark through a fiscal representative must indicate on invoices to Danish customers the representative's name and address and whether the representative is responsible for VAT. Copies of invoices must be kept at the representative's address.

VAT returns

8.24 The VAT return period for companies registered in urban areas is dependent on the size of their turnover:

(*a*) if the turnover is less than DKK 1,000,000 the VAT return is six months (first and second half of the year);

(*b*) if the turnover is between DKK 1,000,000 and DKK 10,000,000 the VAT return is for three months (quarterly);

(*c*) if the turnover is above DKK 10,000,000 the VAT return is monthly.

The filing period depends on the turnover limits given above, respectively:

(i) the first day of the third month after the end of the period;

(ii) the tenth day of the second month after the end of the period;

(iii) the 25th of the month following the end of the period.

When permitted, export companies may opt for a monthly or weekly VAT return period. If so, they may receive in advance from the customs and tax regional authority an amount corresponding to their average VAT refund. This will be either 3/52 of the amount (for monthly returns), or 3/104 (for weekly returns).

EU sales list statements for EU sales are normally submitted for each calendar quarter. They must be submitted, at the latest, one month and ten days after the end of the corresponding quarter.

Finland

Registration

8.25 Any person engaged in a taxable activity must notify the local tax authorities of the requirement to be registered. Foreign taxable persons with no fixed establishment in Finland must register at the regional tax office of Uusimaa in Helsinki.

Records

8.26 Records must be maintained for the purpose of assessing the tax due. All transactions must be recorded in chronological order.

Accounts are prepared in accordance with the Accounting Act.

Accounting records must be kept for at least ten years from the accounting year end, whereas invoices, vouchers and relevant correspondence must be kept for six years.

Invoices

8.27 Every taxable person must issue an invoice for transactions with another taxable person or public body. The invoice must show the price excluding VAT and the VAT at each rate and the text '*Alv rek.*', as indication of the VAT registered status of the supplier. Without an invoice there is no right to deduction.

In the case of intra-Community supplies the VAT number of the purchaser must be shown where appropriate. Finnish VAT numbers start with FI followed by an eight-digit number.

VAT returns

8.28   Registered persons submit monthly returns to regional tax offices and pay VAT due by the fifteenth day of the second month following the return month. The returns include information on:

(*a*)   VAT charged on domestic supplies at each rate;

(*b*)   VAT on taxable intra-Community acquisitions;

(*c*)   deductible VAT;

(*d*)   VAT deducted in the previous return;

(*e*)   amount of tax payable or negative tax to be transferred to the next month;

(*f*)   tax exempt turnover;

(*g*)   value of intra-Community supplies;

(*h*)   value of intra-Community acquisitions;

(*i*)   notification if taxable activity has ceased.

Failure to submit a return leads to an estimated assessment. Primary goods producers (farmers) account for VAT once per year at the end of February following the year in question. Primary producers can however submit monthly returns on application.

Statements

8.29   An EU sales statement must be submitted within one month and 15 days of the quarter end. The Central Liaison Office (CLO) supervises intra-Community transactions. Failure to submit, or an erroneous return, may attract a penalty of at least € 80 but not more than € 1,700.

Intrastat forms for each month must be submitted within ten days of the month end. Taxable persons whose annual acquisition of goods from other member states exceeds € 100,000 or whose annual supplies exceed € 100,000 have to submit monthly intrastat forms within ten working days after the month end.

Release of taxable persons from obligation

8.30   There is no obligation to issue a tax invoice to a private individual, except for the cases of distance selling to Finland.

France

Registration

8.31   All taxable persons operating in France must register for VAT. Foreign businesses are required to register as soon as they make taxable supplies in France.

In France, a VAT identification number has eleven digits and the international prefix is FR.

Non-EU businesses

Foreign businesses may apply for a VAT identification number:

(*a*)   to the competent business centre (e.g. the Chamber of Trade and Commerce);

(*b*)   to the tax office responsible for the fiscal representative.

When a person established outside the EU is liable to VAT or has to fulfil declaration formalities, that non-EU person has to register and appoint a representative liable to VAT and resident in France who undertakes to conduct any and all formalities to which the person is subject, and in the case of taxable transactions to pay VAT on that person's behalf.

Both the tax representative and the non-EU taxable person are jointly liable for payment of VAT and any interest and penalties. For some specific transactions, it is possible to appoint a simplified tax representative.

EU businesses

As from 1 January 2002, the appointment of a tax representative is only limited to the non-EU residents. As a consequence, an EU resident does not have to appoint a tax representative concerning activity in France.

VAT registration formalities

The EU businesses which had a tax representative in France before 1 January 2002 are already registered by INSEE ('French National Institute of Statistics and Economic Surveys') and hold an intra-Community VAT number in France.

Under new rules, EU residents with no tax representative and which are liable to French VAT, or must fulfil declaration formalities, will be registered for VAT purposes in France. In this respect, the French Tax Authorities shall allocate a VAT identification number to each EU resident. This VAT number would be used by the EU resident to declare the transactions carried out by him in France.

Possible appointment of a special representative

From now on, tax representation is not necessary for EU residents, however, they may still appoint a special representative. Whereas both the tax representative and the EU residents were jointly liable for payment of the VAT and any interest and penalties, now the representative is not liable. From now on, only the EU resident is liable.

Records

8.32   The following is required:

(*a*)   reporting the existence, identification or discontinuance of a business;

(*b*)   detailed book-keeping, supported by any evidence or by a ledger;

(*c*)   note of the transactions which are subject to different VAT rates or which are exempt.

Invoices

8.33   All taxable persons must issue invoices. The seller is normally required to issue an invoice immediately upon the sale of goods or services, and the purchaser must demand an invoice.

Invoices must include the following information:

(*a*)   name and address of supplier and recipient;

(*b*)   date and number of invoice;

(*c*)   quantity and description of the goods or services;

(*d*)   price of the goods excluding VAT;

(*e*)   the applicable rate of VAT;

(*f*)   VAT identification number of supplier and customer in case of intra-Community supplies with a specific reference to exemption from VAT;

(*g*)   VAT identification number of customer in case of intra-Community services.

Invoices should normally be issued in euros.

VAT returns

8.34   The normal filing period is monthly, except when the annual amount of VAT due does not exceed € 1,830 in which case the filing period is quarterly. A VAT return must be filed with payment by the 16th day after the end of the filing period.

The VAT return can be filed on the form provided by the French Tax Authorities or on the forms produced by software approved each year by the French Tax Authorities. France has integrated the EC sales list and the Intrastat Declaration into one single document (*Déclaration d'échange de biens entre Etats Membres – DEB*). This document must be submitted on a monthly basis. The filing date is 10 days following the month during which the VAT became chargeable.

Germany

Registration

8.35   Businesses must register with the tax authorities nearest to the principal place of business. A foreign business without a permanent establishment for VAT must be registered with the tax authorities responsible for the district in which the main activities are located. If there is doubt about which is the correct local tax office, the decision is taken by the *Bundesministerium für Finanzen* in Berlin.

In principle, VAT identification numbers are issued on written application to the *Bundesamt für Finanzen* in Saarlouis. The application must include:

(*a*)   the applicant's name and address;

(*b*)   the tax number under which the applicant is registered with the competent German tax office; and

(*c*)   the details of that tax office.

In Germany, a VAT identification number has nine digits and the international prefix is DE. A business resident abroad may appoint a fiscal representative. The fiscal representative must be a tax consultant, lawyer, public accountant or similar qualified person.

Records

8.36   Business records must normally contain the following information:

(*a*)   the basis of taxation for all transactions separated into taxable and non-taxable categories. Taxable transactions must be further split between those liable to the standard and reduced rates. If a business opts for taxation of certain goods and services, it must list these transactions separately;

(*b*)   the amount of money which has been received in advance for goods and services not yet supplied; taxable and non-taxable transactions must be separated;

(*c*)   the basis of taxation for private consumption;

(*d*)   the basis of taxation for all goods and services bought by the business as well as the amount of money which has been paid by the business in advance, in order to receive such goods and services;

(*e*)   the basis of taxation for all imports; and

(*f*)   the basis of taxation for all intra-Community acquisitions.

In general, the taxable person fulfils the above requirements within the scope of his normal bookkeeping. Separate listings are not common. EU sales lists and supplementary declarations are necessary for the supply of goods within the EU.

Invoices

8.37   Invoices must contain the following details:

(*a*)   the name and address of both supplier and customer;

(*b*)   the quantity and a clear description of the goods and services;

(*c*)   date of delivery;

(*d*)   the net consideration for the goods and services supplied, except for invoices with a gross amount which does not exceed € 100;

(*e*)   the amount of VAT or the reference to exemptions;

(*f*)   the VAT reference number;

(*g*)   the VAT identification number of foreign EU customers and reference to the intra-Community supply being non-taxable;

(*h*)   if the liability is transferred from a foreign supplier to the German recipient (see Chapter 9), the reference to the transfer and no VAT being due;

(*i*)   a special qualified electronic signature if it is an electronic invoice.

VAT returns

8.38   All taxable persons in Germany must file periodic tax returns on a special form, showing the net amount of VAT due to or from the local tax authorities.

Until the end of the second year after the establishment of a business, the return period is one month. After this time the return period depends on the total VAT payable in the previous year.

If the total VAT payable in the previous year:

(*a*)   has exceeded € 6,136 the returns must be filed monthly;

(*b*)   has exceeded € 512 up to € 6,136 the returns must be filed quarterly;

(*c*)   has not exceeded € 512 there is no requirement for periodic returns at all.

The filing and VAT payment, if applicable, must be made by the tenth day following the period end. Surcharges are usually applied to late payments.

Statements for intra-Community supplies must be submitted quarterly, within ten days of the end of the quarter.

Greece

Registration

8.39   All taxable persons must register for VAT in Greece. Each person has a single number for all taxes and there is no separate number for VAT.

If a foreign business is legally established in Greece, the business must submit a declaration of commencement of trading to the local tax authorities responsible in the area where the head office of the business is located. This office will issue the tax number.

A foreign business not established in Greece must appoint a fiscal representative who will apply for a tax number. The fiscal representative is appointed upon submission of a copy of the business's authorisation to the local tax office responsible for income tax. The copy must be certified by the Greek consular authority responsible for the location where the trader is established. The representative takes responsibility for all the principal's tax affairs.

If a business opts for taxation it will be registered for at least two years, unless the business ceases trading within this period. However, the tax numbers of individuals are maintained even if trading ceases, whilst those for legal and other persons are cancelled if the legal entity is dissolved or changes format.

In Greece, a VAT identification number has eight digits and the international prefix is GR.

Records

8.40 VAT registered businesses must keep full records for six years of all business transactions which may affect their liability to VAT. The records must be kept up to date and must be sufficiently detailed to facilitate calculation of liability accurately and to enable the Inspector of Taxes to check the calculations if necessary.

Failure to keep proper records may result in a fine of € 2,347.76 (GRD 800,000). The Revenue Commissioners have a general discretionary power to allow any taxable person not to keep records or to reduce the six-year period.

Invoices

8.41 Any individual or legal entity which earns income from commercial, industrial or agricultural activities or a profession in Greece, is obliged to issue, keep and request invoices, when making sales to other businesses.

Invoices must include the following:

(*a*) the name and address of the client;

(*b*) the tax number;

(*c*) a description of the supply;

(*d*) the price of the goods or services excluding VAT; and

(*e*) the rate of and corresponding amount of VAT.

VAT returns

8.42 Businesses with an annual turnover of less than € 5,282.47 (GRD 1,800,000) (goods) or € 1,760.82 (GRD 600,000) (services) are exempt from the requirement to submit provisional returns.

Businesses with an annual turnover of between € 5,282.47 (GRD 1,800,000) and € 52,824.65 (GRD 18,000,000) are required to keep purchase records only and must file a tax return on a quarterly basis by the fifteenth day of the month following the end of the relevant quarter.

Businesses with an annual turnover of between € 52,824.65 (GRD 18,000,000) and € 733,675.75 (GRD 250,000,000) are required to keep income and expenditure records and must file a tax return on a two-month basis by the twentieth day of the month following the end of the period.

Businesses with an annual turnover of more than € 733,675.75 (GRD 250,000,000) are required to keep full records and books and must file a monthly tax return by the twenty-fifth day of the month following the end of the relevant month. Payment of VAT is made directly to the tax authorities or to the post office when returns are filed.

In addition, businesses must submit a consolidated VAT declaration for each calendar year.

EU sales statements for intra-Community supplies are submitted by traders making such transactions every three months.

Ireland

Registration

8.43   Businesses with annual turnover from the supply of taxable goods and services exceeding or likely to exceed the statutory thresholds must register for VAT. Persons who supply taxable goods and services and who are, and expect to remain, below the turnover threshold may opt for taxation.

A foreign business without a permanent establishment in Ireland, and which makes taxable supplies in Ireland, must be registered. There is no obligation to appoint a fiscal representative.

Every person who becomes a taxable person must, within 30 days of so becoming, furnish in writing to the tax authorities the particulars specified in the regulations in order to register. Any changes in the registration particulars must be notified to the tax authorities within a period of 30 days.

Application must be made on a VAT registration application form. The application form must be sent to the tax authorities in the district in which the main place of business is situated. Following registration, the applicant will be issued with a VAT identification number, which will be the same number which is used by the tax authorities for other taxes.

In Ireland a VAT identification number has seven digits followed by a letter and the international prefix is IE.

Records

8.44   Every taxable person shall, in accordance with regulations, keep full and true records of all transactions which affect or may affect his liability to tax for a period of six years.

Invoices

8.45   A taxable person who supplies goods or services to another taxable person where VAT is due, must issue a tax invoice to that other taxable person in respect of each supply.

Invoices must be issued within 15 days of the end of the month during which the chargeable event occurred.

Invoices must include the following:

(*a*)   the name and address of both the supplier and the purchaser;

(*b*)   the VAT registration number of the supplier;

(*c*)   the date of issue of the invoice;

(*d*)   the date of supply of the goods or services;

(*e*)   a description of the goods or services;

(*f*)   the price charged, exclusive of VAT; and

(*g*)   the amount of VAT charged.

VAT returns

8.46   Each taxable person must file a return by the nineteenth day after the end of each taxable period. A taxable period is any two-month period beginning on the first day of January, March, May, July, September and November of any year.

Monthly returns may be submitted in cases where the taxable person, such as an exporter, is in a permanent repayment position. Approval to file monthly VAT returns must be obtained from the local authorities.

Certain businesses may be authorised to file an annual return.

At the end of each year, the bi-monthly return must be accompanied by a detailed analysis of supplies, purchases, imports and acquisitions of goods and services for the previous months.

EU sales statements on intra-Community supplies are submitted every three months by traders making such supplies.

Italy

Registration

8.47   A taxable person who supplies goods or services to another taxable person on which VAT is due, must issue a tax invoice to that other taxable person in respect of each supply.

An invoice must be issued when goods are delivered and services are supplied. If the delivery of goods is properly supported by a 'delivery document', the related invoice may be issued within 15 days from the end of the month during which the delivery is made.

Invoices must include the following:

(*a*) the name and address of both the supplier and the purchaser;

(*b*) the VAT registration number of the supplier and purchaser;

(*c*) the number and the date of issue of the invoice;

(*d*) the date of supply of the goods or services;

(*e*) a description of the goods or services;

(*f*) the price charged, exclusive of VAT;

(*g*) the amount of VAT charged; and

(*h*) reference to the delivery note (if any).

VAT returns

8.48   Since the start of 2002, monthly VAT returns are not requested. A brief annual VAT return must be filed in February and a complete one in October of the following year. Most businesses are required to file their annual VAT return together with their annual income tax return.

VAT payments are made monthly before the sixteenth day of the month following the month to which they refer.

Small businesses may opt to make their periodical VAT payments, every quarter, in which case interest of 1% will be charged on the amount due.

VAT reimbursements may be claimed in the annual VAT return and, if certain conditions are met, by filing a special quarterly return.

EU sales lists must be periodically submitted by any business involved in intra-Community transactions. Supplementary EU sales lists (intrastats) may be filed monthly, quarterly or annually depending on the volume of intra-Community transactions carried out in the prior calendar year.

Luxembourg

Registration

8.49   Businesses must register within 15 days of the start of their activities, unless they are excluded from the requirement to register. The following persons are exempt from registration:

(*a*)   persons who conduct exempt activities;

(*b*)   taxable persons whose annual turnover, excluding VAT, did not exceed € 10,000, for the previous calendar year;

(*c*)   taxable persons who supply goods and services in connection with agricultural activities.

Any individual or legal entity applying for a VAT identification number must first be included in the national register of such persons. An application is sent by the relevant department of the administration to the general registration office. After receiving the VAT registration number, on request, a VAT identification number may be given to be used for any intra-Community acquisitions.

Voluntary registration is not possible. Businesses are not given a VAT registration or identification number until the tax office has received a declaration relating to the commencement of an economic activity. Anyone who is permitted to register receives a registration number.

Foreign businesses which are engaged in economic activities must apply for a licence from the *Ministère des Classes Moyennes* in Luxembourg.

There is no minimum period of registration.

If a foreign business does not appoint a fiscal representative in Luxembourg, the tax authorities may require the payment of security or the issue of a bankers guarantee by an approved bank.

In Luxembourg, a VAT identification number has eight digits and the international prefix is LU.

Records

8.50   Businesses must keep records available for inspection by the tax authorities within Luxembourg for a period of ten years from the date of issue for documents or from the closure or balancing date for books.

Invoices

8.51   Any taxable person must issue invoices in respect of:

(*a*)   goods and services supplied to another taxable person or to a non-taxable legal entity;

(*b*)   intra-Community supplies to other taxable or non-taxable legal entities;

(*c*)   distance sales;

(*d*)   supplies of new means of transport to other EU member states;

(*e*)   transfers of goods in the course of business to another EU country; and

(*f*)   payments on account received from another taxable or non-taxable legal entity before the goods or services are supplied.

Invoices should include the following:

(i)   the date of issue;

(ii)   the name and address of the supplier and the client;

(iii)   the date of supply of the goods or services;

(iv)   the quantity and a description of the goods or services supplied, including the information required to determine the applicable rate;

(v)   the price, excluding tax, and other elements of the taxable base;

(vi)   the applicable rate, the amount of tax due or, in those cases where no VAT is due, the reason for the exemption; and

(vii)   the supplier's VAT registration number.

VAT returns

8.52   A business with an annual turnover of less than € 112,500, must submit an annual tax return which must be filed and paid before 1 March of the following year.

A business with an annual turnover of more than € 112,500, but less than € 625,000, must file a quarterly tax return before the fifteenth of the month following the period end.

A business with an annual turnover of more than € 625,000, must file a monthly tax return. This return must be filed before the fifteenth day of the month following the period end and payments must be made monthly.

Taxable persons who file monthly and quarterly VAT returns are obliged to submit an additional annual VAT return before 1 May each year.

EC sales lists for intra-Community supplies are submitted every three months by traders making such transactions.

The Netherlands

Registration

8.53   Businesses operating under the VAT legislation and making taxable supplies in the Netherlands must be registered with a VAT identification number given by the tax authorities in the district in which their business is located when they commence their taxable activities. There is no registration limit.

Foreign businesses which have no permanent establishment for VAT and which make taxable supplies in the Netherlands must apply for a VAT identification number from the tax authorities for foreign businesses in Heerlen. It is possible to appoint a fiscal representative with joint and several liability to fulfil all VAT obligations for the client, although since 1 January 2002 this is not a requirement.

In the case of distance sales, the business must be registered with a VAT identification number at the tax authorities for foreign businesses in Heerlen.

As regards imports of goods from outside the EU, it is possible to appoint a fiscal representative with limited liability. This representative establishes the VAT liability on the import of the goods and the onward sale. In this case the foreign business need not be registered for VAT.

In the Netherlands, a VAT identification number has twelve digits and the international prefix is NL.

Records

8.54 Businesses must keep records of the goods and services which they supply and receive. The book-keeping system of the business must be clear and arranged so as to facilitate checking by the authorities.

Invoices

8.55 Businesses are required to issue an invoice to other businesses or non-taxable legal entities in respect of supplies of goods and services made by them. Also, invoices must be issued for distance sales and if a private individual supplies a new means of transport to another EU member state.

An invoice must be issued by the fifteenth day following the month in which the supply of goods or services took place.

Invoices must include the following:

(*a*)　the date of supply of goods or services;

(*b*)　the name and address of the supplier and the recipient;

(*c*)　a clear description of the goods or services;

(*d*)　the quantity of goods delivered;

(*e*)　the consideration;

(*f*)   the amount of VAT; and

(*g*)   in the case of intra-Community transport services and supplies of goods, the VAT identification numbers of both the supplier and the recipient.

VAT returns

8.56   Businesses must file VAT returns and pay the appropriate amount of VAT due within one month of the end of the return period. Generally, a return period is three months.

The tax authorities may require a tax return to be filed every month and businesses may opt for monthly returns if they so wish.

An annual return may be accepted for small businesses.

EU sales list statements for intra-Community supplies are submitted every three months by businesses involved in such transactions.

Portugal

Registration

8.57   All businesses carrying on commercial, industrial or professional activities which are not exempt must be registered for VAT purposes. Voluntary registration applies to certain types of business (e.g. translators, interpreters and tourist guides).

From the effective date of registration the business is entitled to reclaim VAT as input tax.

New and foreign businesses applying for a VAT identification number must first obtain a registration number from the National Register of Legal Persons in Lisbon. They must then submit a declaration of commencement of activities to the local tax office in whose area their main activities are centred.

For foreign businesses, the declaration must be submitted to the local tax office responsible for the area where their fiscal representative is based.

A foreign business without a permanent establishment for VAT purposes in Portugal must appoint a fiscal representative to fulfil all VAT obligations.

In Portugal, a VAT identification number has nine digits and the international prefix is PT.

Records

8.58   All businesses must organise their accounting systems in a manner adequate for the clear and precise presentation of the information necessary in order that the tax authorities may assess and supervise VAT.

All records and required supporting documents (e.g. invoices, vouchers, customs release documents, etc.) must be properly filed and retained for ten years or be microfilmed within three years.

Invoices

8.59   Invoices must be issued where the customer is a taxable or exempt person, or in the case of distance sales to another EU member state.

Tax invoices must include the following:

(*a*)   the date and serial number;

(*b*)   the name and address of both the supplier and the receiver;

(*c*)   the tax registration numbers of the businesses involved;

(*d*)   the quantity and description of the goods and services supplied;

(*e*)   the taxable value of the supply;

(*f*)   the applicable VAT rate and the amount of VAT charged; and

(*g*)   the grounds for any VAT relief claimed.

VAT returns

8.60   VAT returns must be filed on a quarterly or monthly basis depending on the turnover of the business. Businesses with an annual turnover less than € 498,797.90 are permitted to file quarterly returns. They may, however, opt for monthly returns.

If turnover exceeds € 498,797.90, businesses must file monthly returns.

Monthly returns should be filed and paid within one month and ten days of the end of each return period, whereas quarterly returns should be filed and paid within one and a half months of the end of each quarter.

EU sales list statements recording intra-Community supplies are submitted every month or every quarter by traders making such supplies.

An annual statement must be filed every year in May or June providing details of all goods and services supplied in the preceding fiscal year. Also

EU sales list statements must be filed every year in May or June providing details of all clients and suppliers for amounts in excess of € 49,879.79.

Spain

Registration

8.61   Spanish businesses must file their declaration form for registration with the local tax authorities immediately they commence their activities.

Foreign businesses with a permanent establishment in Spain must apply for a registration number to the local tax authorities (*AEAT*) responsible for the area in which that establishment is located. Foreign businesses without a permanent establishment in Spain must register through a fiscal representative with the authorities responsible for the location where business activities will be carried on.

There is no minimum level for period of registration, and voluntary registration is not possible.

In Spain, a VAT identification number has nine digits and the international prefix is ES.

Records

8.62   Accounting records must be kept in such a way as to enable the tax administrator to determine the total amount of output VAT charged and input VAT reclaimed. All transactions by a taxable business must be recorded.

A taxable person is required to keep the following records:

(*a*)   invoices and similar documents issued and received;

(*b*)   investment details.

Invoices

8.63   Businesses must issue invoices for each supply and keep a copy. Invoices must be issued within 30 days of the supply of goods or services and must include the following:

(*a*)   the date, place of supply and serial number;

(*b*)   the name and address of both the supplier and his customer or purchaser;

(c)   the tax registration numbers of the businesses involved;

(d)   the quantity and description of the goods and services supplied;

(e)   the taxable base of the supply; and

(f)   the applicable VAT rate and the amount of VAT charged or, if VAT is included in the price, the rate of VAT and a statement that VAT is included.

VAT returns

8.64   Generally businesses must file quarterly returns, although in the following cases the return must be filed monthly:

(a)   businesses with a turnover greater than € 6,010,121.04 (ESP 1,000,000,000) in the preceding year;

(b)   businesses entitled to claim a tax refund at the end of each taxable period because of high value exempt with credit supplies.

In addition to these periodic returns, businesses must also file an annual summary using the appropriate form.

Sweden

Invoices

8.65   A taxable person shall issue an invoice for the supply made specifying the following:

(a)   the consideration;

(b)   the VAT amount for each tax rate;

(c)   the supplier's and the customer's names and addresses;

(d)   type of supply;

(e)   place of supply;

(f)   supplier's VAT registration number or civic registration number/ organisation number; and

(g)   other information of significance in judging the VAT liability and the customer's right to deduct.

VAT returns

8.66   For maximum annual sales of SEK 1,000,000 excluding VAT, the VAT may be accounted for on an annual basis. Otherwise VAT must be accounted for on a monthly basis. Where annual turnover exceeds SEK 40,000,000, the VAT return should be filed and VAT paid at the latest by 26 days after the end of the accounting period. Otherwise the limit is 42 days. Partnerships and others who do not file income tax returns may apply to account for VAT once annually, if annual sales do not exceed SEK 200,000 excluding VAT.

United Kingdom

Registration

8.67   Businesses making taxable supplies in the UK must register if their taxable turnover has exceeded GBP 55,000 in the last twelve months or if it is expected to exceed GBP 55,000 in the next 30 days. See Chapter 12 regarding special rules and the option for a flat rate scheme.

Businesses must notify the authorities of a requirement to register on a standard form, and completed forms should be sent to the local VAT office. Foreign businesses with no UK office or establishment may register at the Special Office for Overseas Traders, Aberdeen. UK business establishments of overseas companies may register in the UK if they make supplies outside the UK which would be taxable if made in the UK. Also, certain companies not otherwise requested, but which dispose of assets in the UK used in the course of business on which VAT has been reclaimed, will be required to register.

Voluntary registration is permissible for businesses making taxable supplies below the threshold or intending to make taxable supplies in the future.

In the UK, a VAT identification number has nine digits and the international prefix is GB.

Records

8.68   Businesses must make the records of their activities available to the authorities upon request, and must keep such records for a period of six years following the activities in question.

Invoices

8.69   Invoices must include the following:

(*a*)   an identifying number;

(*b*)   the time of supply or tax point;

(*c*)   the date of issue;

(*d*)   the name, address and registration number of the supplier;

(*e*)   the type of supply;

(*f*)   a description of the goods or services supplied;

(*g*)   the quantity of goods or nature of services;

(*h*)   the net amount payable;

(*i*)   the total amount payable, before tax;

(*j*)   the rates of tax and the amount of tax at each rate;

(*k*)   the total amount of tax chargeable; and

(*l*)   the rate of any discount.

All amounts are to be expressed in sterling.

Special rules apply to shops and other retailers who are not required to issue VAT invoices. Also, rules are to be introduced for electronic invoicing and storage.

VAT returns

8.70   Once registered, quarterly returns are due if the taxpayer is in a regular payment position, but monthly returns can be submitted if regular repayments are due from the authorities, e.g. for farmers or certain construction businesses.

Certain small businesses may account for VAT on an annual basis making interim payments and submitting one annual return with the balancing payment.

Returns are due one month after the period ends (two months for annual returns).

Monthly payments on account are due from businesses which have paid more than GBP 2,000,000 to the authorities in a given year. Returns, however, are still due quarterly.

Chapter 9

Liability and Chargeable Event

Liability and chargeable event: EU rules

General

9.1   The following persons are liable to pay VAT:

(*a*)   Taxable persons who carry out taxable transactions. However, this does not apply to certain services performed by a taxable person resident abroad. If the taxable transaction is effected by a taxable person resident abroad, EU countries may adopt arrangements whereby VAT is payable by someone other than the taxable person abroad. Inter alia, a tax representative or other person for whom the taxable transaction is carried out may be designated as the liable person. EU member states may also provide that someone other than the taxable person shall be held jointly and severally liable for payment of VAT.

Note that with effect from 1 January 2002, there is no obligation for non-resident businesses to appoint a representative in a member state.

(*b*)   Persons to whom certain services are supplied but which are performed by a taxable person resident abroad. However, EU member states may require that the supplier of services shall be held jointly and severally liable for payment of the VAT.

These include the following services:

(i)   transfer and assignments of copyrights, patents, licences, trade marks and similar rights;

(ii)   advertising services;

(iii)   services of consultants, engineers, consultancy bureaux, lawyers, accountants and other similar services, as well as data processing and information supply;

(iv)   obligations to refrain from pursuing or exercising, in whole or in part, a business activity or a right referred to in this list;

(v) banking, financial and insurance (including reinsurance) transactions, with the exception of the hire of safes;

(vi) supplies of staff;

(vii) the services of agents who act in the name of and on behalf of another, when they procure for their principal the services referred to in this list;

(viii) the hiring out of movable tangible property, with the exception of all forms of transport;

(ix) telecommunication services;

The reverse charge is also extended to the following services:

(x) supplies of services in the intra-Community transport of goods rendered to customers identified for VAT purposes in an EU member state;

(xi) supplies of services involving activities ancillary to the intra-Community transport of goods, rendered to customers identified for VAT purposes in an EU member state;

(xii) supplies of services rendered by intermediaries acting in the name of and on behalf of other persons, where they form part of the supply of services in the intra-Community transport of goods or activities ancillary to the intra-Community transport of goods, where the customer of the services rendered by the intermediary is identified for VAT purposes in an EU member state;

(xiii) supplies of services involving valuations or work on movable tangible property, where the goods are dispatched or transported out of the member state where the services were physically carried out, where the customer is identified for VAT purposes in an EU member state.

This also applies when such services form part of transactions other than the above consultancy services etc., where the customer is identified for VAT purposes in an EU member state.

(c) Any person who mentions VAT on an invoice or other document serving as an invoice.

(d) Any person effecting a taxable intra-Community acquisition of goods. Where such an acquisition is effected by a non-EU person, a tax representative or other person may be designated. Member states may also provide that someone other than the person effecting the intra-Community acquisition shall be held jointly and severally liable for the payment of VAT.

(*e*) On importation of goods into an EU member state, the person or persons designated or accepted as being liable by the EU member states into which the goods are imported.

(*f*) With effect from 1 July 2003 it is proposed that non-EU resident businesses involved in making e-commerce supplies to EU private pensions, should become taxable in the EU member state in which they register for VAT.

[*EC Sixth Directive 77/388, Art 21*].

Chargeable event

General

9.2 A chargeable event occurs and the VAT becomes due when goods are delivered or services are performed.

Deliveries of goods and supplies of services which give rise to successive statements of account or payments shall, in principle, be regarded as being completed at the time when the periods to which such statements of account or payments refer expire.

However, where a payment is to be made on account before the goods are delivered or the services are performed, the VAT shall become chargeable on receipt of the payment and on the amount received. By way of derogation, EU member states may provide that the VAT becomes chargeable, for certain transactions or for certain categories of taxable persons either:

(*a*) no later than the date of issue of the invoice or the document serving as an invoice; or

(*b*) no later than the receipt of payment; or

(*c*) where an invoice or document serving as an invoice is not issued or is issued late, within a specified period from the date of the chargeable event.

Imports of goods

9.3 As regards imported goods, the chargeable event shall occur and the VAT shall become chargeable when the goods are imported. Where goods are placed under one of the customs arrangements on entry into the EU, the chargeable event shall occur and the VAT shall become chargeable when the goods cease to be covered by these arrangements or when the chargeable event for the community customs duties occurs.

Where imported goods are not subject to any such community duties, EU member states shall apply the provisions in force governing customs duties as regards the occurrence of the chargeable event and the time when VAT becomes chargeable.

[*EC Sixth Directive 77/388, Art 10*].

Intra-Community acquisitions of goods

9.4   For intra-Community acquisitions, a chargeable event occurs when a supply of goods takes place.

If an invoice is issued before the fifteenth day of the month following that of the supply, VAT becomes chargeable on the issue of the invoice. If no invoice is issued before the fifteenth day of the month following that of the supply, the chargeable event occurs and the tax becomes due on the fifteenth day of the month, following the supply. For fictitious intra-Community acquisitions, the chargeable event occurs when the supply of similar goods is regarded as being effected and VAT becomes chargeable on the fifteenth day of the month following that of the supply.

[*EC Sixth Directive 77/388, Art 28D*].

Specific rules in the various EU countries

Austria

Liability

9.5   In Austria the supplier is liable for payment of VAT to the tax authorities. If a foreign supplier has no permanent establishment in Austria and provides services to Austrian businesses, the liability is transferred to the Austrian recipient.

Chargeable event

9.6   VAT is due as follows on the supply of goods and services for which a tax invoice is issued:

(*a*)   generally, VAT must be accounted for in the return period in which the supply was made. This date is postponed for one month if the invoice was issued after the end of the month in which the consignment was delivered;

(*b*)   under special conditions, in the return period in which the taxable person receives payment for the supply of goods and services. This applies to businesses which receive income from independent activities.

Belgium

Liability

9.7   For supplies of goods and services the supplier is usually liable for payment of VAT to the tax authorities.

In the case of a foreign business which has applied for a VAT registration, the fiscal representative is liable for payment on behalf of its principal.

It should be noted that customers and clients may also have a liability in respect of VAT, interests and penalties due.

On importation of goods, VAT must be paid to the Customs office at the port of entry unless a deferred payment arrangement has been concluded with the tax authorities.

For intra-Community acquisitions of goods and certain types of contract involving construction work, the purchaser must declare the VAT due on his own VAT return (deferral system). However, the supplier remains fully responsible in the case of non-payment.

Where goods are sold on a consignment basis by a foreign supplier to a consignment holder in Belgium, VAT will be due from the consignment holder on the acquisition of the goods in Belgium.

Chargeable event

9.8   Generally, VAT is due at the time of the supply of the goods or services. However, if part or all of the consideration is invoiced or cash received before the supply of goods takes place, tax is due on the basis of the payment received or invoice issued.

For services, VAT is normally due at the time the service has been completed.

Denmark

Liability

9.9   For supplies of goods and services, the supplier is generally liable for payment of VAT to the tax authorities. In the case of a foreign business, the fiscal representative is jointly and severally liable unless the foreign business is situated in another EU member state, in Greenland, the Faroe Islands, Iceland or Norway.

If a foreign business supplies advisory services or similar, the VAT due is collected from the Danish customer if he is VAT-registered in Denmark.

The liability is also transferred from the foreign supplier to the Danish customer for the supply and installation of goods in Denmark and intra-Community transport services, provided the recipient is VAT registered in Denmark.

If a Danish VAT-registered company purchases goods from countries outside the EU, including Greenland and the Faroe Islands, then the Danish company shall, from 1 April 2001, no longer pay import VAT together with customs duty. If such goods are purchased the calculated VAT amount must be included on the VAT statement.

Chargeable event

9.10   VAT is due on the date of issue of a tax invoice which must be issued before or immediately after a supply. Where a tax invoice is not required, the tax point becomes the receipt of cash.

Finland

General

9.11   VAT is payable when goods are delivered or services performed or when payment is made to the supplier prior to the supply. In the case of a self-supply, the chargeable event is the moment the goods or services are taken for own use.

VAT is reported and paid on a monthly VAT return for invoices received in the month.

VAT returns are completed on the basis of the goods received or services supplied. Certain businesses may use the cash payment basis.

Importation

9.12   The importation of goods is a taxable event when undertaken by any person. VAT is payable at the time of importation. Unregistered persons must pay within ten days of the goods clearing Customs.

Intra-Community acquisition

9.13   The chargeable event is in the month following the acquisition of goods unless the invoice is issued in the same month as the acquisition takes place, in which case the chargeable event is in the same month as the acquisition. VAT is due one month and 15 days thereafter and is accounted for via the VAT return.

France

Liability

9.14   For supplies of goods and services, the supplier is generally liable for payment of VAT to the tax authorities.

If the foreign business fails to account for VAT, the French Tax Authorities are entitled to collect any VAT due, including interest and penalties from its customers.

If a foreign business supplies advisory services or similar, the VAT due is collected from the French customer, provided he is VAT-registered in France. The liability is also transferred from the foreign supplier to the French customer for the supply of intra-Community transport services, provided the recipient is VAT-registered in France.

For imports of goods, VAT is payable by or on behalf of the importer to the French Customs Authorities at the time the goods are imported. In certain cases, VAT payment may be deferred (e.g. for non-ferrous metals, oil and gas).

For intra-Community acquisitions of goods, the purchaser is liable for payment of VAT on its next return. The seller is jointly obliged to pay VAT if the purchaser is not resident in France. For these acquisitions, the VAT is due on the 15th day following the chargeable event.

Chargeable event

9.15   Currently, VAT is payable at the time of supply. For imports, VAT is normally due at importation unless a deferment arrangement exists.

For supplies of goods, the chargeable event is the transfer of ownership.

For supplies of services, the chargeable event is the payment of these services or works. However, if the purchaser pays on account there is a chargeable event upon each advance.

Germany

Liability

9.16   For supplies of goods and services in Germany, the supplier is normally liable for payment of VAT to the tax authorities.

If a foreign business supplies services, or '*Werklieferungen*' (see Chapter 2), and the recipient is a business or a public body, the liability is transferred from the foreign supplier to the German recipient. The foreign supplier is not allowed to show the VAT. The German recipient has to calculate the VAT and pay it to the tax authorities.

For imports of goods, VAT is payable by or on behalf of the importer to the customs authorities. For intra-Community acquisitions of goods, the purchaser is liable to account for VAT on his next return.

Chargeable event

9.17   VAT becomes payable for the supply of goods and services, as follows:

(*a*)   on an invoice basis, at the end of the return period in which the supply was made;

(*b*)   on a cash basis, at the end of the return period in which the taxable person receives payment for the supply of goods and services.

For imports of goods, VAT is normally due at the time the goods are actually imported.

Greece

Liability

9.18   For supplies of goods and services, the supplier is generally liable for payment of VAT to the tax authorities.

In the case of a foreign business, the fiscal representative is jointly and severally liable for payment of VAT. If the foreign business fails to appoint a fiscal representative, the tax authorities are entitled to collect any VAT due, including interest and penalties, from its customers.

If a foreign business supplies advisory services or similar, the VAT due is collected from the Greek customer, provided he is VAT-registered in Greece. The liability is also transferred from the foreign supplier to the Greek customer for the supply of intra-Community transport services, provided the recipient is VAT-registered in Greece.

For imports of goods, VAT is payable by or on behalf of the importer to the customs authorities. For intra-Community acquisitions of goods, the purchaser is liable for payment of the VAT on the next return.

Chargeable event

9.19   VAT becomes due at the time goods or services are supplied to the customer. The actual payment of VAT is made at the time the VAT return is filed.

The tax point is normally the date of issue of a tax invoice or the date when payment is received, whichever is the earlier.

Ireland

Liability

9.20 For supplies of goods and services, the supplier is generally liable for payment of VAT to the tax authorities.

However, in certain instances, the customer rather than the supplier is liable to account for VAT. These are as follows:

Reverse charge services

9.21 Certain services received from outside of Ireland are liable for Irish VAT when they are received for business purposes. These are mainly professional, consultancy and telecommunication services. It is the customer who is liable to account for Irish VAT on these services. These services are known in Ireland as Fourth Schedule' services, as they are listed in the Fourth Schedule to the Irish VAT Act.

Property leases

9.22 In certain instances involving the grant of a property lease, permission can be obtained for the lessee to account for VAT on the transaction. In certain circumstances where a lease is being surrendered to a landlord, the landlord is obliged to account for the VAT on the transaction.

International transport services

9.23 Where an Irish VAT-registered entity receives international transport services from a transport operator registered for VAT in another EU state, the Irish customer must account for the VAT on the transaction.

Importation of goods

9.24 When goods are imported into Ireland from outside of the EU, the importer must pay VAT at the point at which the goods are imported into Ireland.

Intra-Community acquisitions

9.25 Where an intra-Community acquisition occurs, VAT is accountable by the fifteenth day of the month following the date of the transaction. However, if the supplier issues an invoice prior to that date, VAT is accountable on the date of the invoice.

Chargeable event

9.26   A liability to VAT normally arises at the time when a VAT invoice is issued. Where a person is entitled to account for VAT on the cash basis, VAT is due when he receives a deposit or payment from his customer.

A VAT invoice must be issued to all VAT-registered customers by the fifteenth day of the month following that in which the supply takes place. Taxable persons not entitled to account for VAT on the cash basis must account for VAT in respect of all invoices issued, by the nineteenth day of the month following the VAT period.

Where the customer is not a VAT-registered person, VAT is due on the date that the supply is made.

Italy

Liability

9.27   For supplies of goods and services, the supplier is generally liable for payment of VAT to the tax authorities.

By February 2002, the Italian parliament had approved the EU Directive relating to the appointment of fiscal representatives but a government decree, which is required to legally enforce the new rules, remains outstanding and therefore currently the old rules on the need to appoint a fiscal representative apply.

When the new rules come into force, EU businesses carrying on activities within Italy will no longer be required to appoint resident representatives as they may register themselves with the local VAT office. If a fiscal representative is appointed the representative will not be liable for payments for VAT nor have any other responsibility as the VAT duties and responsibility remain with the principal.

If a foreign business supplies advisory services or similar, VAT due is collected from the Italian customer, provided the recipient is VAT-registered in Italy. The liability is also transferred from the foreign supplier to the Italian customer for the supply of intra-Community transport services provided the recipient is VAT-registered in Italy.

For imports of goods, VAT is payable by or on behalf of the importer to the customs authorities. For intra-Community acquisitions of goods, the purchaser is liable for payment of the VAT on the next return.

Chargeable event

9.28   For supplies of goods, VAT becomes due at the date of delivery or, if earlier, when payment is received or when an invoice is issued. For services, VAT becomes due when the payment is received or, if earlier, when the invoice is issued. Special rules apply to supplies of real estate, supplies to public entities and supplies of goods where the transfer of their ownership occurs later than consignment.

Luxembourg

Liability

9.29   For supplies of goods and services, the supplier is generally liable for payment of VAT to the tax authorities. If a customer cannot prove that he has paid VAT to his supplier, he will, in principle, be liable for payment. In the case of a foreign business, the fiscal representative is jointly and severally liable for payment of VAT.

If a foreign business supplies intra-Community transport services which are taxable in Luxembourg, the liability is deferred to its customer provided the recipient is a VAT-registered business.

For imports of goods, VAT is payable by or on behalf of the importer to the customs authorities.

For intra-Community acquisitions of goods, the purchaser is liable for payment of the VAT on his next return.

Chargeable event

9.30   VAT becomes due:

(*a*)   for supplies of goods or services for which an invoice must be issued:

    (i)   at the time of issue of the invoice, where the time limits for issuing an invoice are observed;

    (ii)   at the time the invoice should have been issued, where the time limits for issuing an invoice are not observed;

    (iii)   at the time of receipt of cash where payments are received prior to the issue of an invoice;

(*b*)   at the time of supply of goods or services for which an invoice need not be issued. If an invoice is nevertheless issued or a payment is made before the supply, there is a deemed supply and VAT is payable on the amount shown on the invoice or the payment received;

(*c*)   for imports at the time the goods are actually imported.

The Netherlands

Liability

9.31   For supplies of goods and services, the supplier is generally liable for payment of VAT to the tax authorities.

If a foreign business supplies goods or services in the Netherlands, VAT due will be collected from the customer, provided the customer is either a taxable or exempt business or a non-taxable legal entity.

For imports of goods, VAT is payable by or on behalf of the importer to the customs authorities. Unless the foreign business has appointed a fiscal representative with limited liability, the representative will be liable for payment of VAT due. A foreign business involved in distance sales to the Netherlands will pay VAT due through a fiscal representative who has joint and several liability.

For VAT due on intra-Community acquisitions of goods, the purchaser is liable for payment of VAT on the next VAT return.

In certain cases (e.g. supplies of existing property, construction work and supplies in the textile industry and for supplies by Dutch resident businesses) the VAT liability may be transferred to the recipient.

Chargeable event

9.32   VAT becomes payable:

(*a*)   for supplies of goods and services for which an invoice must be issued, on the date of issue of the invoice, or at the latest, by the fifteenth day of the month following the month in which the supply was made;

(*b*)   for supplies of goods and services for which an invoice need not be issued, at the time of supply of the goods or services.

Portugal

Liability

9.33   The supplier is generally liable for payment to the tax authorities of VAT on supplies of goods and services.

In the case of a foreign business, the fiscal representative is jointly and severally liable for the VAT payment. If the foreign business fails to appoint a fiscal representative, the tax authorities are entitled to collect any VAT due, including interest and penalties, from the business' customers.

Where a foreign business supplies goods and services, the VAT due is collected from the Portuguese customer, provided he is a VAT-registered business in Portugal.

For imports of goods, VAT is payable by or on behalf of the importer to the customs authorities.

For intra-Community acquisitions of goods, the purchaser is liable to account for VAT on the next return.

Chargeable event

9.34   VAT becomes chargeable:

(*a*)   at the time of supply of goods or services;

(*b*)   for imports, when the related customs release documents are issued.

Spain

Liability

9.35   The supplier of goods or services in Spain is usually responsible for paying VAT to the tax authorities. If a foreign business supplies goods or services in Spain, the tax is usually collected from the customer. If a fiscal representative is appointed, he will be jointly and severally liable.

VAT is payable by the importer on imported goods when they are cleared into free circulation. The acquirer of intra-Community goods must account for acquisition VAT on the VAT return.

Since 1 January 2002, the directors are liable in cases of fraud or omission leading to the failure to pay the correct amount of tax.

Chargeable event

9.36   A chargeable event generally occurs when goods are delivered to the customer, which is the point at which the risk on the goods is transferred from vendor to purchaser. The chargeable event for services is when they are performed.

Special rules apply in the following situations:

(*a*)   delivery of goods without transfer of title: although the goods still belong to the supplier, for VAT purposes there is a deemed supply of goods and the general rule is followed;

(*b*)   delivery of goods from commission payers to commission receivers both on selling and buying commissions: VAT is not due until the goods are delivered to the final customer;

(*c*)   contracts involving estimated prices: VAT is not due until the goods are delivered to the final customer;

(*d*)   advance payments on delivery of goods or performance of services: VAT becomes due whenever a payment is made even though the goods have not been delivered and the service has not been performed;

(*e*)   contracts of work for the Public Administrations: at the time of payment;

(*f*)   Successive invoicing: when the price has not been established or covers a period greater than one year, income is treated as earned on 31 December pro-rata to the period covered.

Sweden

Liability, chargeable event and usage of the right to deduct

9.37   The supplier's VAT liability and the customer's right to deduct VAT arises when a supply and the corresponding acquisition are made. Prior to this taxable event there is no liability to account for VAT or right to claim VAT.

Output tax must be accounted for in the VAT return of the accounting period under which a supply, in accordance with generally accepted accounting principles, has been or should be accounted for. However, where a payment is to be made on account before the goods are delivered or the services are performed, VAT becomes chargeable on receipt of the payment and according to the amount received. The customer has a corresponding right to deduct input tax. Deduction may be claimed in the VAT return of the accounting period during which an invoice carrying VAT has been received for a cost, acquisition or import made and according to accounting principles has been, or should have been, booked. In the case of a payment on account, the customer may claim deduction of input tax in the VAT return of the accounting period under which payment was made, provided a VAT invoice has been received.

A person is liable to pay VAT in Sweden in the following cases:

(*a*)   when making supplies of goods or services subject to VAT within Sweden and as part of the business activity;

(*b*)   when making an intra-Community acquisition of goods comprising movable tangible property;

(*c*)   on importation of goods from a location outside the EU.

In general, tax liability arises when two conditions are fulfilled: a supply takes place within Sweden, and the supply is made by an 'entrepreneur'. Both conditions must be fulfilled, otherwise there is no tax liability within Sweden. The taxable person may be an 'entrepreneur' in Sweden or a foreign 'entrepreneur'. A foreign 'entrepreneur' who makes supplies in Sweden on an occasional basis must be registered for VAT in Sweden. New rules came into effect from 1 July 2002 regarding certain supplies made in Sweden to a taxable person by an entrepreneur from another EU member state in relation to the appointment of VAT representatives. The tax authorities normally accept a VAT representative without making a close investigation, but are entitled by law to request security from the VAT representative. The VAT representative must be able to present the tax authorities with original documentation regarding the principal's business activities in Sweden.

In the case of intra-Community acquisitions, the purchaser (if a taxable person) shall apply a reverse charge and calculate and account for VAT on the agreed price (calculated in SEK) and may, when entitled to credit for input tax, directly make an equivalent deduction for input tax. A reverse charge must also be made by a non-taxable person (e.g. a private person) for intra-Community acquisitions of certain new means of transport (e.g. passenger cars). With reference to imports, anyone that reports an importation to the Swedish Customs shall pay to them VAT on the value of the goods calculated on the basis of cost, insurance and freight. When entitled to credit for input tax, the purchaser may, upon receipt of the relevant invoice or at the earliest date stated by a forwarding agent, make a deduction equivalent to the VAT paid to Customs. In both cases, this is provided that the goods are subject to Swedish VAT.

United Kingdom

Liability

9.38   The supplier of goods or services in the UK is usually responsible for paying VAT to the tax authorities.

If a foreign business supplies goods or services in the UK, the tax is usually collected from the customer. If a fiscal representative is appointed, the representative will be jointly and severally liable, although there is now no requirement to appoint a representative.

For imports of goods, VAT is payable by or on behalf of the importer either at the port of entry or deferred until the fifteenth day of the following month. However, for intra-Community acquisitions, the acquirer accounts for the tax on his next return.

To the extent that the services are of the type listed in the *Sixth Directive, Article 9(2)(e)*, and deemed as being supplied where received, the 'reverse charge system' applies and this now covers nearly all imported services.

Chargeable event

9.39   VAT payments are due with returns except for monthly payments on account. If the authorities receive payment late, the taxpayer is regarded as in default.

The time of supply is known in the UK as the tax point. For goods, the basic tax point is the date of removal of the goods or when they are made available to the customer. The basic tax point can be superseded by the receipt of payment or the issue of a tax invoice which can be issued up to 14 days after the basic tax point unless an extension is agreed with the authorities. For goods supplied on a sale or return basis, the tax point is the date the customer indicates he wishes to adopt the goods, or twelve months after the initial supply, whichever is the earlier.

The basic tax point for services is when they are performed which is the date on which all work except invoicing is completed. However, certain services are regarded as continuous which means they do not have a basic tax point. VAT then becomes due when payment is received or a tax invoice is issued, whichever is the earlier.

The tax point for EU acquisitions is the fifteenth day of the month after the goods are removed or the date of issue of an invoice, whichever is the earlier.

The tax point for imports is the date the goods are cleared by customs, although taxpayers have the facility to defer duty and VAT payments until the fifteenth day of the following month unless the goods are warehoused, in which case VAT becomes due when they are removed from the warehouse.

Chapter 10

Penalties

Penalties: EU rules

General

10.1   For penalties there are no harmonised common EU rules. Penalty provisions and amounts are established separately by each EU member state.

Specific rules in the various EU countries

Austria

Administrative penalties

Late filing of VAT returns

10.2   For the late filing of VAT returns tax authorities may levy a fine of up to 10% of the tax due.

Late payment of tax

10.3   For late payment, a fine of 2% of the unpaid VAT is due if the unpaid VAT exceeds € 50, in a single VAT return period.

Criminal penalties

10.4   For tax evasions, the maximum fine is 200% of the evaded amount. In addition, a prison sentence may be imposed of up to one year.

Belgium

Administrative penalties

10.5   Failure to file VAT returns, to declare or to pay the VAT due on time, or to provide the required documentation may incur:

(*a*)   interest on the amounts due on the twentieth day following each monthly or quarterly period;

(*b*)   administrative fines which may be as high as twice the VAT due. These fines are fixed by administrative legislation and will depend on the type of violation.

Where professionals, such as accountants, tax consultants, etc., are involved, they may be suspended by their professional body for up to five years.

The VAT authorities may normally only take action within five years of the relevant period.

Penalties may also be incurred for:

(i)   fraud;

(ii)   incorrect import documents;

(iii)   insufficient taxable turnover declared;

(iv)   violation of import laws.

Criminal penalties

10.6   In addition to incurring civil penalties, deliberate or fraudulent violations of the VAT legislation are punished by fines of between € 250 and € 12,390 or prison sentences of between eight days and five years.

Denmark

Administrative penalties

Late filing and payment of VAT returns

10.7   VAT returns must be filed on time regardless of whether any VAT is actually due for the period. Where the due date is not observed, the following penalties will be imposed:

(*a*)   in the case of late returns, VAT due is increased by 1% with a minimum of DKK 500 and a maximum of DKK 1,100. In certain cases a surcharge of DKK 150 is applied;

(*b*)   late payments of VAT will carry a monthly interest rate of 1.3% for each month from the due date. The minimum is DKK 50 with a reminder fee of DKK 65.

Should a company repeatedly fail to pay VAT due on time, over a short period, a reduction of the company's credit will be introduced according to a specific scale.

Non-registration

10.8   If a business fails to register for VAT, the following fines may be imposed:

(*a*)   deliberate violation:

  (i)   evasions up to and including DKK 30,000: the stated amount of VAT;

  (ii)   evasions of between DKK 30,000 and DKK 100,000: DKK 30,000 plus twice the additional amount;

  (iii)   evasions above DKK 100,000: demand for imprisonment and a fine of the amount;

(*b*)   gross negligence:

  (i)   errors of up to and including DKK 30,000: 50% of the stated amount;

  (ii)   errors of more than DKK 30,000: DKK 15,000 plus the additional amount.

Criminal penalties

10.9   Danish legislation provides for fines and penalties for failure to comply with the regulations regardless of whether non-compliance is deliberate or the result of gross negligence. Deliberate violations may incur imprisonment for a period of up to two years. Complicity with evasion on the part of third parties also leads to penalties.

In general, any evasion of duties and taxes exceeding more than DKK 100,000 will be brought before the courts and, normally, imprisonment and an additional penalty of 100% of the amount evaded will be demanded.

Finland

10.10   A penalty is assessed if a taxable person has paid less tax than is due. The amount of penalty depends on the number of past failures, on the amount of unpaid VAT and on the length of the period for which tax remains unpaid. A person failing to submit monthly returns may be assessed to a penalty of 20% of the tax.

In the case of a failure to submit a VAT return, the authorities may issue estimated assessments which must be made no later than three years after the end of the calendar year in which the liability arose. Additional assessments may be made to recover tax not wholly or partly paid, or if too much VAT has been refunded.

Interest will also be charged on late payments on a daily basis. The annual rate for the year 2002 is 11%.

Failure to submit a VIES statement or submission of a faulty statement can give rise to a penalty of a minimum of € 80, up to a maximum of € 1,700. A similar penalty arises for failure in the case of intrastat statements.

France

Administrative penalties

Late filing of VAT returns

10.11   For late filing, a 5% flat penalty plus late payment interest of 0.75% per month applies. In the case of fraud, a 40% penalty applies (in addition to 0.75% late payment interest). This is increased to 80% in the case of serious fraud.

Late payment of tax or additional assessment

10.12   For omissions or late payment of tax, 0.75% per month interest for late payment is due, increased by a penalty of 5% of the tax due. In the case of fraud the above rates apply.

Incorrect VAT returns

10.13   If a business files an incorrect VAT return but has acted in good faith, the amount of tax will be increased by interest at the rate of 0.75% per month. In the case of fraud the above rates apply.

Refusal to give information

10.14   Refusal to give information to the tax authorities or provide books or other financial records for their inspection is subject to a fine of € 150.

Document defaults

10.15   The omission or late filing of forms or other documents required by the tax authorities for verification procedures is subject to a penalty of € 15. This penalty applies to each document due to be submitted and may be increased to € 150 per document if the documents are submitted later than 30 days after the receipt of a first warning notice. However, if the business voluntarily, or at the first warning notice from the tax authorities, submits the documents within three months after the due date, no penalty will be imposed.

Criminal penalties

10.16   If a business commits a second offence of the type listed above within three years of receiving a fine, the court may apply an 80% increase in the tax due and/or a prison sentence of six months maximum.

In cases of tax fraud, the offender is liable to a maximum fine of € 37,500, and a prison sentence of five years maximum.

Germany

Administrative penalties

Late filing of VAT returns

10.17   If a taxable person does not file a periodic or annual tax return on time, the tax authorities may charge a fine of up to 10% of the tax due. The penalty is payable together with the tax and shall not exceed € 25,000.

Failure to pay VAT

10.18   If a business fails to pay VAT due on time, a fine of 1% of the unpaid VAT is due for every month the delay continues. If a business does not pay VAT, the maximum fine which can be imposed in this case is 50,000.

Document defaults

10.19   A taxable person may be charged a fine up to € 5,000 by the tax authorities for failure to:

(*a*)   keep a copy of a tax invoice issued in connection with an intra-Community supply; or

(*b*)   properly fulfil the quarterly listing requirements (EU sales lists).

Criminal penalties

10.20   For tax evasion, the maximum prison sentence is five years, and in aggravated cases up to ten years. For smuggling, imprisonment may be for a period of three months to five years.

Fines are imposed in the following cases:

(*a*)   for minor cases of tax evasion;

(*b*)   irregularities regarding taxes;

(*c*)   failure to pay the right amount of VAT;

(*d*)   errors resulting in an unjustified reduction of tax liability. (The maximum fine which can be imposed in this case is € 50,000).

Greece

Administrative penalties

Failure to submit 'provisional' VAT returns

10.21   If a taxpayer does not file a provisional return then the taxpayer is subject to:

(*a*)   additional tax amounting to 150% of the assessed tax;

(*b*)   a fine proportional to the amount of the assessed tax.

Incorrect 'provisional' VAT returns

10.22   If a taxpayer submits an incorrect provisional return then the taxpayer is subject to:

(*a*)   additional tax equal to the non-declared amount of the principal tax;

(*b*)   a fine proportional to the difference between the tax paid on the return and the tax assessed by the tax inspector.

Submitting 'provisional' VAT returns late

10.23   If the taxpayer does not file the provisional return on time then the taxpayer is subject to:

(*a*)   additional tax amounting to 10% of the principal tax for every month of delay;

(*b*)   a fine which may not be less than one-tenth of the tax due on the return, if the return is filed later than ten months after the due date.

Failure to submit 'final' VAT returns and incorrect 'final' VAT returns

10.24   The penalties for non-compliance regarding final VAT returns are the same as for provisional returns.

Criminal penalties

10.25   Tax evasion is punishable by imprisonment for a term between one month and five years.

Tax evasion is committed if the taxpayer:

(*a*)   does not submit a tax return;

(*b*)   makes tax deductions without proper supporting documentation or in the knowledge that such documentation is false;

(*c*)   does not issue the special receipt which is required if he is a farmer.

Ireland

Administrative penalties

10.26   Penalties for non-compliance with or breach of a provision of VAT law are confined to lump sum fines. Offences such as failure to register, late filing, failure to produce records, late payment, failure to issue invoices, unauthorised charging of VAT, etc., are punished with penalties of up to € 1,520 and/or twelve months' imprisonment.

Criminal penalties

10.27   For fraudulent actions by a taxpayer, there are penalties up to € 12,697 and/or five years' imprisonment.

Italy

Administrative penalties

10.28   The most important administrative penalties under VAT law are:

(*a*)   for non-payment or partial payment of annual VAT, a fine of 30% of the amount of the tax not paid;

(*b*)   for non-payment of the monthly (or for small businesses the quarterly) prepayment, a fine of 30% of the amount of tax not paid;

(*c*)   for failure to file a VAT return, a fine ranging between 120% and 240% of the unpaid tax;

(*d*)   for filing an incorrect VAT return, a fine ranging between 100% and 200% of the unpaid tax;

(*e*)   for omitting to issue an invoice, one to two times the amount of tax not paid; and

(*f*)   for not keeping books and records or keeping them in an inadequate form, a fine of between € 1,032.00 and € 7,746.00.

Fines may be reduced in extenuating circumstances.

Criminal penalties

10.29   The most serious offences with their corresponding penalties are:

(*a*)   the destruction and concealment of books and documents to reduce the VAT liability: imprisonment between six months and five years;

(*b*)   fraudulent VAT return declaring false invoices: imprisonment between six months and two years; if the false invoices are over € 154,937.10: imprisonment between eighteen months and six years;

(*c*)   fraudulent VAT return for other reasons, if the amount of the tax that should have been declared is over € 77,468.53 and the value of the supplies not declared are over 5% of the total amount of supplies, or over € 1,549,370.70: imprisonment between eighteen months and six years;

(*d*)   incorrect VAT return, if the amount of the tax that should have been declared is over € 103,291.38 and the value of the supplies not declared are over 10% of the total amount of supplies or over € 2,065,827.60: imprisonment between one and three years;

(*e*)   failure to file a VAT return, if the amount of the tax that should have been declared is over € 77,468.53: imprisonment between one and three years;

(*f*)   producing false invoices: imprisonment between six months and two years; if the false invoices are over € 154,937.10: imprisonment between eighteen months and six years;

(*g*)   fraudulent actions on the use of own assets and not paying the tax: imprisonment between six months and four years.

Luxembourg

Administrative penalties

10.30   Any violation of rules on accounting, administration, registration of non-resident taxpayers not having a permanent establishment in Luxembourg, books, records, investigations etc., is punishable by a fine of between € 125 and € 1,250 for each violation. Late payment or failure to pay VAT due is subject to a fine of not more than 10% of the tax due.

Criminal penalties

10.31   Fraudulent actions render the taxpayer liable to fines of between € 25 and € 1,250 and, in addition, to criminal law proceedings. Penalties must be paid within one month of notification in writing by the director of the administration or his delegate, regardless of whether or not an appeal against the penalty has been filed. A penalty of one month to five years imprisonment may be imposed for fraud.

The Netherlands

Administrative penalties

Failure to submit VAT returns

10.32 If a business fails to file its tax return on time or at all, the tax inspector can impose a penalty. The assessed tax is increased by penalties of:

(*a*) 0% for the first default;

(*b*) 5% for the second default (maximum € 2,268 (NLG 5,000));

(*c*) 10% for the third and any subsequent default (maximum € 4,537 (NLG 10,000)).

There must be seven periods during which no defaults occur for the default record to be removed.

Incorrect VAT returns

10.33 Where an additional assessment is made because incorrect returns are filed, the penalties are as follows:

(*a*) 25% of the tax due in the case of error or negligence;

(*b*) 50% of the tax due in the case of bad faith;

(*c*) 100% of the tax due for serious fraud.

If the offence is repeated, the penalties are doubled, but will not be higher than 100% of the tax due.

The tax authorities can impose assessments and penalties up to five years from the end of the calendar year in which the tax liability arose.

A decision of the Supreme Court in the Netherlands states that the entitlement to impose penalties must be in accordance with the Treaty of Rome. This essentially requires that the reason for imposing a penalty should be explained to the offender before it is issued.

Criminal penalties

10.34 In cases of fraud (e.g. failure to submit VAT returns, failure to supply information), imprisonment for up to four years and a fine of € 11,344 (NLG 25,000) is possible.

Portugal

Administrative penalties

10.35   Administrative penalties are confined to fixed sum fines, which are generally set according to the type of taxpayer and nature of offence involved.

The minimum amount of administrative penalties is € 150, unless otherwise determined by law.

A penalty of up to € 30,000 is applicable to negligent offences; a penalty of up to € 110,000 is applicable to fraudulent offences. For individuals these amounts are reduced by 50%.

The most important administrative penalties are:

(*a*)   non-payment in the prescribed period:

    (i)   negligent: 10% to 50% of tax due;

    (ii)   fraudulent: the same penalty and it may be treated as a fiscal crime;

(*b*)   refusal to make accounting records available, not keeping records or refusal to give reasonable assistance to the tax controller: € 250 (minimum) up to € 25,000 (maximum); it may be considered fiscal fraud;

(*c*)   non-filing or late filing of returns: € 100 up to € 2,500;

(*d*)   accounts not organised as prescribed: € 50 up to € 1,750, unless it is considered a criminal offence.

Criminal penalties

10.36   Misconduct may also constitute a criminal offence.

Where a business is found guilty of tax fraud or evasion by a court, in certain cases a penalty may include publication of the identity of the offender together with a summary of the court case, including the judgement, in two major newspapers in Portugal and in a local journal.

Spain

Administrative penalties

10.37   Broadly speaking, Spanish VAT law does not impose specific penalties, and therefore the general penalty regime of the Spanish general fiscal law (*Ley General Tributaria*) usually applies.

This legislation distinguishes between minor and major offences. Minor offences attract light penalties. Failure to comply with any of the following requirements is regarded as a minor offence:

(*a*)   declaration of commencing, altering or ceasing business activities;

(*b*)   requesting a Spanish VAT registration number, where appropriate;

(*c*)   issuing invoices;

(*d*)   fulfilling legal accounting requirements;

(*e*)   filing VAT returns;

(*f*)   appointing a tax representative as necessary.

Penalties vary between € 6.01 (ESP 1,000) to € 1,202.02 (ESP 200,000) per error, with a limit to the total fine of 3% of previous year's sales. Where the offence is committed in the first year of activity, the fine may not be higher than € 30,050.60 (ESP 5,000,000). If the tax authorities are unable to obtain the required information due to the business's failure to cooperate, the fine will vary between € 901.51 (ESP 150,000) to 3% of the previous year's sales, or € 48,080.96 (ESP 8,000,000) in the first year of business activity.

Failure to file a tax return and pay tax on time is subject to a 5%, 10%, or 15% surcharge respectively on the amount of tax due where this is filed or paid within three, six or twelve months after the time due. The surcharge is 20% plus interest if the due amount is paid over twelve months after the limit date.

Major offences include unduly obtaining tax benefits, exemptions or deductions, incorrect declaration of the VAT, or falsely claiming tax credits.

Major offences are subject to penalties of between 75% and 150% of the amount due, although a reduction of 30% of the penalty applies on mitigation.

The following factors are taken into account by tax inspectors in order to determine the exact percentage of the penalty:

(i)   whether the same offence has been committed in the past;

(ii)   the cooperation of the tax payer;

(iii)   whether fraud is involved;

(iv)   whether the offender has deliberately concealed information from the authorities.

Criminal penalties

10.38   It is a criminal offence if a taxpayer deliberately evades VAT of
€ 90,151.81 (ESP 15,000,000) or more.

Sweden

General

10.39   If the VAT return is filed after the relevant deadline, a penalty fee
of SEK 1,000 is charged (from 1 January 2003, SEK 500). The tax
authorities calculate interest on late payments. They may also charge a
penalty of 20% if they discover an error in the VAT return. If a supply or
an acquisition is accounted for in the wrong period the penalty is 5% of
the amount of the error made.

United Kingdom

General

10.40   The civil penalty system in the UK is constantly under review.
The principal penalties currently in force are described below.

Default surcharge

10.41   When amounts shown on returns as due are paid late, or returns
submitted late, the business receives a surcharge liability notice (SLN). If
payments are made on time and returns submitted on time for the next
twelve months, the SLN is withdrawn. However, in the case of further
defaults, the first default carries a 2% surcharge of the tax due, the next
5%, then 10% and a maximum of 15% applies to future defaults.

Misdeclaration penalty

10.42   Where the authorities discover errors on returns, normally as a
result of a routine visit to check records, a misdeclaration penalty is due if
the error is greater than the lesser of GBP 1,000,000 and 30% of the gross
amount of tax (GAT). GAT is the aggregate of output tax and input tax
in the relevant tax period.

Late registration penalty

10.43   If the authorities receive late notification of a requirement to
register, the penalty is 5% of the VAT due if notification was up to 9
months late; 10% for notification between 9 and 18 months late, and
15% for notification more than 18 months late.

Conduct involving dishonesty

10.44   Otherwise known as civil fraud, the basic penalty is up to 100% of the amount due. Criminal penalties may apply in the case of serious fraud.

Mitigation

10.45   Most penalties may be mitigated, but not generally in cases where excuses are made on the grounds of lack of funds, no tax loss to the authorities, or an action taken in good faith.

248

Chapter 11

Objections and Appeals

Objections and appeals: EU rules

General

11.1   There are no harmonised common EU rules regarding objections and appeals. Tax payers' rights are established by the authorities for each EU member state separately. Ultimately, the European Court of Justice may decide a case referred to it by the national authorities.

Specific rules in the various EU countries

Austria

11.2   All taxable persons have the right to submit an appeal to the local tax authorities if unsatisfied with any decisions made concerning their VAT affairs.

Where local authorities uphold the original decision, a further appeal may be made to an independent superior tax authority. Under certain circumstances, a final appeal to the Supreme Court is allowed where constitutional rights are affected.

Belgium

11.3   There are no specific rules providing for administrative appeal procedures in cases of litigation.

If no amicable agreement can be reached with the VAT administration, the matter may have to be brought before the courts.

Denmark

11.4   If a business is unable to agree with an assessment issued by a customs and tax regional authority, an action may be brought before the Inspector.

The complaint must be submitted in writing normally within four weeks of the company receiving the assessment. The business may query the extent of the VAT liability, the taxable amount, deduction of input VAT, exemption for vessels, aeroplanes, newspapers and public supplies. The local customs and tax regional authorities will rule in most cases.

Cases which may not be brought before the VAT Commissioner, may be appealed to the Customs and Tax Board (*Told & Skattestyrelsen*).

In addition, most disputes may be taken to court. If a business is not willing to accept a fine, the dispute will automatically be dealt with by the courts.

Finland

11.5   Regional tax offices will provide information on VAT if requested. On application, an advance ruling can be obtained either from the regional tax office or from the Central Tax Board on how the VAT Act will be applied in the circumstances of a particular transaction. A fee will be charged for this service.

Where a decision is made and then appealed by the business, if the decision was wrong the regional tax office may correct it by itself. An appeal from a regional tax office decision may be made to the Administrative County Court of Helsinki. The appeal may relate to any matters to do with monthly tax returns, refund applications, assessments, corrections and advance rulings.

The time limit for appeal is generally three years from the end of the financial year to which the erroneously treated transaction relates, or in the case of additional assessments at least 60 days from the serving of the assessment to the business, and in the case of registration matters and advance rulings 30 days. A decision may be appealed to the Supreme Administrative Court in certain cases.

VAT must generally be paid even if it is subject to appeal.

Penalties and interest on the tax due may, in certain cases, be mitigated on appeal to the National Board of Taxes or Customs.

France

11.6   If a business is not satisfied with an assessment or if a refund is refused, an appeal can be made to the tax inspector or tax director.

The deadline for submitting this claim depends largely upon the reason for it. If the appeal arises from a mistake made by the taxpayer (such as omission of VAT credit), it must be submitted before 31 December of the second year following the overpayment.

For VAT deductions, omitted credits can be claimed directly on the tax return, without filing a special claim. If the claim relates to an additional assessment the taxpayer normally has three years after its issue to lodge an appeal.

Appeals to the Tax Administrative Court, the Court of Appeal and the Supreme Court (*Conseil d'Etat*) are possible.

Germany

11.7   A taxable person may raise an objection to the tax authorities' decisions, and in certain cases an action may be filed to the local tax court or the federal tax court.

In specific circumstances, an appeal may be made to the Supreme Court where the constitutional rights of the taxable person are affected.

Greece

11.8   An appeal against an assessment must be submitted within 20 days of the disputed decision. Businesses may appeal before a court, or agree to a compromise with the tax authorities.

Further appeals are permissible before a higher court and, under certain circumstances, before the Supreme Court.

Ireland

11.9   Where a taxable person is not satisfied with any formal determination of the Revenue Commissioners, with any assessment of the amount payable by him, or with any refusal or restriction of a repayment claim made by an Inspector of Taxes, he may appeal to the Appeal Commissioners within 21 days of receipt of the notice.

The Appeal Commissioners are independent from the Revenue Commissioners. If a taxpayer is dissatisfied with the decision of the Appeal Commissioners, the taxpayer may appeal that decision to the Circuit Court. A decision of the Circuit Court may only be appealed to the High Court on a point of law.

Any appeal heard before the Appeal Commissioners or in the Circuit Court is held in private. Appeals heard before the High Court are heard in open court.

Where a taxpayer is dissatisfied with a decision taken by the Revenue authorities, the taxpayer may ask to have the matter reviewed by an independent panel. If the panel decides in favour of the taxpayer, the Revenue's decision may be overturned.

This procedure does not in any way affect the taxpayer's right to lodge an appeal against a determination or a decision of the Revenue.

Italy

11.10 A taxpayer may file an appeal to the first level Tax Commissioner against a VAT assessment within 60 days of its issue.

Appeals against the decision of the first level Tax Commissioner may be made to the second level Tax Commission within 60 days of the first decision.

Thereafter, appeals may be submitted to the Court of Cessation. This final court decides solely on questions of law, not on questions of fact.

Luxembourg

11.11 An appeal against an assessment of tax must be made within three months of its issue. Further appeals can be made within three months to the District Court and then to the Supreme Court.

The Netherlands

11.12 If a business is not satisfied with an assessment or a decision of the tax inspector regarding penalties or a refusal of a request for a refund, a notice of objection may be filed with the Inspector within six weeks of the date of the assessment or the disputed decision.

A decision on the objection raised is given by the Inspector who issued the contested assessment or decision.

Further appeals are permissible to the tax court and then the Supreme Court.

Portugal

11.13 Taxpayers who are individually or jointly responsible for payment of tax may contest a VAT assessment, either with the tax authorities or in the courts, according to the terms of the Tax Procedural Code.

Spain

11.14 An appeal may be lodged against any assessment issued by a Spanish tax official within 15 days of its notification, either to the same local office or to the provincial administrative court (*Tribunal Económico Administrativo*).

The regional court deals with assessments less than € 15,025.30 (ESP 25,000,000) or where there is an adjustment of € 1,803,036.31 (ESP 300,000,000) or more to the taxable base.

Where larger amounts are involved, the decision of the regional court may be appealed before the Central Court. This is the final stage of the administrative appeal procedure.

Once an administrative appeal is concluded, the decision may be appealed before the ordinary Courts of Justice within two months of notification of the administrative decision. The decision given by these courts may only be challenged in certain circumstances and by appeal to the Supreme Court.

Sweden

11.15   A taxable person is entitled within six years after the year in which a decision concerning VAT liability is made, to request reconsideration by the tax authorities. An appeal of the decision may be submitted to the country's administration court within the same time limit.

United Kingdom

11.16   The normal appeal procedure in the UK would be as follows.

Where a person disagrees with a decision, a request for reconsideration may be made. A reconsideration can be requested at any time, but a notice of appeal must normally be served within 30 days of the disputed decision. If the original decision is confirmed, the person has a further 21 days from the date of confirmation to lodge an appeal. If a revised decision is given, the person has a further 30 days to lodge an appeal.

Requests for reconsideration are made to the local VAT office. Appeals are made to an independent VAT Tribunal which will hear the case and provide a ruling. Certain decisions may be appealed to the High Court and the more complex cases may be further appealed to higher courts or finally to the European Court of Justice.

Chapter 12

Special VAT Rules

Special VAT rules: EU rules

General

12.1   EU member states may apply special rules to small businesses, farmers, travel agents, transactions in second-hand goods, works of art, collectors' items, antiques and investment gold. The additional reliefs available to them are explained below.

Small businesses

12.2   EU member states may introduce special VAT arrangements for small businesses. In addition, they may introduce exemptions and graduate tax reliefs.

Member states which, in 1977, already applied an exemption or tax relief to small businesses may, in principle, continue those arrangements. Those countries which applied an exemption from VAT to businesses with annual turnover of less than the equivalent in national currency of ECU 5,000 at the conversion rate of the day this Directive was adopted, may increase the threshold by ECU 5,000.

Member states which, in 1977, applied a graduated tax relief may neither increase their threshold nor render the conditions for their application more favourable.

Member states which did not apply an exemption for small businesses in 1977 may grant an exemption from tax to businesses with annual turnover up to ECU 5,000. They may also grant a graduated tax relief to taxable persons whose annual turnover exceeds the threshold fixed for the application of the exemption.

Member states which, in 1977, applied an exemption to small businesses with turnover equal to or higher than ECU 5,000, may increase it in order to maintain its value in real terms.

Each member state may also exclude certain transactions from the exemption for small businesses. However, every EU member state must exclude the supply of real estate from the exemption.

The turnover taken into account for the exemption is the aggregate excluding VAT of all taxable goods and services supplied by the business. The transfer of a business as a going concern shall not be included in turnover.

Businesses which use the exemption for small businesses are not entitled to deduct VAT, nor to show VAT on their invoices. They may either opt for the exemption or for the normal VAT rules.

Businesses using graduated relief shall be treated as taxable persons subject to the normal VAT rules.

Until the EU Council introduces a special system for small businesses, EU member states may retain their own schemes provided they are in accordance with the above rules.

[*EC Sixth Directive 77/388, Art 24*].

Farmers and agricultural activities

12.3   EU member states may allow farmers to apply a flat rate scheme.

This scheme applies to agricultural products and services by agricultural, forestry or fisheries businesses.

EU member states shall fix the flat rate compensation percentages, where necessary, and shall notify the Commission before applying them. Such percentages shall be based on macro-economic statistics for flat rate farmers alone for the preceding three years. They may not be used to obtain for flat rate farmers refunds greater than the VAT charged on inputs.

Each member state may reduce such percentages to a nil rate or the percentage may be rounded up or down to the nearest half point. Also, each member state may fix varying flat rate compensation percentages for forestry, for the different sub-divisions of agriculture and for fisheries.

The tax authorities within each member state may release flat rate farmers from the obligation to maintain records etc.

The flat rate percentages shall be applied to the price (excluding VAT) of agricultural products and services supplied by the flat rate farmers to taxable persons other than flat rate farmers. This compensation shall exclude all other forms of deduction.

EU member states may provide for the flat rate compensation to be paid:

(*a*)   by the taxable person to whom the goods or services are supplied, in which case that person shall be authorised, following the procedure laid down by each country, to deduct from the VAT for which he is liable, the flat rate compensation he has paid to the flat rate farmers; or

(*b*)   by the public authorities.

They shall also take all necessary steps to check properly the payment of the flat rate compensation to eligible farmers and may exclude from the scheme certain categories of farmers and farmers for whom the application of the normal VAT rules would not give rise to administrative difficulties.

Every eligible farmer may opt for application of the normal VAT rules instead of the flat rate scheme subject to the rules and conditions laid down by each member state.

[*EC Sixth Directive 77/388, Art 25*].

Travel agents

12.4   A special VAT regime exists for the services of tour operators and travel agents that do not act in the name of their principal but in their own name.

Under this scheme, the package of services is always regarded as one single service supplied by the travel agent to the traveller. It is taxable in the member state in which the travel agent has established his business.

The taxable basis for this service is the margin between total turnover for designated supplies and the net costs. As a consequence, no VAT on associated expenditure is deductible as input tax.

[*EC Sixth Directive 77/388, Art 26*].

Second-hand goods, works of art, collectors' items and antiques

12.5   Member states shall apply special arrangements for taxing the profit margin made by a taxable dealer on a supply of any of the above. The goods must have been supplied to the taxable dealer within the Community:

(*a*)   by a non-taxable person; or

(*b*)   by another taxable person where the goods did not give rise to a deduction of input tax; or (*c*)   by another taxable person of capital assets where that person is covered by a special scheme for small undertakings; or

(*d*)   by another taxable dealer of goods covered by this scheme.

The taxable amount shall be the profit margin less the amount of VAT relating to the profit margin.

Member states shall entitle taxable dealers to opt for the special arrangements for supplies of works of art, collectors' items or antiques which they have imported themselves, works of art supplied to them by the creators or their successors in title, or works of art supplied to them by a taxable person where the supply was subject to the reduced rate of VAT on import. The option shall apply for at least two years.

Taxable persons shall not be able to deduct the VAT due or paid in respect of the goods supplied to them where the goods are subject to the special arrangements.

The taxable dealer may not indicate on invoices issued, or any other document serving as an invoice, tax relating to the supply of goods which are subject to the special arrangements. In order to simplify the procedure for charging tax, the margin for the total of all goods sold subject to the same rate of VAT may be taken to be the taxable amount. A taxable dealer may apply the normal VAT accounting arrangements to any supply otherwise subject to the margin scheme.

[*EC Sixth Directive 77/388, Art 26A(B)*].

Special arrangements may apply by way of derogation in the case of supplies of second-hand goods, works of art, collectors' items or antiques at public auction by an organiser acting in his own name where commission is payable, and the sale is on behalf of:

  (i)   a non-taxable person; or

 (ii)   another taxable person where the goods did not give rise to a deduction of input tax; or

(iii)   another taxable person of capital assets where that person is covered by a special scheme for small undertakings; or

(iv)   a taxable dealer where the goods are subject to the special margin scheme arrangements.

In this case the taxable amount is the difference between the invoice value to the purchases being the auction price plus taxes, dues, levies and charges, plus incidental expenses such as commission, packing, transport and insurance, less the difference between the price of the goods and the organiser's commission, and the amount of tax due by the organiser in respect of the supply.

The invoice to the purchaser must not indicate VAT separately. The organiser must issue to his principal a statement which shows the auction price less commission due. A statement so drawn up shall serve as the invoice which the principal, where he is a taxable person, must issue.

[*EC Sixth Directive 77/388, Art 26A(C)*].

Note that new means of transport are excluded from the above special arrangements.

Investment gold

12.6   Investment gold means bars or wafers of purity equal to or greater than 995 thousandths and certain gold coins, a list of which is published in the Official Journal of the European Communities.

Member states shall exempt from VAT, the supply, intra-Community acquisition and importation of investment gold. This includes trade in investment gold represented by certificates for allocated or unallocated gold or traded on gold accounts, gold loans and swaps, futures and forward contracts. Member states shall also exempt the services of agents.

Member states shall allow taxable persons in certain circumstances the right of option for taxation of supplies of investment gold to another taxable person which would otherwise be exempt under the special arrangements. In such cases an agent may also opt to tax.

Taxable persons shall be entitled to deduct tax due or paid on gold supplied to them where the supplier has exercised the right of option, on an intra-Community acquisition or importation of gold transformed into investment gold, and in respect of services supplied to them in the case of gold, if their subsequent supply is exempt.

Member states shall, as a minimum, ensure trades keep account of all substantial transactions and keep the documentation to allow identification of the customer for a period of at least five years.

In the case of certain gold supplies, member states may designate the purchaser as the person liable to pay tax under the reverse charge procedures.

Where a supply of investment gold takes place within a member state the exemption provided for by the special scheme may be disapplied. For transactions between taxable persons who are members of a regulated bullion market the tax may be suspended. Where the taxable person is not a member the reverse charge applies, or if the non-member is not registered, the member shall fulfil the fiscal obligations.

[*EC Sixth Directive 77/388, Art 26B*].

Specific rules in the various EU countries

Austria

Small businesses

12.7   Businesses with a taxable turnover of not more than € 22,000, may opt for VAT exemption, although doing so will mean they also give up the right to deduct input VAT.

Agricultural and forestry enterprises

12.8   Agricultural and forestry enterprises are not usually required to file VAT returns as the tax authorities assume that output VAT will equal input VAT.

Travel agencies

12.9   Travel agencies and tour operators acting in their own name, are subject to special tax treatment insofar as they buy in goods and services or use other taxable persons to assemble their packages.

The service is taxable in the country of the supplier, and the taxable basis is the margin between the selling price of the package and its cost.

Belgium

Small businesses

12.10   Small businesses, usually in the retail sector, are taxed on a fixed amount in order to ease administrative burdens.

A small business is an individual, partnership, or other association which sells directly to consumers and whose annual purchases and imports do not exceed € 62,000. Corporations and limited partnerships are excluded from the small business definition.

The special provisions only apply if the small business sells food products, shoes, certain textile products, pharmaceutical products, goods used for general maintenance, paint, books and newspapers. Excluded are mail order services and certain specialised retailers. These businesses may not deduct any input VAT on services and goods received.

Small businesses may opt to be subject to the normal VAT rules, in which case they may not revert to the special arrangements.

Agricultural and forestry businesses

12.11   There exists a special scheme for such entities. They are excluded entirely from VAT for their farming, horticulture, fruit growing, floriculture and forestry activities unless they opt to be subject to the ordinary VAT regime.

A farmer applying for the exemption is not entitled to reclaim input VAT. The customers are, however, allowed to reclaim input VAT under a special regime.

However, these businesses will be excluded from the exemption if they:

(*a*)   take on corporate form; or

(*b*)   conduct other activities.

Other special regimes

12.12   Special regulations are set out for:

(*a*)   tobacco and alcohol;

(*b*)   products from fishing;

(*c*)   contents of the personal luggage of travellers;

(*d*)   art and antiques;

(*e*)   travel agencies;

(*f*)   second-hand cars, etc.

Denmark

Small businesses

12.13   No special rules apply to small businesses in Denmark other than the rule stating that no company is obliged to register for VAT purposes unless its annual sales exceed DKK 20,000.

Farmers etc.

12.14   No special rules apply to farmers or similar businesses in Denmark.

Special exemptions

12.15   The Minister of Taxation may grant tax exemption to certain groups of companies or persons, such as:

(*a*)   blind people, on the sale of goods and services not exceeding an annual amount of DKK 110,000;

(*b*)   stamp collectors' clubs which exchange stamps for other stamps with no money involved;

(*c*)   second-hand shops with charitable objectives;

(*d*)   company canteens where certain conditions are met, e.g. annual sales must not exceed DKK 30,000.

Finland

Small businesses

12.16   A small business is not liable for VAT provided annual turnover does not exceed € 8,500.

Farmers

12.17   Primary producers are liable to VAT. Finland does not apply a flat rate scheme to farmers. Most farming products attract a reduced rate of 17%.

Travel agents

12.18   Finland applies a margin scheme to travel agents. Agencies can deduct 82% of the purchase price (including VAT) of services or goods purchased from other businesses from the price of their own supplies (excluding VAT) to arrive at the tax base for the 'commission'.

Second-hand goods

12.19   Special margin scheme rules apply to the sale of second-hand goods when the goods have not been acquired on a tax invoice. This includes also works of art, antiques and collectors' items. If the scheme is not applied then VAT is due in the usual way on sales.

France

Small businesses

12.20   Since 1 January 1999, the regime for small businesses provides as follows:

Thresholds

(*a*)   For small businesses whose turnover for the previous year does not exceed € 76,300 exclusive of VAT (for suppliers of goods) or € 27,000 exclusive of VAT (for supplies of services), they are exempt from filing VAT returns and unable to recover VAT. They can opt for VAT. This option is for 2 years and it is renewable for the same period.

(*b*)   Since 30 December 1998, small businesses with annual turnover below € 763,000 (for supplies of goods) or € 289,000 (for supplies of services), can introduce a quarterly accounts system.

Each year, these businesses have to file a VAT summary return with the tax due for the year and the amount of quarterly VAT which was paid.

Businesses falling within these limits may elect to remain within the normal VAT regime.

Agricultural activities and flat rate farmers

12.21   Agricultural activities are generally not subject to VAT. These activities include any activity which is directed at obtaining products during or at the end of an arable or animal production cycle, e.g. viniculture. Fishing is also included in the definition of agricultural activities.

Farmers are entitled to a fixed refund of VAT calculated as a certain percentage of the aggregate amount received in the preceding year from their sales of agricultural and exported products to persons subject to VAT.

In the following cases, farmers are subject to VAT:

(*a*)   when average annual turnover in two consecutive years exceeds € 46,000;

(*b*)   when they perform other non-agricultural activities;

(*c*)   when the nature or scale of their activities is comparable to that of other trades or industries even if these activities are a mere extension of their agricultural activities.

Farmers may opt to apply the normal VAT rules. The option is valid for three years and may be extended to five years.

Oil and gas

12.22   A special regime applies to certain oil products.

Travel agents

12.23   Licensed travel agents are only subject to VAT on services supplied within the EU member state. Services supplied outside the EU are exempt. The taxable basis is the difference between receipts and expenses.

Although travel agencies are exempt from VAT in respect of services rendered outside the EU member states, they benefit from a full deduction of input VAT on their overhead costs.

Germany

Small businesses

12.24   Businesses with taxable turnover of:

(*a*)   not more than € 16,620 in the previous year;

(*b*)   not more than € 50,000 expected in the current year;

may keep the VAT invoiced for supplies of goods and services, but forfeit the right to deduct any input VAT.

Nevertheless, small businesses may opt to apply the normal rules in order to retain the right to deduct.

Agricultural and forestry enterprises

12.25   There are special rules for agricultural and forestry enterprises according to which reduced VAT rates apply.

VAT is levied at a reduced rate on businesses engaged in agriculture and forestry. Credit for input tax is calculated in the same way.

Leasing of an agricultural or forestry business does not qualify for the special provisions.

Agricultural and forestry activities include horticulture, viticulture, nurseries, fish farming and breeding, beekeeping, breeding of animals and growing seeds.

Travel agencies

12.26   Travel services to a business are taxed according to the normal rules.

Special rules apply to travel agents who act in their own name. If such a travel agent supplies a package to a customer, these services must be regarded as a single service.

The service is taxable in the country of the supplier, and the taxable basis is the margin between the selling price of the package and its cost.

Credit for input tax is possible on pre-travel services which are exempt in connection with export. Input tax on other pre-travel services may not be deducted.

Greece

Small businesses

12.27   Small businesses are defined as businesses whose annual income does not exceed € 17,608.22 (GRD 6,000,000) and which are not required to keep records. Excluded from the 'small business' definition are farmers, to whom other special arrangements apply and businesses which realise at least 60% of their income from wholesale or export sales.

Small businesses with an annual income not exceeding € 2,934.70 (GRD 1,000,000) are exempt from the obligation to file returns and pay tax. This exemption, however, does not apply to start-up businesses. Exempt businesses may not claim deduction of input VAT on purchases, and must issue invoices exclusive of VAT.

The income of small businesses, other than of businesses which are exempt, is determined on a deemed basis, applying gross profit coefficients to the cost of sales excluding VAT. The coefficients are determined by the Ministry of Finance and any business affected must file returns in the normal way.

Small businesses may opt to apply normal VAT rules and exempt businesses may opt to apply either the small business provisions or the normal rules.

Agricultural activities

12.28   Farmers are entitled to request a refund of net VAT due for the supply of agricultural products and services. The refund of VAT is made by the government through the application of lump sum tax rates on the value of the agricultural goods or services.

Agricultural activities include the following:

(*a*)   farming in general;

(*b*)   animal breeding in general;

(*c*)   forestry in general;

(*d*)   fishing;

(*e*)   the processing activities of farmers performed within the framework of the agricultural business.

Travel agencies

12.29   Travel agencies and tour operators, acting in their own name, are subject to special tax treatment insofar and to the extent that they use goods and services or other taxable persons to assemble a travel package.

All transactions performed by the travel agent in respect of any journey are treated as a single service provided by the travel agent to the traveller. Such service is taxable in Greece if the place of establishment of the travel agent by whom the service is provided is in Greece.

The taxable amount in such cases is the difference between the amount paid by the travel agent's customer, exclusive of VAT, and the actual cost to the travel agent of the supplies and services, including VAT, provided by others where these supplies are for the direct benefit of the customer.

The above provisions are not applicable to the fees of travel agents for the provision of services supplied exclusively as agents. In this case, the commission only is taxable.

Ireland

Small businesses

12.30   Businesses with turnover not exceeding the statutory limit (€ 51,000 for goods and € 25,500 for services) in any continuous period of twelve months are not obliged to register. However, they may elect to become taxable persons, in which case all the rights and obligations of taxable persons apply.

Agricultural activities and flat rate scheme farmers

12.31   Farmers are exempt from VAT liability but may elect to be taxable.

Farmers who do not make this election are obliged to operate the flat rate scheme of 4.3%. This scheme is designed to compensate such persons for the tax they are charged on their business purchases and for which they receive no credit or refund. Under the flat rate scheme, farmers make an addition of 4.3% to the price paid for the supply of agricultural produce or agricultural services to registered persons. The customer treats this addition as input tax, but the farmer is not required to hand it over to the Revenue Commissioners.

The definition of 'farmer' is extremely wide and also includes foresters and fishermen.

Travel agents

12.32 Travel agencies and tour operators are exempt from VAT.

Italy

Small businesses

12.33 Special provisions for small businesses exist only in respect of a simplified process for filing tax returns and the removal of obligation to issue invoices.

Small businesses which sell goods in certain authorised premises through vending machines or door-to-door, may not reclaim VAT on costs but only a fixed percentage.

Agricultural activities and flat rate scheme farmers

12.34 Farmers, forestry enterprises and fishermen are subject to VAT on their supplies, although they may apply for a reduced rate. In this case, they may claim an amount equal to a percentage of their sales against their VAT liability, instead of claiming the actual input tax paid.

The products which benefit from this treatment are mainly common types of fish, vegetables and cattle, etc. The taxpayer has no liability for VAT where turnover is not more than € 2,582.28 per annum and provided two-thirds of turnover consists of products to which the flat rate applies.

All of the above types of business may elect to be taxed in the normal way.

Travel agencies

12.35 A special scheme exists for travel agencies carrying on the sale and the organisation of travel and holiday packages. The special regime is also applicable to travel agencies acting in their own name for the re-sale of holiday packages organised by third parties. Ordinary VAT rules apply for travel agencies acting on behalf and in the name of the client (e.g. booking services).

The VAT taxable base is the price paid by the client less costs (inclusive of VAT) incurred by the organiser for acquiring goods and services for the benefit of the traveller and commissions paid to independent agents. No credit for input VAT is allowed. Services provided outside EU are not subject to VAT.

Luxembourg

Small businesses

12.36   Businesses with annual turnover not exceeding € 10,000 in the preceding calendar year and not having yet exceeded that amount in the current tax year, are not subject to VAT.

If the turnover of the small business exceeds the limit, it is subject to VAT from the first day of the month following the month in which the limit was exceeded.

The above businesses may, however, opt for normal treatment. The option applies normally for a period of at least five years and only in special cases is a return to the exemption system for small businesses allowed.

Special tax reductions are given to other small businesses with annual turnover less than € 25,000. Businesses with turnover in the current calendar year not exceeding € 25,000 may reduce the amount of VAT payable by 1% of the difference between € 25,000 and the actual amount of annual turnover. The reduction may not exceed the VAT liability for the year (after credit for input tax) and cannot be greater than € 150.

Agricultural activities and flat rate scheme farmers

12.37   Agricultural and forestry enterprises are excluded entirely from VAT. They are not entitled to a credit for input tax. However, an option to be taxed as normal businesses can be made.

Special rates apply as follows:

(*a*)   4% of the taxable base for supplies normally produced by forestry businesses;

(*b*)   8% of the taxable base for:

   (i)   supplies of goods normally produced by agricultural businesses;

   (ii)   supplies of services that contribute to agricultural or forestry exploitation and its commercialisation;

   (iii)   supplies of goods that have been used by the taxpayer for his agricultural or forestry activities.

Fishing enterprises, fish-breeding and the breeding of frogs are subject to the normal VAT rules.

Travel agencies

12.38   Special rules apply to activities carried out by travel agencies.

Travel agents including tour operators are deemed to supply single supplies of services to individual clients, provided they make these supplies in their own name, even though they actually use goods and services directly supplied to the travellers by other businesses relating to transport, lodgings, consumption of food and drink, and entertainment.

Travel agencies that deal with the traveller in the name of the business actually supplying the goods or services are thus excluded. They must only charge VAT on their commission if the place of supply is in Luxembourg.

The Netherlands

Small businesses

12.39   A special tax reduction provision exists for small businesses which are either individuals or associated groups of individuals (e.g. partnerships) and which pay an amount of no more than € 1,883 (NLG 4,150) per year after credit for input tax.

If the normal amount of VAT due does not exceed € 1,883 (NLG 4,150), the amount due is reduced by an amount equal to 2.5 times the difference between € 1,883 (NLG 4,150) and the normal amount of tax. The reduction cannot exceed the amount of VAT due.

Small businesses may show VAT separately on their invoices, thus allowing the customer to claim input VAT. In order to be allowed to operate the tax reduction, the business must maintain records in accordance with the applicable statutory provisions.

If, according to the above rules, a business does not pay any VAT, the business must not show VAT as a separate item on its invoices and, as a result, its customers not having been charged any VAT, are not able to reclaim input VAT.

Agricultural activities

12.40   Special provisions exist with respect to agriculture, which includes farming, horticulture, husbandry and forestry. These enterprises are excluded entirely from the main VAT system, but they may opt to be taxed.

Businesses purchasing agricultural goods and services from these exempt enterprises are granted a VAT credit of 5% of the price charged by the farmer.

Fishing enterprises

12.41   A special zero rate applies to the importation and supply of fish to a fish auction house.

Travel agencies

12.42   The Netherlands has not yet implemented the 'margin scheme' for travel agencies. However, special provisions do exist in the Netherlands for travel agencies.

Travel agents are, in principle, subject to the normal VAT provisions, although the Dutch Ministry of Finance does allow a margin scheme under certain guidelines which travel agents are not obliged to apply. The guidelines permit that all travel supplies be considered as one single service which is treated as if it were a transportation service. This means that supplies are zero-rated, but input VAT remains fully recoverable.

Portugal

Small businesses

12.43   Two different schemes apply to small businesses, comprising an exemption scheme for very small businesses and a simplified scheme for small businesses.

Very small businesses with annual turnover in the preceding year not exceeding € 9,975.96 or, in the case of retail businesses, up to € 12,469.95 are exempt from VAT and treated as final consumers. They may, nevertheless, opt to be taxed under the general VAT regime or under the simplified scheme.

Small businesses which meet certain criteria are taxed under a simplified scheme, unless they opt to be taxed under the general VAT system. To be eligible for the simplified scheme, they must meet the following conditions:

(*a*)   the total amount of purchases must not exceed € 49,879.79 (excluding VAT);

(*b*)   at least 90% of turnover must come from the sale of goods bought ready for re-sale;

(*c*)   the business must not be involved in export, import, intra-Community transactions or in the provision of taxable services exceeding an annual turnover of € 249,40;

(*d*)   the business is not subject to the income tax legislation that imposes specific obligations for the organisation of its accounting records, nor has it opted to follow the rules for such legislation.

Under the simplified scheme, VAT is assessed on 25% of the total VAT paid on purchases.

Agricultural activities

12.44 Businesses supplying goods and services in the course of their agricultural or forestry undertakings are excluded from VAT entirely unless they have opted to be taxed.

Once this option takes effect the taxable business must remain taxable under the simplified or normal VAT scheme for a minimum period of five years. If it then wishes to resume an exempt status, it must notify the local tax inspector. In this case, exemption takes effect from 1 January of the following year.

Travel agencies

12.45 Special rules exist for travel agencies.

If a travel agent acts as an intermediary between his principal and the customer, his commission only will be subject to VAT at the reduced rate.

A travel agent is treated as having carried out a transaction as a principal where the supply includes goods and services supplied in his own name but for the direct benefit of his customer.

Under the special provisions, all services are treated as a single service by the travel agent who is taxable in the country of the supplier of the service. The taxable basis will be the margin between the selling price and purchase price of the package.

Spain

Small businesses

12.46 A special scheme is applicable to small businesses with an annual turnover of taxable and exempt supplies in the preceding year not exceeding € 450,759.08 (ESP 75,000,000). This limit may be modified in the annual budget. Small businesses may opt to be treated according to the normal rules.

Agricultural activities and flat rate scheme farmers

12.47 A special scheme applies to agricultural, forestry, livestock and fishing enterprises.

Businesses are compensated for VAT which they are charged on their purchases by means of a flat rate addition at a level of 8% for agricultural and forestry activities and 7% for cattle or fishing activities, to the price at which they sell their products to taxable persons. Taxable persons to whom the goods or services are supplied are obliged to pay such compensation but may reclaim it as input VAT.

This scheme is not normally applicable to legal corporations, co-operatives, SATs (Special Agricultural Companies), and taxable persons whose turnover is more than € 450,759.08 (ESP 75,000,000), although there are a few exceptions.

Travel agencies

12.48   A special scheme applies to travel agencies and tour operators which deal in their own name and use the supplies and services of other taxable persons for the provision of travel facilities.

All transactions performed by the travel agent in respect of a journey are treated as a single service supplied to the traveller. The supply is deemed to take place where the travel agent has a fixed establishment from which the service is provided. The taxable base is the travel agent's margin, i.e. the difference between the total amount to be paid by the traveller, exclusive of VAT, and the actual cost to the travel agent of supplies of goods and services (including VAT) provided by other taxable persons when these supplies are for the direct benefit of the traveller.

Travel agents' services are partly exempt with credit when the transactions entrusted to other taxable persons, for the benefit of the traveller and used for travelling purposes, are performed both inside and outside the EU. Only that part of the service relating to transactions outside the EU is exempt; but there is still entitlement to full input VAT credit.

Second-hand goods

12.49   Special schemes exist for antique dealers and traders in certain second-hand goods. Under these schemes, the taxable person may choose how to determine the taxable base; either by way of the individual margin of every operation or on a global basis for a large number of items with individual low value.

Special scheme for retailers

12.50   A compulsory special scheme applies to retailers (taxable persons who supply goods purchased for resale where more than 80% of their turnover relates to supplies to final consumers).

Under this scheme, the retailer need not pay VAT or file returns for the transactions within the special scheme but suppliers to the retailer must charge and pay an additional amount of VAT. The surcharge is 4% for goods subject to 16% VAT, 1% for goods subject to the 7% rate, and 0.5% for goods subject to VAT at 4%.

Sweden

12.51   Special arrangements for calculating and accounting for VAT apply to the following cases:

Margin schemes for second-hand goods and travel agents

12.52   When calculating VAT the taxable amount shall, under the conditions set out below, be the profit margin rather than the price excluding VAT. The following illustrates where the margin scheme is mandatory and where it is permitted to opt to apply the scheme rather than the general rules.

A dealer in second-hand goods, works of art, collectors' items and antiques may opt to apply the scheme on sales if the goods were supplied to him within the EU by:

(*a*)   a non-taxable person (e.g. a private person);

(*b*)   a taxable person accounting under the scheme in Sweden or in another EU member state;

(*c*)   a taxable person transferring equipment exempt from VAT;

(*d*)   an artist exempt from tax liability;

(*e*)   a taxable person in another EU member state, where the goods are his equipment and he is exempt from liability to account for VAT in his country according to local rules for small enterprises.

If a business applies the margin scheme, invoices should not indicate VAT separately relating to supplies, and the purchaser is prohibited from deducting VAT as input tax.

Travel agents

12.53   Travel agents dealing with customers in their own name and using the supplies and services of other taxable persons for the provision of travel facilities for the direct benefit of the traveller are obliged to apply the margin scheme. An agent may only opt not to use the scheme where the traveller (i.e. the customer) has the right to deduct input tax. The travel service is deemed to be supplied in the country where the travel agent has established his business or has a fixed establishment. However, there is a deemed export (no Swedish VAT) on that part of the travel agent's service relating to transactions performed by a taxable person outside the EU.

The Swedish National Tax Board considers that the standard tax rate of 25% should apply to travel services, although supplies purchased from others might be subject to reduced tax rates. The travel agent's purchase of goods and services which are not for the direct benefit of the traveller follow general rules in respect of the right to deduct input tax.

Where supplies are made strictly as agents (those not acting in their own name) for a principal, VAT is due on the agent's commission. When the agent's service relates to trips beginning or ending abroad or accommodation in hotels abroad, the agent does not levy VAT because the place of supply of his services is also considered to be abroad.

Artists' supply of own works of art

12.54 An artist has a special VAT status with reference to his own works of art. Where these supplies do not amount to more than SEK 300,000, excluding VAT for the financial year, the artist is not liable to VAT. He may, however, opt for taxation.

United Kingdom

Optional flat rate scheme

12.55 From 25 April 2002, an optional scheme applies for businesses with a turnover of up to GBP 100,000 (to be increased to GBP 150,000 from April 2003) whereby VAT may be accounted for at a flat rate percentage on income. The percentage applicable depends on the nature of the business.

Retailers

12.56 There are special schemes available for retail businesses, to enable them to choose a basis on which to calculate the tax due on their supplies but these have been restricted in recent years.

Second-hand (used) goods

12.57 The margin scheme applies to works of art, antiques or collectors' items, motor vehicles, second-hand goods and goods sold at auction.

Generally, dealers cannot claim input tax on purchases for resale but only pay output tax on the margin between the purchase and selling price.

Tour operators/travel agents

12.58 There is a special scheme which must be used by businesses which buy in services used by travellers from third parties and resell them as principals. The scheme allows them to account for tax on the difference between the purchase and selling price of the package, rather than on the full selling price.

Accounting schemes

12.59   There are also schemes designed to assist smaller businesses with accounting for VAT and to ease cash flow problems. Cash accounting requires VAT to be accounted for on the basis of cash received and paid, rather than invoice dates. Annual accounting allows a single VAT return to be submitted each year, with payments made throughout the year by bank debit. Such schemes have conditions attached to their use.

Flat rate scheme for farmers

12.60   As an alternative to registering for VAT, a scheme is available for farmers under which VAT is not accounted for on certain activities, and no input tax is recovered on purchases. Instead, a flat rate charge is made to registered persons which is retained by the farmers but reclaimed as input VAT by the customers.

Racehorse owners scheme

12.61   A scheme is also available under which persons owning racing horses with a view to seeking sponsorship and prize money may be registered for VAT.

Investment gold

12.62   A special scheme provides for investment gold to be treated as exempt. An option to tax is available for producers and refiners of investment gold and, subject to certain conditions, other suppliers, if in the course of their business, they sell investment gold for an industrial use, e.g. jewellery.

Chapter 13

Non-European Union Countries

Introduction

13.1   In order that a comparison can be made between VAT systems in the EU and outside, this chapter analyses the principle VAT provisions in a number of non-EU member states. Subject to the meeting of certain criteria, the EU may commit in the near future to allowing the accession of Bulgaria, Cyprus, Czech Republic, Estonia, Hungary, Latvia, Lithuania, Malta, Poland, Romania, Slovakia, Slovenia and Turkey.

Cyprus

General

13.2   The VAT legislation is based on the UK legislation and therefore generally in line with EU law. VAT is administered by the VAT Commissioner and the VAT Department is part of the Ministry of Finance. A new law was enacted which came into operation on 1 February 2002, whose main purpose was to streamline the VAT legislation of Cyprus with that of the *EU Sixth Directive*, while retaining its origins based on UK law.

Taxable persons and registration

13.3   A taxable person is a person who makes or intends to make taxable supplies, and who is, or is required to be, registered.

A taxable person may be either a natural person or a legal person (limited company, partnership, club, association, etc).

Registration applies to any person operating in the course or furtherance of business.

A person is obliged to register either:

(*a*)   at the end of the month in which its turnover has exceeded CYP 9,000 in the twelve months preceding that month; or (*b*)   at any time when it is expected that its turnover will exceed CYP 9,000 in the thirty days which follow.

VAT is chargeable on taxable supplies and is reclaimable on costs incurred.

When completing a VAT return the trader accounts for all the output and input tax relating to the VAT period covered by the return. Returns are normally for periods covering three months, with the exception of the first return which may be longer, for administration purposes.

When the input tax exceeds the output tax the trader is entitled to a repayment from the State.

Group registration

13.4   Two or more companies may apply for group registration provided they are both registered in Cyprus and as follows:

(*a*)   one controls the other; or

(*b*)   one person (legal or physical) controls all of them; or

(*c*)   two or more persons (which act together as a partnership) control all of them.

The application to register a group must be filed at least ninety days prior to the suggested commencement of operation of group registration. The registration is carried out in the name of the representative person.

Cyprus non-resident companies

13.5   (a)   Prior to February 2002

The activities of non-resident business entities fell outside the scope of Cyprus VAT legislation and therefore such entities were not required or permitted to register for VAT purposes. Therefore, they could not recover any VAT suffered and this was treated as a cost to the company.

The following supplies to such companies were and still are zero-rated:

(i)   telecommunication services;

(ii)   importation of goods which such companies or their expatriate personnel are entitled to import free of import duty.

(b)   After February 2002

With the introduction of the new legislation there is no distinction between non-resident business entities and local companies, with the effect that if the rules prescribe that there is a taxable supply of goods then such companies should register for VAT purposes.

In practice, non-resident companies are companies which are beneficially owned by non-Cypriots. Transactions are carried out exclusively abroad, and therefore they are not required to register with the VAT authorities of Cyprus because of the operation of the VAT rules regarding the place of supply. In accordance with VAT legislation, transactions that are carried out outside Cyprus (i.e. the place of supply is deemed to be outside Cyprus) are considered outside the scope of VAT legislation. The rules covering the place of supply are detailed further below.

Supplies to embassies and United Nations forces

13.6 Supplies made to embassies and United Nations forces are subject to VAT. However, certain arrangements allow the VAT suffered by embassies and UN forces in Cyprus to be refunded.

Taxable activities

13.7 VAT is charged on importation and on any supply of goods or services which is a taxable supply made by a taxable person in the course or furtherance of any business carried on by that taxable person.

Exemptions

13.8 Certain goods and services are exempted from VAT, including:

(*a*) hospital and medical treatment;

(*b*) educational services;

(*c*) supply of services by non-profit organisations;

(*d*) supply of services related to athletics;

(*e*) supply of services of a cultural character;

(*f*) sale of postage stamps;

(*g*) transport of injured persons with passenger vehicles;

(*h*) insurance and reinsurance services;

(*i*) importation of gold by the Central Bank of Cyprus;

(*j*) supply of lottery tickets.

Supplies of goods

13.9 A taxable supply of goods includes the normal transfer of goods on payment by one taxable person to another. Goods are defined as all

movable and immovable objects with minor exceptions. Supplies which
are not subject to VAT include:

(*a*)   letting of immovable property, with certain exceptions;

(*b*)   supply of immovable property;

(*c*)   supply of food by hospitals to patients or by schools;

(*d*)   supplies of human organs, blood and human milk;

(*e*)   importation of goods under a declaration for transit arrangement
or temporary importation arrangement;

(*f*)   importation of goods put into the following Customs' regimes:

   (i)   temporary retention in Customs areas;

   (ii)   free zones;

   (iii)   Customs warehousing.

Supplies of services

13.10   Under Cypriot legislation anything which is not a supply of
goods but is made for a consideration is a supply of services. Supplies of
services, unless specifically exempted (or outside the scope), are chargeable to VAT if the place of supply is deemed to be Cyprus.

Place of supply

13.11   To determine whether the place of supply is considered to be in
Cyprus or not the following rules apply:

(a) Sale of goods:

The place of supply is the place that the goods are located when they are
supplied to the customer.

(b) Services rendered:

The basic rule is that the supply of services is taxed where the business is
based.

A business is considered to be based in Cyprus if:

(i)   it has a business activity or other permanent presence in Cyprus;

(ii)   it has no such presence but its usual place of residence is in Cyprus
(usual place of residence for companies is the place of registration);

(iii)   it has a presence in both Cyprus and abroad but the presence with
which the service is most connected with is Cyprus.

There are important exceptions to the above basic rules:

Certain services are deemed to be supplied in the country where the recipient is based and not where the person performing those services is based. These exceptions include:

(i)   transactions involving intellectual property;

(ii)   advertising services;

(iii)   services of consultants, engineers, lawyers, accountants, data processors;

(iv)   banking, finance and leasing services;

(v)   provision of personnel;

(vi)   leasing of movables (except vehicles);

(vii)   telecommunications;

(viii) services of commission agents and intermediaries in relation to the above services.

Under the old legislation the above services were considered VAT exempt, with the result that no input VAT in relation to those services could be recovered. Under the new legislation, the above services are considered outside the scope of VAT (instead of exempt) and therefore the VAT expenses incurred in the furtherance of those services may be recovered.

It is important to note that if such services are rendered from abroad to a Cypriot person, then a reverse charge applies. In this case the recipient calculates output VAT on the service enjoyed and also claims credit for input VAT of the same value to the extent taxable supplies are made.

The other important exception to the basic rule is in connection with:

(i)   services relating to property – these are deemed to be rendered where the property is situated;

(ii)   services of transport of passengers or goods – these are deemed to be rendered where the service is rendered;

(iii)   services of intermediaries – these are deemed to be rendered where the originating transaction is rendered.

Taxable basis

13.12   VAT is due on the total price paid for the goods or services, excluding the VAT itself.

Special cases

13.13   Certain categories of business are taxed according to a different system including farmers, tour operators, hotels, restaurants, second-hand cars, motorcycles, caravans, boats, aircraft, etc., works of art, antiques and collectors' pieces, etc.

Tax rates

13.14   The legislation provides for the following tax rates:

(*a*)   zero rate – 0%;

(*b*)   reduced rate – 5%

(*c*)   standard rate – 10%.

A proposal is presently being discussed at the House of Representatives by which the standard rate of VAT will be increased from 10% to 13%. Cyprus has given assurances to the EU that the VAT rate will be increased to 15% prior to the country's entry to the EU and within the year 2003.

Zero rate

13.15   Zero-rated supplies include the following:

(*a*)   exports;

(*b*)   supply of unbottled water;

(*c*)   food, except the supply of food in the course of catering;

(*d*)   supply of medicines;

(*e*)   supply of newspapers, periodicals and books;

(*f*)   supply of gas cylinders;

(*g*)   supply of children's clothing and footwear;

(*h*)   ship management services;

(*i*)   services offered by urban and rural buses, etc.

Zero rate versus exemption

13.16   Suppliers making exempt supplies may not register for VAT purposes and are not entitled to reclaim input tax. Suppliers making zero-rated supplies must register and may reclaim any input tax incurred.

Reduced rate

The following services are subject to the reduced rate of 5%:

(*a*)   services of restaurants and other services in relation to catering (with the exception of alcoholic drinks which are charged at the standard rate);

(*b*)   provision of hotel accommodation, accommodation in tourist resorts and similar establishments including the leasing of camping sites;

(*c*)   delivery of coffins;

(*d*)   services rendered by funeral directors;

(*e*)   services rendered in connection with road cleaning and garbage disposal;

(*f*)   services of authors, composers or writers of plays as well as the royalties relating to those services.

VAT returns

13.17   VAT returns must be submitted quarterly within 40 days from the end of the VAT period.

Delays in the submission of VAT returns incur penalties, currently amounting to CYP 30.

Administrative obligations

13.18   Payments of tax due should be made within 40 days from the end of the VAT period to which they relate. Delays are subject to a fixed penalty of 10% of the amount of the tax and, after 30 days, interest at 9% per annum on both the amount of the tax outstanding and the fixed penalty.

Criminal penalties

13.19   In addition to civil penalties, deliberate or fraudulent violation of the VAT laws and regulations is punishable by fines up to CYP 50,000 or prison sentences of up to three years.

Payment/repayment of tax

13.20   Where input tax exceeds output tax and therefore a repayment is due, the amount repayable is repaid to the taxable person.

Input tax which cannot be reclaimed

13.21   A trader may reclaim VAT charged on business expenditure or imports. However, VAT charged on the following may not be reclaimed:

(*a*) on the purchase or importation of tobacco and alcohol products except if acquired for resale;

(*b*) on entertainment and hospitality generally, with the exception of staff entertainment;

(*c*) on housing, food, drinks, transport and entertainment of representatives of a business;

(*d*) on the purchase or importation of private saloon cars;

(*e*) on the purchase or importation of boats or aircraft for private use or sport except where purchased for resale.

VAT invoices

13.22 All taxable persons, except retailers, must issue VAT invoices when making supplies to other persons.

An invoice should include the VAT registration number of the supplier, the charge before VAT in Cypriot pounds, the rate of VAT in Cypriot pounds and the total amount due in Cypriot pounds.

Objections and appeals

13.23 Legislation provides for objections and appeals against decisions of the VAT Commissioner to be raised either with the VAT Commissioner himself, the Minister of Finance or the Supreme Court of Cyprus, or finally a complaint to the Administrative Ombudsman.

Czech Republic

General

13.24 The Czech VAT system (DPH) is similar to the EU system. VAT must be charged at each stage of the production and distribution process, unless it is specifically relieved, and the final consumer bears the real cost. Supplies of goods, imports of goods and services are subject to VAT.

Taxable persons

13.25 Taxable persons are individuals and legal entities in business in the Czech Republic or undertaking activities which have the attributes of a business enterprise according to the Czech law.

Registration for VAT is not required unless taxable turnover exceeds CZK 750,000 in any three-month period.

This rule is valid for all entities including charitable, religious and sports organisations. Non-registered businesses must not charge VAT on supplies nor may they recover input tax.

Taxable activities

Supplies of goods

13.26   All supplies of goods are subject to VAT except those specified in the legislation. The definition of goods for VAT purposes is wide, including tangible property, electric power, gas, heat, livestock, etc. Bank notes and coins are deemed to be outside the scope of Czech VAT, except where specified in Czech VAT legislation.

Imports of goods

13.27   Imports of goods are subject to VAT.

Supplies of services

13.28   Supplies of services are subject to tax in the Czech Republic except for those specified in VAT legislation.

Place of taxable transactions

13.29   The place of supply of goods is deemed to be where and when risk associated with the goods (e.g. damage) is transferred from supplier to buyer. The place of supply of services is normally considered to be where the supplier is established.

Services supplied abroad by a Czech company are normally deemed to be outside the scope of Czech VAT.

Exemptions

13.30   There are two kinds of exemptions recognised by the Czech VAT legislation. If the goods or services are purchased for effecting taxable supplies included in the first group (Group 1), no recovery of VAT is permitted. However, if the goods or services are purchased for taxable supplies included in the second group of exemptions (Group 2), recovery of VAT is permitted – see paragraph, Credit for input tax, 13.33, below.

Group 1 contains the following taxable supplies which are exempt from VAT under the conditions specified in the Czech VAT legislation:

(*a*)   postal services;

(*b*)   radio and television broadcasting;

(*c*)   financial services;

(*d*)   insurance services;

(*e*)   transfer and lease of land and buildings;

(*f*)   training and education (supply of goods and services rendered as part of training and educational activities by specified entities and individuals);

(*g*)   health care services and products provided by authorised individuals and entities;

(*h*)   social welfare services;

(*i*)   lotteries and similar games of chance;

(*j*)   sales of enterprises.

Group 2 contains the following activities, which are exempt from VAT under the conditions specified in the Czech VAT legislation:

(*a*)   export of goods;

(*b*)   services provided to foreign countries;

(*c*)   international transportation of goods and monies and scheduled international transportation of passengers.

Taxable basis

13.31   The basis of taxation for a particular transaction is the price calculated including all costs whether these are invoiced separately or not.

Where a transaction is between related parties, the VAT legislation requires use of open market value in specified transactions.

In general, the VAT liability is based on tax documents issued and received. Deposits are not subject to VAT unless the transaction as such is partly or fully completed.

Tax rates

13.32   The standard VAT rate for supplies of goods is 22%. The Czech VAT legislation specifies some exceptions at the reduced 5% rate. The standard VAT rate for supplies of services is 5%. The Czech VAT legislation specifies some exceptions which are at the 22% rate.

Credit for input tax

13.33   The right to deduct input VAT arises at the time the recipient (registered taxable person) of taxable goods or services receives a proper tax document (invoices, custom declaration in case of import) from the supplier. The taxable supplies (supplies of goods or services) must be used for generating turnover from the provision of taxable supplies, exempted activities included in Group 2, or supplies outside the scope of VAT.

The date of making a taxable supply as stated on the tax document (for example, an invoice) will indicate the period in which VAT recovery can be made. VAT cannot be recovered on the following supplies:

(*a*) food and beverage in hotels, restaurants, railways, ships and air-craft;

(*b*) purchase of passenger cars (if not purchased for trading);

(*c*) goods and services for an exempt activity;

(*d*) goods and services not for business purposes;

(*e*) goods used as gifts (except for promotional goods with a company logo up to the price CZK 200 per item).

Partial recovery is permitted where goods and services are purchased for both exempt (only included in Group 1 of exemptions) and for taxable activities, exempt activities included in Group 2, or activities outside the scope of VAT legislation.

Legal entities whose registered offices are located abroad, and who are not authorised to carry on a business activity on the territory of the Czech Republic, can claim an entitlement to a refund of the tax on selected goods and services purchased in the Czech Republic, if this is provided for under a bilateral agreement, within the scope and under the conditions stipulated in such an agreement. Those selected goods and services are:

(*a*) lubricants and similar products for the operation of motor vehicles, with the exception of fuels;

(*b*) diesel oil and bio-oil;

(*c*) repair of means of transport and their spare parts and accessories;

(*d*) towing away of a means of transport;

(*e*) repairs under guarantee.

Foreign individuals (not entities) are entitled to a refund of VAT relating to the goods bought in the Czech Republic if the goods are exported within 30 days from the purchase date, and the export of the goods is declared by the Czech Custom Office on a special declaration document.

The Czech VAT legislation recognises some other cases for VAT refunds.

Administrative obligations

Registration

13.34   Every taxable person or entity must notify the tax authorities and complete the necessary forms when commencing or ceasing taxable activities.

Records

13.35   Businesses are obliged to keep proper records for ten years and make them available for inspection by the VAT authorities.

Invoices

13.36   All transactions must be documented by the issue of an invoice specifying the name, address and the tax identification number of both the supplier and customer. The invoice must also contain:

(*a*)   the serial number of the invoice;

(*b*)   the nature of the supply of goods and services;

(*c*)   the total price excluding the tax;

(*d*)   the amount and rate of any VAT payable;

(*e*)   the date of issue of the invoice;

(*f*)   the date when the taxable supply was rendered.

VAT returns

13.37   VAT returns must be completed every month or every three months depending on the taxable period relevant for the taxable person. The taxable period is one month for individuals or entities whose turnover for the last calendar year exceeded CZK 10,000,000. If the turnover was below CZK 2,000,000, the period is calendar quarter. In other cases the taxable person can choose either a calendar month or a calendar quarter period.

The VAT return shows the total for output VAT (for 5% VAT rate and for 22% VAT rate), total VAT, total exempted activities (for those included in Group 1 and those in Group 2), total tax for input VAT (for each VAT rate, separating domestic purchases and imports), total input VAT and the net VAT payable or due.

The VAT return must be completed and reported up to 25 days after the end of the tax period.

Penalties

Administrative penalties

13.38 A surcharge of 10% of net tax due is applied when returns are submitted late or not in the prescribed form.

If payment of VAT is made after the due date, interest is calculated at a rate of 10% per day from the due date. If VAT due has been increased on assessment, interest is calculated at a rate of 5% per day from the due date.

If input VAT is over-deducted or output VAT under-declared, and an assessment is issued by the VAT authorities, interest is calculated at a rate of 20% per day from the due date.

Criminal penalties

13.39 In addition to civil penalties, deliberate or fraudulent violation of VAT law is punishable by fines or prison sentences of up to six years.

Objections and appeals

13.40 The administrative appeals procedures are fixed by law and appeals are usually submitted to the office of the tax administrator (Local Tax Office, Regional Directorate of Taxes and in some cases the Ministry of Finance) whose decision may be contested by appeal. This tax administrator shall decide on the appeal himself if he fully or partly concurs with it.

The administrator can also reject the appeal if it is inadmissible, submitted after the stipulated time limit, or submitted by an unauthorised person. If the tax administrator does not make a decision himself according to the rules, he shall pass the appeal to the Appeal Authority which is the immediately superior authority to the tax administrator whose decision is being contested.

Under the conditions of Czech Law, decisions of tax administrators and Appeal Authorities can be reviewed by the court.

Hungary

General

13.41 Hungarian VAT law is similar to the *EC Sixth Directive* in all important respects, e.g. taxable transactions, tax base, a mechanism for tax refunds etc. However, there are minor differences between the Hungarian VAT system and the EU model.

Taxable persons

13.42   In Hungary, taxable persons are individuals, legal entities, and organisations, which undertake a business activity in their own name. Foundations, churches and other social organisations are also taxable persons. However, the tax authority permits VAT refunds to such bodies only under special procedures, in view of the fact that their activities are generally free of VAT.

If a non-resident individual or legal entity, wishes to conduct business activities in Hungary, they must have a Hungarian establishment. This would include domestically established business organisations, branches, permanent establishments and commercial representations that are subject to tax in Hungary.

Taxable activities

13.43   The activities taxed in Hungary are supplies of goods and services and imports of goods.

Supplies of goods

13.44   The main rule is that the transfer of ownership of goods, in exchange for consideration giving the recipient the right to dispose of the goods as owner, gives rise to a supply.

Imports of goods

13.45   The importation of goods from abroad, gives rise to a tax obligation concurrently with the customs clearance. The tax is levied by the customs authority jointly with the customs duty.

Supplies of services

13.46   According to the main rule, all activities performed in exchange for consideration, which are not deemed to be a supply of goods, are a supply of services.

Place of taxable supply

13.47   In relation to supplies of goods, the place of supply is the place where the product is actually located on the date the tax obligation arises. This obligation arises on the date on which the right of disposal over the product is transferred.

In relation to the supplies of services, the place of supply is where the service provider is established or has its permanent business premises. In some special instances, the place of supply is determined by the belonging of the customer. This applies in relation to, for example:

(*a*)   the leasing of products (excluding real estate);

(*b*)   transfer of rights related to intellectual products;

(*c*)   intellectual rights;

(*d*)   legal services;

(*e*)   accounting and tax-related etc., services.

There are some specific services where the place of supply is deemed to be the place where the service is actually provided. Such services include, for example:

(*a*)   cultural;

(*b*)   artistic;

(*c*)   scientific;

(*d*)   educational services;

(*e*)   ancillary services related to transportation, such as warehousing, guarding of transportation facilities, the assembly, repair, maintenance etc., of products, excluding real estate.

Exemptions

13.48   There are two forms of tax exemption:

(*a*)   Subject tax exemption – this exemption may be chosen by the taxpayer if his revenue in the tax year does not exceed HUF 2,000,000. These taxpayers are not obliged to pay tax, but they cannot exercise their right of deduction;

(*b*)   Activity tax exemption – the law exempts certain activities from tax. If someone conducts such activities, there is no right to deduct VAT.

Supplies of goods

13.49   In Hungary, there are some activity tax exempt supplies of goods (see below), and a range of products come under the 0% or 12% lower tax rate. These are typically health products. Upon accession to the EU, the 0% tax rate will probably be removed.

Supplies of services

13.50   Journal and book publishing, hotel services, shipping and warehousing are services provided with a 12% tax rate. Services typically provided in the health sector have a 0% tax rate.

Activity tax exemptions

13.51   A wide range of services and goods come under the aforementioned activity tax exemption. No tax is payable on activity tax exempt services. However, if someone undertakes only such activities, VAT on purchases may not be deducted.

Some typical examples:

(*a*)   sale of residential property, excluding sales prior to completion of construction, and the first sale following the completion of construction;

(*b*)   financial services and ancillary services, with a few exceptions;

(*c*)   assignment of securities, business shares and certain other financial arrangements;

(*d*)   renting of residential real estate, irrespective of intended use;

(*e*)   assignment and assumption of debt;

(*f*)   activities exclusively performed by attorneys, legal representation;

(*g*)   sports and recreational services;

(*h*)   gambling services;

(*i*)   intermediary roles and provision of services if these are made on behalf of and to the benefit of someone else.

Taxable basis

13.52   The base of the tax in relation to both supplies of goods and services is the consideration paid. The consideration includes all that is received or must be received by the taxpayer from the customer or a third party. This includes: price supplements, other central budget subsidies, and incidental costs related to performance, even if these are part of a separate agreement. Such incidental costs are typically agency, commission, insurance and transportation costs.

Where the supply is between connected parties, the consideration is the market value of the goods sold or service provided.

Tax rates

13.53   The general rate is currently 25%; with the reduced rates of 0% and 12% in relation to certain goods and services. The zero rate is for exports and certain supplies of goods, and for supplies of goods and services related to international transportation.

Credit for input tax

13.54 The right to deduct tax related to the amount of tax payable may only be exercised if in the possession of an invoice or a document certifying the amount of tax. The date of the right to deduct tax is the date of supply indicated on the invoice.

Tax may not be deducted in the following cases:

(*a*) the taxpayer does not use the goods in whole or in part for the purpose of the business activity;

(*b*) the goods or services fall under the scope of the activity tax exemption;

(*c*) in certain instances for fuel purchases;

(*d*) in relation to passenger cars, if the purchase is not for resale purposes;

(*e*) in relation to the use of a passenger taxi service.

The tax refund generally depends on sales revenue. In relation to the purchase of tangible assets, taxes paid may be refunded if these exceed € 822.82 (HUF 200,000). With the exclusion of some special cases, tax may be refunded only if the tax has also been paid.

VAT refunds for non-residents

13.55 In Hungary, foreign legal entities may apply for VAT refunds depending on reciprocity with the foreign country. The refund is conditional on certification issued by the competent foreign tax office stating that the refund applicant is obliged to pay VAT in the given country. Such documents are valid for one year from the date of issue and additional certification is not required within the above period. The tax refund application may be made in the six months following the relevant year to 30 June. Foreign private individuals may apply for a tax refund for product purchases from a retailer.

Administrative obligations

Registration

13.56 All taxpayers, prior to the commencement of a business activity, must report to the tax authority for the purpose of receiving a tax number.

Records

13.57   Taxable persons must keep documents for five years from the last date of the calendar year in which the tax had to be returned and paid.

Invoices

13.58   Taxpayers must issue invoices for supplies of goods and services performed by them. The invoice must indicate the base of the tax and the amount of tax in detail according to the tax rate charged, as well as the aggregate amount.

VAT returns

13.59   Taxpayers, depending on the amount of tax payable and the sales revenue of the previous year, must prepare VAT returns on a monthly, quarterly or yearly basis. Investment companies and taxpayers conducting activities with reduced tax rates (e.g. shipping firms, exporters, etc.) may request the tax authority to accept tax returns prepared twice a month or bi-monthly.

Penalties

Administrative penalties

13.60   Late payment of tax, gives rise to a charge payable from the due date. The amount of charge equals for each calendar day, 1/365th of the double prime interest rate valid on the date of the charge.

A tax fine is payable for unpaid taxes. The amount of the fine equals 50% of unpaid taxes. The tax authority also determines a fine if the taxpayer did not have the right to deduct VAT. In such a case, the base of the fine equals the amount illegally applied for.

If the taxpayer submits the tax return after the return deadline, but prior to the notice issued by the tax authority, the taxpayer must pay a default fine depending on the period of default, but no more than HUF 100,000. In relation to incorrectly submitted returns, the default fine equals 5% of the difference between the correct and incorrect tax amount, but at least HUF 5,000 and no more than HUF 100,000. If the taxpayer has not met the tax return obligation, the tax authority imposes a default fine of up to HUF 200,000.

Criminal penalties

13.61   Tax fraud is committed by the taxpayer if, in relation to the taxpayer's obligation, the taxpayer misrepresents material facts to the tax authority, or conceals the facts, thereby reducing tax due. The penalty depends on the amount of tax for which the crime is committed. The penalty may be imprisonment, public work or a fine.

The taxpayer may not be penalised if the tax debt is settled prior to indictment procedures.

Objections and appeals

13.62 Rulings by the tax authority in the first instance may be appealed, and in the second instance to the superior body of the tax authority, and a review of the tax authority's resolution requested from a court. The court may be asked to suspend the ruling of the tax authority.

Norway

General

13.63 The Norwegian VAT system *(Merverdiavgift)* is similar to the EU system although the legislation is structured differently. VAT must be charged at each stage of the production and distribution process, unless it is specifically relieved, and the final consumer bears the VAT cost. Supplies of goods, imports of goods and certain services are subject to VAT.

Taxable persons

13.64 A taxable person is any person or entity supplying goods or services subject to VAT according to Norwegian law. A foreign company or a person residing abroad carrying out such activities within Norway, must register through a fiscal representative, a resident individual or a company established in Norway.

Registration for VAT is not required unless taxable turnover exceeds NOK 30,000 in any twelve-month period.

Charitable, religious and sports organisations need not register for VAT unless taxable turnover exceeds NOK 140,000 in any twelve-month period.

Group registration is permitted between parent companies and subsidiaries where the parent company owns more than 85% of the subsidiary and there is commercial cooperation between the companies. Group registration will give each company joint and several liability for payment of VAT.

Non-registered businesses must not charge VAT on supplies nor may they recover input tax.

Taxable activities

Supplies of goods

13.65   All supplies of goods are subject to VAT except those exempted by the VAT legislation.

The definition of goods for VAT purposes is wide, including tangible property, electric power, gas, heat, livestock, trees and crops where these are not sold together with land, the right to exploit land for minerals or stone, hunting and fishing rights and the right to show cinematographic films.

Supplies of services

13.66   Most supplies of services are subject to tax in Norway.

The definition of services is everything which can be sold and which is not considered as goods. Limited rights to tangible objects or real estate, as well as the use of intangibles, are also included in the term services.

Imports of goods and services

13.67   Imports of goods and services are subject to VAT.

Place of taxable transactions

13.68   The place of supply of goods is deemed to be where and when risk associated with the goods (e.g. damage) is transferred from supplier to buyer.

The place of supply of services is normally considered to be where the supplier is established.

Services supplied abroad by a Norwegian company are normally deemed to be outside the scope of Norwegian VAT.

Exemptions

Supplies of goods

13.69   The following supplies of goods are exempt from VAT:

(*a*)   original works of art when supplied by or on behalf of the artist;

(*b*)   goods supplied in connection with medical care by dentists, dental technicians and doctors;

(*c*)   sales of programmes, catalogues, postcards and souvenirs by museums, theatres, cinemas, exhibitions and concerts;

(*d*)   sales of postcards, calendars and other items of insignificant value (less than NOK 100 per item) by charitable and sports organisations;

(*e*)   sales and leases of cinematographic films for public exhibition;

(*f*)   stamps, bank notes and coins as collectors items.

Supplies of services

13.70   The following are exempt from VAT:

(*a*)   health services;

(*b*)   social services;

(*c*)   education;

(*d*)   financial services;

(*e*)   insurance;

(*f*)   financial services, although not a financial lease;

(*g*)   payment services/bank services;

(*h*)   financial instruments and intermediary commissions in this respect;

(*i*)   custodian of investment funds;

(*j*)   theatre, opera, ballet, cinema, circus, concerts and sport arrangements, exhibitions in galleries and museums, and admission to amusement parks etc.;

(*k*)   lotteries;

(*l*)   public services;

(*m*)   ceremonial services at funerals;

(*n*)   public and private transport of passengers (special rules for air transportation);

(*o*)   intermediary commissions regarding transportation and hotel accommodation;

(*p*)   guiding and intermediary services in this respect;

(*q*)   services from student canteens;

(*r*)   artist performance and intermediary services in this respect;

(*s*)   safety alarm service.

Taxable basis

13.71   The basis of taxation for a particular transaction is the price calculated including all costs whether these are invoiced separately or not.

Where a transaction is between related parties, the VAT authorities may determine open market value if the cost has been artificially reduced. In general, VAT liability is based on tax invoices issued and received.

Deposits are not subject to VAT unless the transaction as such is partly or fully completed.

Tax rates

13.72   The standard VAT rate is 24%.

Certain transactions are zero-rated, such as the supply of:

(*a*)   books and newspapers;

(*b*)   second-hand cars;

(*c*)   export of goods and services;

(*d*)   international transport;

(*e*)   supply of goods and services to ships and aircraft engaged in international transport (goods and passengers);

(*f*)   supply of goods and services to foreign ships and aircraft;

(*g*)   supply of goods and services to oil exploration and exploitation activities offshore;

(*h*)   the supply of services in connection with the building and repair of public roads and railways;

(*i*)   assets transferred in connection with the sale of the whole or part of a business as a going concern;

(*j*)   privately owned goods which have not been subject to VAT recovery;

(*k*)   car ferry services;

(*l*)   certain services to public service infrastructure;

(*m*)   electric cars.

Entitlement to input tax is reduced as a result of investment tax (currently 7%) which is payable on the acquisition of goods to be used in the business of the tax entity. Therefore, the net input tax recovery is restricted to 17%.

Investment tax is payable by the acquirer of the goods provided the business is registered for VAT purposes and is entitled to reclaim VAT. This tax applies only to investment goods and not to goods bought for resale. There is a proposal that investment tax be removed by the end of 2002.

The import of cars and some luxury articles are taxed by special fiscal rules which are not part of the VAT system.

Credit for input tax

13.73   The right to deduct input VAT arises at the time the recipient of taxable goods or services receives a proper tax invoice from the supplier. The date of the invoice will indicate the period in which VAT recovery can be made.

VAT cannot be recovered on the following supplies:

(*a*)   food and beverage in hotels, restaurants, railways, ships and air-craft;

(*b*)   works of art and antiques, unless the buyer is a trader in arts or antiques;

(*c*)   purchase, rent and maintenance of passenger cars;

(*d*)   payment in kind;

(*e*)   goods and services used for making property available for rent (certain exemptions exist);

(*f*)   recreational supplies;

(*g*)   goods and services for an exempt activity.

Partial recovery is permitted where goods and services are purchased for both exempt and taxable activities.

Foreign businesses are entitled to a refund of VAT relating to services or goods bought in Norway or imports of goods to Norway. The following conditions must be fulfilled to qualify for a refund:

(i)   the VAT relates to a business carried on outside Norway;

(ii)   the business would have been liable to registration in accordance with the Norwegian VAT Act if it had been carried out in Norway; and

(iii)   the input VAT would in that case have been deductible.

Administrative obligations

Registration

13.74   Every taxable person or entity must notify the tax authorities and complete the necessary forms when commencing or ceasing taxable activities.

Records

13.75   Businesses are obliged to keep proper records for ten years and make them available for inspection by the VAT authorities.

Invoices

13.76   All transactions must be documented by the issue of an invoice specifying the name and address of the supplier and customer and the nature of the supply of goods and services.

Invoices should also show the tax exclusive price, the amount and rate of any VAT payable and the supplier's VAT registration number.

VAT returns

13.77   VAT returns must be completed every second month showing total sales, sales not subject to VAT, output VAT, input VAT, investment tax and net amount payable or due.

However, farmers and fishermen need only complete one return per year. The same rule applies to charitable, religious and sports organisations (upon application) if annual turnover does not exceed NOK 200,000.

Businesses in a net repayment position, e.g. exporters, may apply for tax periods as short as one week.

The VAT return must be completed and filed one month and ten days after the end of the tax period.

Penalties

Administrative penalties

13.78   A surcharge of 3% of net tax due is applied when returns are submitted late or not in the prescribed form. The maximum penalty is NOK 5,000.

If payment of VAT is made after the due date, interest is calculated at a rate of 15% per annum. If VAT due has been increased on assessment, interest is calculated at a rate of 1.25% per month from the due date.

If input VAT is over-deducted, or if investment tax or output tax are calculated incorrectly, and an assessment is issued by the VAT authorities, a civil fine of up to 100% of the error may be assessed. However, the usual rate applied is 30%.

Criminal penalties

13.79   In addition to civil penalties, deliberate or fraudulent violation of VAT law is punishable by fines or prison sentences of up to six years.

Objections and appeals

13.80   The administrative appeals procedures are fixed by law and appeals are usually submitted to an independent government appointed body known as the *Klagenemnda for merverdiavgiften.*

Other civil offences, e.g. failure to register, may be appealed to the Directorate of Taxes.

However, as the civil appeal body now requires two to three years to settle an appeal, there is an increasing tendency to take such cases directly to the courts.

Poland

General

13.81   The Polish VAT system is gradually being brought into line with the EU system.

Taxable persons

13.82   Every person, organisation or legal entity, which conducts taxable activities with the intention of continuing such activity, is a taxable person for the purposes of Polish VAT. A commercial or profit motive is not required.

Each taxable person is obliged to register for VAT prior to commencing any taxable activities. If annual sales do not exceed a specific registration limit the taxpayer may choose to register and pay VAT on a voluntary basis or may register as a VAT exempt entity. The registration limit for the year 2002 is PLN 35,786.91.

If a foreign business makes taxable supplies to other businesses in Poland the VAT liability is transferred to the customer. Foreign businesses may choose to register for VAT in Poland, in which case they must obtain a tax identification number, open a bank account and appoint a fiscal representative.

Taxable activities

13.83   Taxable activities include:

(*a*)   the supply of goods and services in the territory of the Polish Republic;

(*b*)   import and export of both goods and services;

(*c*)   supply of services or use of goods for the purpose of advertising;

(*d*)   transfer of goods for personal use;

(*e*)   services supplied free of charge.

From March 2002 the transfer of certain intangible assets such as rights, licences and computer software constitute a taxable activity.

VAT does not apply to the sale of a company's business, lotteries and similar activities, which are subject to separate tax regulations, nor to activities which are not subject to legally valid agreements.

Exemptions

13.84   Certain supplies are exempt from VAT. The most important ones are as follows:

(*a*)   most basic agricultural products (meat, poultry, fish, milk, grain, vegetables, and other non-processed agricultural products), if supplied by farmers who are not registered VAT payers;

(*b*)   agricultural services, forestry, fishing;

(*c*)   post and taxi services;

(*d*)   financial services (banking);

(*e*)   public services, including administration, defence, social and health care and education.

Farmers reporting annual sales exceeding PLN 19,086.34 may choose to register as VAT payers.

Tax on the import of services is accounted for by the importer. From the year 2000 importers may offset the VAT due on imported services against an equal amount of input VAT.

Sales of buildings and constructions are exempt from VAT if the buildings are at least five years old and the seller has no right to deduct input VAT in respect of such sales.

Place of supply

13.85   Supplies of goods and services are regarded as taxable activities if they are carried out in the territory of the Polish Republic.

The services rendered outside Poland may be regarded as exports. Services rendered in Poland to a foreign entity, for example agency commissions, advertising, marketing services etc., do not constitute exports for the purposes of the VAT legislation.

The supply of services by a foreign entity to a Polish business are regarded as imports only if they are rendered in Poland and the consideration is paid to an entity which has its head office or is established abroad. Services rendered outside Poland are not regarded as imports.

Taxable basis

13.86   The taxable basis is 'turnover', defined as an amount receivable from sales of goods excluding the amount of VAT due. For imports of goods the customs value including the customs duty is taken as the taxable basis.

In real estate transactions the value of land is not included in the taxable basis. For non-monetary supplies, such as donations, gifts and advertising purposes, comparative prices based on transactions with the business's main commercial customers, or average local market prices, should be used to calculate the taxable basis.

Where a transaction is between related parties, the VAT authorities may substitute open market value where the cost has been artificially reduced.

Tax rates

13.87   There are four different rates of VAT in Poland: 22%, 7%, 3% and zero:

(*a*)   the standard rate of 22% applies to all supplies of goods and services which are not specifically exempt or subject to a reduced rate;

(*b*)   a reduced rate of 7% applies for supplies such as: energy, coal, gas, distribution of energy, construction materials and services for housing, municipal services, passenger transport services, food, selected children's supplies, medicines, newspapers, hotel services and restaurant services with the exception of alcoholic beverages, coffee and certain other drinks;

(*c*)   a reduced rate of 3% applies to agricultural products supplied by registered VAT payers;

(*d*)   zero rating is limited in scope. The main examples are books, certain medical supplies, fertilisers, animal feed, and agricultural machinery. Some services (legal, accounting, construction design, data processing) may be taxed at zero rates, if supplied to foreign entities and paid within the prescribed deadline of 90 days.

Certain reduced rates are valid for a limited duration only, for example for specialist magazines and books. The rates will increase unless the government extends existing regulations.

Credit for input tax

13.88   With certain exceptions, the right to deduct input VAT arises at the time the purchaser of taxable goods or services receives a formal tax invoice. The right to deduct input VAT may not be exercised if the recipient has not received the goods or services in question or if the invoice is incorrect.

From the year 2000 the right to deduct input VAT for supplies of energy, gas and water as well as telecommunication services arises in the month the payment is due as indicated on the invoice.

With some exceptions VAT recovery may be made in the month of receipt of the invoice or in the following month. For imported services the recovery can be made only in the month following the month when the import VAT has been reported.

VAT may not be recovered on the following supplies:

(*a*)   restaurant bills;

(*b*)   hotel bills;

(*c*)   purchase and/or leasing of passenger cars;

(*d*)   fuel for passenger cars;

(*e*)   any other supplies which do not constitute costs deductible against income tax.

VAT may not be recovered on supplies of goods and services for an exempt activity. Partial recovery is permitted where goods and services are purchased for both exempt and taxable activities. Where no clear separation of supplies is possible, the input VAT for a given month is split according to the ratio of taxable and exempt sales for the month between deductible and non-deductible.

VAT may not be recovered on purchases of services imported from the 41 tax heaven countries listed in an attachment to the VAT Act.

Non-resident businesses may, under conditions, claim a refund of VAT paid on purchases of goods and services in Poland. The refund can be granted if the claiming entity has an establishment in the country with mutual arrangements in respect of Polish companies. The claiming entity has to state that it carried out no business activities subject to Polish VAT in the period for which the claim is made.

There are no other refund provisions except for sales to tourists and certain foreign assistance and support programs.

Administrative obligations

Registration

13.89   Every taxable person must notify the tax authorities and complete the necessary forms when commencing or ceasing taxable activities. Businesses are obliged to keep proper records for five years and make them available for inspection by the tax authorities.

Invoices

13.90   All transactions must be documented by the issue of an invoice specifying the name and address of the supplier and customer, date of the invoice, date of sale and the nature of the supply of goods and services. Invoices should also show the tax exclusive price, the amount and rate of any VAT payable and both the supplier's and recipient's VAT registration numbers. The customer's VAT number is not required for retail and export sales. Invoices documenting sales of goods and services at reduced rates must include the statistical classification number of the goods.

With some exceptions, invoices must be issued within seven days from the date of the sale of goods, the supply of the service, or receipt of an advance payment where the amount exceeds 50% of the contract value.

All invoices must be signed by the representatives of both parties. The buyer may permanently authorise the seller to issue invoices without his signature.

Internal VAT invoices must be issued to document the use or transfer of goods for gifts, advertising, donations or private non-business purposes.

Minor errors may be corrected via a correction note. Errors relating to quantity, price, value, VAT rates etc., must be corrected using correction invoices. Debit or credit notes are not allowed to document transactions which are subject to VAT.

VAT returns

13.91   VAT returns must be completed and filed every month by the twenty-fifth day after the end of the previous month together with payment. No annual summary statements are required.

Penalties

13.92 If a taxpayer does not keep proper VAT records the tax authorities may assess any undocumented sales and claim the tax due at the 22% rate, with no right to deduct input VAT.

If the taxpayer under-declares the amount of VAT due or over-recovers input VAT, the tax authorities may impose an additional charge equal to 30% of the difference.

Penalty interest is applicable for late payments of VAT. Such interest does not constitute a deductible cost for income tax purposes.

More severe offences against tax law, including criminal acts, are considered according to the Penalty Code.

Objections and appeals

13.93 Administrative appeals procedures are fixed by law and are usually submitted to a superior tax authority.

Cases subject to the Penalty Code may be appealed to higher courts.

Special VAT rules

13.94 Companies employing handicapped persons may be entitled to a full or partial refund of input VAT, provided they are properly registered according to specific regulations governing the employment of handicapped persons.

Switzerland

General

13.95 The Swiss VAT system follows EU directives with certain variations.

At each stage of the production and distribution process, VAT is due and the final consumer bears the cost of VAT. Goods and services supplied in Switzerland, as well as goods and services imported into Switzerland, are subject to VAT.

Certain services supplied to customers residing outside Switzerland are tax exempt (zero-rated).

Taxable persons

13.96 Any individual carrying on an independent business or other economic activity in Switzerland is a taxable person, whether or not a profit is made. A business comprises all commercial or professional activities undertaken by an individual or a legal entity.

Public legal entities are also taxable in respect of their commercial activities.

Foreign businesses supplying goods or rendering services within Switzerland must register for VAT. Businesses without a presence in Switzerland and with no permanent establishment are included in this category and must appoint a fiscal representative.

A taxable person is not subject to VAT if annual turnover is less than CHF 75,000.

Furthermore, VAT registration is not required for businesses with an annual turnover of less than CHF 250,000 if the net VAT amount due does not exceed CHF 4,000 after deduction of recoverable VAT.

Taxable activities

Supplies of goods

13.97   VAT is levied on all commercial sales of goods other than the transfer of real estate.

Electric power, gas, heating and cooling are considered to be goods.

Supplies of services

13.98   VAT is chargeable on all services other than those specifically listed as exempt under Swiss VAT legislation.

Exemptions

13.99   Supplies which are not exempt are referred to as taxable supplies.

The rental income from real estate is usually exempt from VAT. However, the owner may voluntarily register for VAT if the building is used for taxable activities or if the tenant is a taxable person.

Exemptions apply, inter alia, to the following supplies:

(*a*)   certain banking services;

(*b*)   insurance and financial services;

(*c*)   property transactions;

(*d*)   educational and health services;

(*e*)   certain non profit-making activities;

(*f*)   social services;

(*g*)   certain cultural services.

Place of supply

13.100   As a general rule, the place from which goods are supplied or where the provider of services is established determines whether an activity takes place in Switzerland.

However, the following services are exceptions, for example:

(*a*)   in respect of immovable property – where the property is located;

(*b*)   movable property – where the goods are located;

(*c*)   conferences, exhibitions, entertainment, training and education – where the service is performed;

(*d*)   financial services, consulting services, most leasing of equipment, use of intellectual property and advertising – where the recipient is located.

Supplies which do not take place in Switzerland are treated as being 'outside the scope' of the legislation.

VAT is due on goods and services imported into Switzerland. Certain services supplied to customers residing outside Switzerland are tax exempt (zero-rated).

Taxable basis

13.101   The taxable basis for VAT is the total price paid for the supply, excluding VAT.

When transactions take place between related parties, the VAT authorities may apply open market value if the cost of supplies has been artificially reduced.

Tax rates

13.102   There are three rates of VAT in Switzerland: 2.4%, 3.6% and 7.6%.

(*a*)   the VAT rate of 2.4% is applicable to, inter alia, tap water, non-alcoholic beverages and food, medication, printed items and livestock;

(*b*)   the VAT rate of 3.6% is a reduced rate applied to supplies such as hotel services and camping;

(*c*)   the standard VAT rate of 7.6% applies to all supplies of goods and services which are not specifically exempt or subject to reduced rates.

Credit for input tax

13.103 Businesses supplying taxable goods and services in Switzerland may normally fully deduct input VAT on goods purchased or services received from another Swiss registered business. VAT is also deductible on imported goods and services.

VAT may not be recovered on the following supplies:

(*a*)   entertainment expenses;

(*b*)   purchase and maintenance of motorcycles, sailing boats and sports aircraft.

Only 50% of input VAT may be recovered for food and beverages.

Partial recovery of VAT is allowable where goods and/or services are purchased for both exempt and taxable activities.

Non-resident businesses may claim a refund of VAT through a fiscal representative. Such claims must be filed at the latest by 30 June of the calendar year following the business year concerned.

Administrative obligations

Invoices

13.104 Invoices must include the following items and the authorities are strict regarding fulfilment of these conditions:

(*a*)   the name and address of the supplier and recipient;

(*b*)   the supplier's VAT registration number;

(*c*)   a description of the goods and services supplied;

(*d*)   the date or period of delivery;

(*e*)   the price;

(*f*)   the applicable rate and the amount of VAT.

VAT returns

13.105 As a general rule, VAT returns must be filed within two months of the end of each civil quarter.

Any net amount due must be paid at the same time.

Penalties

13.106   Civil penalties are applied to late payments. The interest rate for late payment varies, but is usually in the region of 5%.

Objections and appeals

13.107   Every taxable person has the right to submit an appeal to the federal tax authorities within 30 days after any particular decision taken by the VAT authorities.

However, should the authorities not reverse their original decision, a further appeal may be made to an independent superior tax commission. A final appeal to the Supreme Court is allowed.

Special VAT rules

13.108   Small and medium sized companies with an annual turnover of up to CHF 1,500,000 may choose to declare VAT on a net basis applying a special rate.

Turkey

General

13.109   The Turkish tax system charges VAT on the supply and the importation of goods and services. Turkish VAT is known as *Katma Deger Vergisi,* abbreviated to KDV.

The liability for VAT arises:

(*a*)   when a person or entity performs commercial, industrial, agricultural or independent professional activities within Turkey;

(*b*)   goods and services are imported into Turkey.

VAT is levied at each stage of the production and distribution process. Liability for tax falls on the person who supplies or imports goods or services. However, the real burden of VAT is borne by the final consumer. This result is achieved by a tax credit method where the computation of the VAT liability is based on the difference between the VAT liability of a business's sales (output VAT) and the amount of VAT the business has already paid on purchases (input VAT). This follows the *EC Sixth Directive.*

The Turkish VAT system employs multiple rates which may be amended on the authority of the Council of Ministers within certain limits.

Taxable persons

13.110 A VAT taxpayer is defined under VAT law as being engaged in taxable transactions irrespective of the taxpayer's legal status or nature or liability for other taxes.

In the event that the taxpayer is not resident, or does not have a place of business in Turkey, or head office or place of management in Turkey, the Ministry is authorised to hold responsible for the payment of tax any one of the persons involved in a taxable transaction.

The following persons or entities are liable for VAT:

(*a*)   those engaged in the supply of goods and services;

(*b*)   those that import goods or services;

(*c*)   those required to fulfil the customs formalities for the transit of goods through Turkey;

(*d*)   authorised public lottery bodies, including *Spor Tolo* and national lottery;

(*e*)   postal services (PTT) and radio and television administration (TRT);

(*f*)   organisers of horse races and other betting activities;

(*g*)   organisers of shows, concerts and sporting events involving the participation of professional artists and professional sportsmen;

(*h*)   lessors of goods and rights. These include immovable property such as land, buildings, mines and rights which are in the nature of immovable property, and other goods and rights such as those which relate to motor vehicles, machines and equipment, ships, literary, artistic and commercial copyrights, commercial or industrial know-how, patents, trade marks, licences and similar intangible properties and rights.

Importation of goods and services

13.111 For VAT purposes, any importation of goods and services into the Turkish territory is a taxable transaction regardless of the status of the importer or nature of the transaction.

To equalise the tax burden on importation and domestic supply of goods and services, VAT is levied only on the importation of goods and services that are liable to tax within Turkey. Accordingly, any transaction exempted in Turkey is also exempted at import. The VAT on importation is imposed at the same rates applicable as for the domestic supply of goods and services. In the case of importation, the taxable event occurs at the time the goods pass the frontier customs control.

Tax liability for imported goods

13.112 The VAT on importation of goods is assessed by customs authorities on each individual import and is payable together with customs duty. Where the transaction is exempt from customs duty, VAT is assessed upon a special declaration made at the customs frontier and is payable at the time the taxable event occurs. The taxpayer is whoever owns the title to the imported goods.

Tax liability for imported services

13.113 Services purchased abroad are taxable only if utilised or accounted for in Turkey. Therefore, a Turkish acquirer of such services is required, as the withholding agent, to declare and pay the VAT.

Tax liability for export of goods

13.114 The export from Turkey of goods and ancillary services related to such export are exempt from VAT. An export is exempt from VAT if the following conditions are met:

(*a*)   the delivery of the goods must be made to a customer (foreign recipient) outside the domestic territory of Turkey (deliveries to free zones are considered to be export deliveries since free zones are outside the customs area); and

(*b*)   the goods to be delivered must pass through the Turkish customs frontier and reach a foreign destination.

Although the export of goods is exempt from VAT, any input VAT paid may be credited and any excess amount refunded.

Sale of goods destined for export

13.115 Where goods are sold by their producer to an exporter, subject to the condition that they are to be exported, the exporter will pay no VAT to the producer. However, the producer must include the amount of VAT normally due in his periodic returns, but the computed VAT is deferred. If the goods are exported within three months from the beginning of the month following the date of the delivery to the exporter, the deferred VAT is cancelled.

Taxable activities

13.116 Taxable activities defined in VAT law include the supply of goods and services and other transactions.

The following transactions carried out in Turkey are subject to VAT:

(a) supply of goods and services within the scope of commercial, industrial, agricultural or independent professional activities;

(b) importation of all kinds of goods and services;

(c) other activities:

   (i) postal, telecommunications services, radio and television services;

   (ii) organisation of all kinds of betting, gaming and lotteries including authorised public lotteries;

   (iii) organisation of shows, concerts and sporting events with the participation of independent professional artists and professional sportsmen;

   (iv) sales and bonded warehouses and auctions;

   (v) transportation of petroleum and gas and their products through pipelines;

   (vi) leasing of goods and rights;

   (vii) supplies of a commercial, industrial, agricultural or professional nature by enterprises belonging to national and local government agencies and establishments, universities, associations, foundations and all kinds of professional organisations;

   (viii) supplies deemed to be taxable upon application for optional liability, in order to avoid distortions of competition.

Exemptions granted under other tax laws will not be valid for VAT purposes where the business performs an activity that falls within the scope of VAT.

Foreign trade: imports and exports

13.117 An importation of goods and services is a taxable transaction whether or not the importation is made a business purpose.

Export transactions are exempt from VAT with a credit and refund available for input VAT in respect of the goods exported.

Exemptions

Immovable property

13.118 The following are exempt from VAT:

(a) supplies of land and workplaces by business enterprises within small industrial sites and organised industrial regions;

(*b*) supplies of houses and buildings to members of housing construction co-operatives;

(*c*) the leasing of immovable property, except for immovable business assets.

Financial transactions

13.119 Transactions carried out by banks and insurance companies that fall within the scope of banking and insurance transaction tax are exempt without credit from VAT.

Services rendered by banks, bankers and insurance companies are subject to a banking and insurance transactions tax.

Supplies of unprocessed gold and silver, foreign exchange, money, tax and duty stamps, valuable documents, vehicle tax stamps, stocks and bonds are exempt from VAT.

Supplies by public institutions of banknotes, coins and official stamps and documents are exempt from VAT.

Transportation and communication

13.120 International transportation is exempt from tax.

Transportation of foreign crude oil, gas and their products through pipelines is exempt from VAT.

Machinery and equipment under investment incentive certificate

13.121 Importation of machinery and equipment under an investment incentive certificate (IIC) are exempted from VAT.

Importation of goods

13.122 Exemptions at importation granted under VAT law are set out below:

(*a*) the import of goods and services that are exempt from VAT if supplied in Turkey (e.g. importation of unprocessed gold and silver; importation of machinery and equipment under IIC);

(*b*) the import of certain goods that are exempt from customs duties, with reference to customs law (e.g. samples and models of products that are of no commercial value);

(*c*) goods and services to which transit, transhipment, bonded warehouse, temporary storage, customs area and free zone regimes are applied.

Temporary importation of goods for re-exportation

13.123 The temporary importation of goods for re-exportation is exempt from tax which is secured by a deposit.

Temporary exportation for re-importation

13.124 Goods temporarily exported for re-importation are exempt from tax provided that they have not been worked on or treated in any way. An increase in the value of the goods exported due to work performed abroad will be subject to tax at re-importation.

Other

13.125 The supply of water for agricultural purposes and land improvement services rendered by public institutions, agricultural co-operative societies and farmers unions are exempt from VAT.

Credit for input tax

13.126 Certain transactions are not taxable and at the same time the taxpayer has the right to claim a credit and a refund. This mechanism operates under the name 'exemption with credit for previously paid VAT' and is used principally for exports.

The following supply of goods and services are exempt from VAT with credit for previously paid VAT:

(*a*) export supplies;

(*b*) supply of sea, air and railway transportation to be used for business purposes and supplies related to their maintenance and repair;

(*c*) supplies to people engaged in petroleum exploration activities within the scope of petroleum law;

(*d*) services supplied at harbours and airports for vessels and aircraft;

(*e*) supplies to embassies, consulates and diplomatic and consular agents subject to the condition of reciprocity;

(*f*) supplies to international institutions and foreign agents connected with such institutions to the extent that the exemption is granted by an international agreement;

(*g*) supplies of machinery and equipment under the IIC granted to the buyer.

Tax mechanism

13.127 The tax mechanism operates on the basis of tax returns filed by taxable persons within the period allowed by VAT law. The business may credit the VAT charged on goods and services supplied, and on importation, against the VAT on the supply of goods and services made by the business, and pay the difference due. If the amount of credit exceeds the amount charged by the business the excess credit may either be carried forward or refunded.

To be eligible to claim VAT, the invoice or similar documents must identify separately the VAT charged on the supply, and must be recorded in the business accounts. However, it is not required that the VAT should actually have been paid, i.e. VAT liability and deductibility is computed on an accruals basis.

VAT is collected at every stage of production and distribution from the first sale by the producer to the last sale to the consumer. At each of these stages, the amount of tax payable is the difference between the total amount of tax charged on the invoices issued by the taxpayer and the total amount of tax charged on invoices issued to the taxpayer during the same period. Thus the VAT is initially computed by applying the appropriate rate of taxation to the taxable base for goods and services supplied by the taxpayer during a taxable period. This amount is then reduced by a credit for VAT previously paid on importation and on goods and services supplied to the taxpayer.

Non-deductible VAT

13.128 No credit for VAT may be claimed in the following cases:

(*a*) VAT on the purchase of cars (which are recorded as an expense or cost);

(*b*) missing or stolen stocks;

(*c*) VAT on non-deductible expenses.

Taxable basis

13.129 The taxable base of a transaction is generally the total value of the consideration received excluding the VAT itself. VAT law deals with the taxable base under four headings, namely taxable base for deliveries and services; importation; international transportation; and special cases.

Where there is no consideration, or consideration is in a form other than money, the taxable base is the market value. Market value is the average price due in the market for similar goods and services and is determined with reference to the Tax Procedural Law.

Exclusions from the taxable base

13.130 The taxable base for goods delivered and services rendered does not include the VAT itself and allows for discounts provided that they are

316

at a commercially reasonable rate and explicitly listed on all invoices or similar documents.

Tax rates

Standard rate

13.131 The standard rate of VAT on taxable transactions is 18%.

Special rates

13.132 For the deliveries and the services noted in List No.1, the VAT rate is 1%. List No.1 includes agricultural products such as raw cotton, dried hazelnuts and the supply and leasing of goods within the scope of the Financial Leasing Law.

For the deliveries and the services noted in List No.2, the VAT rate is 8%. List No.2 includes basic food stuffs and books and similar publications.

For the deliveries and the services noted in List No.3, the VAT rate is 26%. List No.3 includes luxury goods, e.g. hairspray, cosmetics, make-up, electric shavers and video cassettes.

For the deliveries and the services noted in List No.4, the VAT rate is 40%. List No.4 includes the delivery of automobiles with cylinder capacities exceeding 2,000, 2,500 and 3,000 cc depending on the Customs Tariff classification.

Administrative obligations

Registration

13.133 Any person or entity engaged in an activity within the scope of VAT law must notify the tax office local to the place of business. Where there is more than one place of business, registration is made at the tax office that is authorised with respect to individual or corporate income tax.

Records

13.134 Taxpayers must keep records in such a way as to enable the computation and control of VAT by the authorities.

Invoices

13.135 Invoices must include the following information:

(*a*) invoice number;

(*b*) date of supply;

(*c*) name, address and the tax registration number of the company receiving the supply;

(*d*) name, address and the tax registration number of the supplier;

(*e*) description of the goods or services supplied;

(*f*) quantity and price;

(*g*) date of delivery of the goods and the quantity of goods dispatched;

(*h*) VAT must be shown separately on invoices and similar documents for the purpose of the credit mechanism.

Taxable period and submission of VAT return

13.136 Taxpayers must file and submit their returns to the local tax office within twenty-five days following the end of each taxable period.

For taxpayers engaged in the international transportation of goods and goods in transit, the tax period is quarterly.

The tax point for the international transportation of goods and goods in transit is the moment the goods cross the customs frontier.

Payment of VAT

13.137 VAT payments are made at the same time as the submission of the VAT return to the related tax office.

Nexia contacts by country

Austria	Vinzenz Hamerle *EWB Revisions-und* *Treuhandgesellschaft* *mbH*	Telephone: Facsimile: email:	+ 43 (1) 712 4114 + 43 (1) 712 411420 office@hamerle-partner.at
Belgium	Edward van Rijswijck *Delvaux, Fronville,* *Servais et Associés* *(DFSA)*	Telephone: Facsimile: email:	+ 32 (02) 352 0490 + 32 (02) 351 0487 reception@dfsa.be
Cyprus	John P. Poyiadjis *Nexia Poyiadjis*	Telephone: Facsimile: email:	+ 357 (2) 2456 111 + 357 (2) 2666 276 np@nexia.com.cy
Czech Republic	Vladimir Králicek *Audit Plus*	Telephone: Facsimile: email:	+ 42 (02) 2278 2492 + 42 (02) 2278 0435 audit.plus@volny.cz
Denmark	Nigel Hodges *Nexia International* *Secretariat*	Telephone: Facsimile: email:	+ 44 207 487 4648 + 44 207 487 3484 nhodges@nexia.com
Finland	Frej Lobbas *Tilintarkastus Logos Oy*	Telephone: Facsimile: email:	+ 358 (9) 7744 8122 + 358 (9) 7744 8139 frej.lobbas@tilintarkastuslogos.fi
France	Jean Marcel Denis *Auditeurs & Conseils* *Associés*	Telephone: Facsimile: email:	+ 33 (0) 1 47 66 77 88 + 33 (0) 1 47 66 77 80 jm.denis@aca.nexia.fr
	Yves Sevestre *Tax lawyer*	Telephone: Facsimile: email:	+ 33 (0) 1 47 66 76 10 + 33 (0) 1 47 66 77 14 ysevestre@wanadoo.fr
Germany	Thomas Rohler *BTR Breratung und* *Treuhand Ring GmbH*	Telephone: Facsimile: email:	+ 49 (0211) 595 150 + 49 (089) 595 1555 rohler.dhpg@datevnet.de
Greece	Nigel Hodges *Nexia International* *Secretariat*	Telephone: Facsimile: email:	+ 44 207 487 4648 + 44 207 487 3484 nhodges@nexia.com
Hungary	Péter Galambos *Metrum Auditing Ltd*	Telephone: Facsimile: email:	+ 361 209 4922 + 361 209 4923 metrum@metrum.hu
Ireland	Dermot Troy *Oliver Freaney &* *Company*	Telephone: Facsimile: email:	+ 353 (01) 614 2500 + 353 (01) 614 2555 dtroy@ofc.ie
Italy	Massimo Milan *Arietti & Co*	Telephone: Facsimile: email:	+ 39 (011) 561 2722 + 39 (011) 561 9114 massimo.milan@studioarietti.com
Luxembourg	Marc Van Hoek *Luxfiducia Sàrl*	Telephone: Facsimile: email:	+ 352 26 43 29 97 + 352 26 43 29 98 mvhoek@luxfiducia.com

Nexia contacts by country

Netherlands	Ton Krol *Horlings, Brouwer &* *Horlings Tax Consultants*	*Telephone:* *Facsimile:* *email:*	+ 31 (20) 670 6159 + 31 (20) 670 6205 tkrol@hbh.nl
Norway	Jon Wiggen *Kjelstrup & Wiggen AS*	*Telephone:* *Facsimile:* *email:*	+ 47 (23) 11 4200 + 47 (23) 11 4201 wiggen@kjelwig.no
Poland	Jerzy Pawilno-Pacewicz *Multiexpert Sp z.o.o.*	*Telephone:* *Facsimile:* *email:*	+ 48 (22) 826 0415, 826 0417 + 48 (22) 826 2431 multiexp@medianet.pl
Portugal	H. Lisboa Afonso *Camacho Palma &* *Lisboa Afonso – SROC*	*Telephone:* *Facsimile:* *email:*	+ 351 (21) 722 1330 + 351 (21) 722 3673 h.lisboa.afonso@cpla-sroc.pt
Spain	Carlos Sahunquillo *P B Auditores S.L.*	*Telephone:* *Facsimile:* *email:*	+ 34 (93) 414 2402 + 34 (93) 201 1740 carlos.sahuquillo@bcn.pbauditores.com
Sweden	Anders Landsjö *Nexia Revision* *Stockholm KB*	*Telephone:* *Facsimile:* *email:*	+ 46 (8) 562 561 00 + 46 (8) 562 561 99 anders.landsjo@nexia.se
Switzerland	Roland Schaer *NSL Audit & Consulting* *Sàrl*	*Telephone:* *Facsimile:* *email:*	+ 41 (22) 908 0150 + 41 (22) 908 0151 firex@bluewin.ch
Turkey	Metin Etkin *GYM – Güreli Yeminli* *Mali Müsavirlik A.S.*	*Telephone:* *Facsimile:* *email:*	+ 90 (212) 286 1212 + 90 (212) 276 6702
United Kingdom	John Voyez *Smith & Williamson*	*Telephone:* *Facsimile:* *email:*	+ 44 (0) 20 7637 5377 + 44 (0) 20 7631 0741 JHV@smith.williamson.co.uk

Nexia International Secretariat:

Nigel Hodges
Executive Director

36 Manchester Street
London
W1U 7LH
United Kingdom

Telephone: + 44 (0) 20 7487 4648
Facsimile: + 44 (0) 20 7487 3484

e-mail: nhodges@nexia.com
Website: www.nexia.com

Index